한국 인권문제

제 사안 1

한국 인권문제

제 사안 1

| 머리말

일제 강점기 독립운동과 병행되었던 한국의 인권운동은 해방이 되었음에도 큰 결실을 보지 못했다. 1950년대 반공을 앞세운 이승만 정부와 한국전쟁, 역시 경제발전과 반공을 내세우다 유신 체제에 이르렀던 박정희 정권, 쿠데타로 집권한 1980년대 전두환 정권까지, 한국의 인권은 이를 보장해야 할 국가와 정부에 의해 도리어 억압받고 침해되었다. 이런 배경상 근대 한국의 인권운동은 반독재, 민주화운동과 결을 같이했고, 대체로 국외에 본부를 둔 인권 단체나 정치로부터 상대적으로 자유로운 종교 단체에 의해 주도되곤 했다. 이는 1980년 5·18광주민주화운동을 계기로 보다 근적인 변혁을 요구하는 형태로 조직화되었고, 그 활동 영역도 정치를 넘어 노동자, 농민, 빈민 등으로 확대되었다. 이들이 없었다면 한국은 1987년 군부 독재 종식하고 절차적 민주주의를 도입할 수 없었을 것이다. 민주화 이후에도 수많은 어려움이 있었지만, 한국의 인권운동은 점차 전문적이고 독립된 운동으로 분화되며 더 많은 이들의 참여를 이끌어냈고, 지금까지 많은 결실을 맺을 수 있었다.

본 총서는 1980년대 중반부터 1990년대 초반까지, 외교부에서 작성하여 30여 년간 유지했던 한국 인권문제와 관련한 국내외 자료를 담고 있다. 6월 항쟁이 일어나고 민주화 선언이 이뤄지는 등 한국 인권운동에 많은 변화가 있었던 시기다. 당시 인권문제와 관련한 국내외 사안들, 각종 사건에 대한 미국과 우방국, 유엔의 반응, 최초의 한국 인권보고서 제출과 아동의 권리에 관한 협약 과정, 유엔인권위원회 활동, 기타 민주화 관련 자료 등 총 18권으로 구성되었다. 전체 분량은 약 9천여 쪽에 이른다.

2024년 3월

한국학술정보(주)

| 일러두기

· 본 총서에 실린 자료는 2022년 4월과 2023년 4월에 각각 공개한 외교문서 4,827권, 76만
여 쪽 가운데 일부를 발췌한 것이다.

· 각 권의 제목과 순서는 공개된 원본을 최대한 반영하였으나, 주제에 따라 일부는 적절히
변경하였다.

· 원본 자료는 A4 판형에 맞게 축소하거나 원본 비율을 유지한 채 A4 페이지 안에 삽입
하였다. 또한 현재 시점에선 공개되지 않아 '공란'이란 표기만 있는 페이지 역시 그대로
실었다.

· 외교부가 공개한 문서 각 권의 첫 페이지에는 '정리 보존 문서 목록'이란 이름으로 기록물
종류, 일자, 명칭, 간단한 내용 등의 정보가 수록되어 있으며, 이를 기준으로 0001번부터
번호가 매겨져 있다. 이는 삭제하지 않고 총서에 그대로 수록하였다.

· 보고서 내용에 관한 더 자세한 정보가 필요하다면, 외교부가 온라인상에 제공하는 『대한
민국 외교사료요약집』 1991년과 1992년 자료를 참조할 수 있다.

| 차례

머리말 4

일러두기 5

한국 인권문제와 관련한 제 사안, 1985-86 7

한국 인권문제와 관련한 제 사안, 1987 217

정 리 보 존 문 서 목 록

기록물종류	일반공문서철	등록번호	21737	등록일자	1995-06-13
분류번호	701	국가코드	US	보존기간	영구
명 칭	한국 인권문제와 관련한 제 사안, 1985-86				
생 산 과	북미과	생산년도	1985~1986	담당그룹	북미국
내용목차	1. Jackson목사 기자회견, 1985.6.6 - 광주사태 진상조사 측구 2. Int'l Luman Rights Law Group 사무국장 방한, 1986.1.27-31 3. California 주 Berkeley 시, 광주의 날 선포 문제, 1986.4.-5 4. 미국 South California주 교회협의회 인권조사단 방한, 1986.6 5. Amnesty Int'l 인사 면담, 1986.8.11 6. 미국 유학생(양동화, 김성만, 황대권) 간첩사건, 1986.6-11 7. 한국NCC 인사 출국규제문제, 1986.11-12				

0001

1. Jackson 목사 기자회견, 1985.6.6
   - 광주사태 진상조사 촉구

관리 번호 *** 대 외 비 ****

*** 대 외 비 ****

종 별: 지 급

번 호: NYW-0581   일 시: 50531 1730

수 신: 장 관(미북, 영재, 해외, 사본:주미대사-직송필)

발 신: 주 뉴욕 총영사

제 목: JACKSON 목사 광주사태 진상조사위 구성 촉구

1. 전 민주당 대통령 후보였던 JESSIE JACKSON 목사는 5.
30. 맨하탄 소재 UN 감리교회 센타에서 가진 기자회견에서, 레이건 행
정부는 대필리핀 군사원조를 삭감해 마르코스 대통령의 독재정권에 대한 지지
를 철회하고, 한국의 광주사태와 연관된 미국의 개입 및 책임여부를 공정히
밝힐 의회 진상조사위원회를 구성하라고 촉구했음.

2. 동 기자회견에는 뉴욕지구 아시안-아메리칸 커뮤니티 인사들이 동석하
여 한국의 광주사태를 비롯하여 필리핀내의 인권상황을 발표하였음.

3. JACKSON 목사는 대학생 미문화원 농성이 진행중이던 지난 5.
25. 슐츠 국무장관과 한국 전국교회 협의회에 서한을 보내, 그가 주도하
는 "전국 무지개연합(NRC)" 은 광주사건시의 한국 군부와 미국정부의
역할을 조사, 규명.공개할것을 요구하는 한국 대학생들의 주장을 전적으로
지지한다고 밝힌바 있다고 하였음.

4. 한인사회에서 나온 목요 기도회의 김윤국(장로)은 미문화원을 점거.
농성하여 광주사태 진상규명을 요구한 한국대학생들의 입장에 지지와 함께 연
대감을 나타내고, 잭슨목사의 미의회 조사단 구성 요구를 환영한다고 하였음
. 동인은 또한 성과 인종, 국적을 초월하여 모든 미국 친구들이 수백명의
무고한 광주 시민.학생들이 희생된 광주사태에 대한 미국정부의 책임을 밝
혀내는데 동참할 것을 호소하였음.

5. 동 기자회견 석상에는 민승연(민주구락부), 한중직 목사(후크카든

배 부 처	장관실	의전실	아태가국	총구과	청와대	재무부	보안사
	차관실	아주국	국기국	감사관	총리실	치령위	물공실
1차		미주국 O	경제국	공보관	안기부	처육부	
2차보		구주국	경문국	외연원	법무부	SLOCC	
기획실		승등국	영교국	상장실	상공부	국방부	

1

0003

회 ）， 유종근（인권 연구소）， 김효신（재민 한국청년연합회）등 반정부 인사
들이 동석하였음 . 끝 .

(총영사 김태지 - 장관)

엮고： 85 . 12 . 31 까지

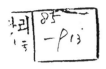 

＊＊＊ 대　외　비 ＊＊＊＊

번　호: USW-2690　　　　　일　시: 50605 1902

수　신: 장　관(미북)

발　신: 주 미 대사

제　목: 잭슨목사 접촉

　　　대: WUS-1905

　　　연: NYW-0581

　1. 국무성 한국과에 의하면 연호 3 항 잭슨 목사가 슐츠장관에게 보냈
다는 서한은 접수한 사실이 없다고 하며, 잭슨목사의 5.30. 기자회견
사실도 알지못하고 있음.

　2. 본직은 적절한 기회에 잭슨목사와 접촉, 진상을 설명, 설득하겠음.

(대사류병현)

여고문 1985.12.31. 까지

85.1.1 호

- PAGE: 1 -

0005

발 신 전 보

WHS-1905

번 호: WNY-0624   일 시: 06041630   전보종별: _____

수 신: 주 미 대사 / 壽慶씨 (사본 : 주뉴욕총영사)

발 신: 장 관 (미북)

제 목: 잭손 목사 접촉

연 : NYW-0581

1. 연호 주뉴욕총영사 보고와 관련, 귀하는 주뉴욕총영사와 협의하여 잭손목사를 접촉, 광주사태는 <ins>외 정상을 설명하고 동사더는</ins> 국가의 안위를 위태롭게 했던 상황이었으며 순수한 국내문제라는 점에서 미국에서 간여할 사항이 아님을 지적하고 동인이 광주사태와 관련한 더이상의 활동을 벌이지 않도록 설득 바람.

2. 이와 관련, 미국무성측과도 협의 바라며 또한 필요시 잭손 목사의 광주사태 진상조사위 구성 요구를 배후에서 선동하고 있는 교포 목사들에 대한 대책도 강구 바람. (장관 이원경)

검토필 (1986. 6. 30)

보안 통제

<table>
<tr><td rowspan="2">앙고재</td><td rowspan="2">85년 6월 4일</td><td rowspan="2">보 미 과</td><td>기안자</td><td>과 장</td><td>심의관</td><td>국 장</td><td>제2차관보</td><td>차 관</td><td>장 관</td></tr>
<tr><td>김성환</td><td></td><td></td><td></td><td></td><td></td><td></td></tr>
<tr><td colspan="3"></td><td colspan="7">외신과   접수자   통제</td></tr>
</table>

종 별: 보 통

번 호: USW-2709　　　　일 시: 50606 1857

수 신: 장 관 (미북, 사본: 주뉴욕총영사)

발 신: 주 미 대사

제 목: 잭슨 목사 기자회견

　　　　대 : WUS-1905

　　　　연 : NYW-581

1. JESSE JACKSON 목사는 금 6.6 11:00 시 당지 미
국 연합 감리교회관에서 이신범, 서유웅 및 비율빈 반정부 인사들과 함께 기
자회견을 갖고 주로 비율빈에 대한 원조 중단을 촉구하였으며, 아국관련 사항
으로서는 의회가 광주사태의 진상을 조사해야한다는 주장을 간략히 언급함.

2. JACKSON 목사는 비율빈 반정부인사 2인 연설후 성명을 낭독하고
질문에 답한바 아국관련 답변요지를 아래 보고함.

　　가. 광주사태

　1)미국정부의 성실성과 한국국민의 생명및 자유에 관한 문제임.

　2)의회는 국가안보및 정부의 신뢰성에 관련된 문제를 조사할 권한을 갖고
　　있는바, 광주사태에 대한 미국정부관련 주장및 가능성은 미국의 국가적 도
　　덕적 이익에 직결되는 문제이므로 의회가 공개적인 진상조사를 행하여
　　야함.

　　나. 미국문화원 점거 농성

　1)학생들에대한 한국정부의 처벌계획은 철회되어야함.

　2)농성은 정당한 요구를 비폭력적 수단으로 주장한 것으로서 마하드마 간
　　디, 마르틴두터 킹등이 행하였던 효과적인 항의 방법임.

배부처	장관실	의전실	아교과국	총무과	청와대	재무부	보안사
	차관실	아주국	국기국	감사관	총리실	핵협위	문공부
	1차보	미주국 ○	경제국	공브관	아기부	체육부	PAGE. 1 -
	2차보	구주국	정문국	외연원	민주부	SLOOC	
	기획실	중동국	영교국	상창실	상부	국방부	

검토필 (85 6.30)

85.6.7.

0007

　　　　　　　※※※

　3)의회는 농성학생들 주장 및 한국정부의 처벌계획을 조사해야함.

　3. 금일 회견어는 약130명이 참가한바, 미국인이 약 2/3, 비율빈이
약 4분의1, 나머지는 아국계 반정부 인사및 교포 신문기자였음.

　4. 금일회견은 주로 비율빈문제에 촛점이 맞추어졌는바, 일부 아국계 반정
부 인사들이 JACKSON 목사어게 아국관련 사항을 포함시키도록 한것으로
보이며 동 목사도 자신이 주도하는 무기재 연합에 아시아계를 끌어들이기
위한 수단의 일환으로 아국 반정부 인사들을 이용하고 있는것으로 관찰됨.

　5. 본직과 JACKSON 목사와의 면담을 주선중어 있는바, 동 면담시 아
국 실정을 상세히 설명하겠음.

　6. 주최측은 한국인권 북미연합회가 작성한 PRESS PACKET 를 금
일 회견 참석자들어게 배포한바, 정파편 1부 송부하겠음

(대사 류병현)

여고 :　85.12.31까지

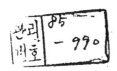

위(爲)
要 도약 보

관리
번호 85
-990

주 미 대 사 관

미국(정) 700 - 210   1985. 6. 7.

수 신 : 장 관
참 조 : 미주국장
제 목 : 잭슨 목사 기자 회견

공 람 인	충 당	과 장	심 의 관	국 장	차관보	차 관	장 관

연 : USW - 2709 (85. 6. 6)

85.6.6. Jesse Jackson 목사 기자회견 참석자들 에게 배포된
한국인권 북미연합회 작성 Press Packet   를 별첨 송부 합니다.

첨 부 : 상기 자료. 끝.

발송
1985. 6. 07
주미대사관

주 미 대 사

0009

외 무 부		
접수	1.85. 6시	지시사항
번호	2826 호	
주자		
담당자		
취급 임자		

처리할 것   년   월   일 까지

0010

PRESS CONFERENCE

11 a.m., Thursday, June 6, 1985
100 Maryland Avenue NE (Methodist Bldg.;
    beside Supreme Court)

REV. JESSE JACKSON

CHANGING U.S. POLICY TOWARD THE PHILIPPINES AND SOUTH KOREA

Also speaking:

Lee, Shin Bom
Director of Asia Commission
Center for Development Policy

Dr. Walden Bello
National Staff
Philippine Human Rights Lobby

Charito Planas
National Council
Friends of the Filipino People

So, Yu Ung
General Secretary
United Movement for Democracy and
Unification in Korea

National Rainbow Coalition, Inc.   955-5795
Philippine Human Rights Lobby   296-8152

North American Coalition for Human Rights in KOREA

110 Maryland Avenue NE, Washington, DC 20002 ● (202) 546-4304
475 Riverside Drive, Room 1538, New York, NY 10115 ● (212) 870-3693
"Korea-phone" (202) 546-NEWS ● Telex 292001 HR WASH

P R E S S   P A C K E T

F O R

N E W S   C O N F E R E N C E

W I T H

T H E   R E V E R E N D   J E S S E   J A C K S O N

JUNE 6, 1985

WASHINGTON, D.C.

0012

Kim Chai-choon, Honorary Chairperson ● Peggy Billings, Chairperson ● Pharis J. Harvey, Executive Director

minds, as well as bodies." Flora McManning, and many others like her, remain vital and want to remain active. We must recognize that ability and desire, and find ways to ensure the continued involvement of nursing home residents in our society.

The over 1 million nursing home residents in this country hold a heritage too vast to be forgotten. Let us today honor our oldest generation of Americans and thank them for their ongoing leadership and contributions to our great country.●

THE NEED FOR DEMOCRACY IN KOREA

● Mr. KENNEDY. Mr. President, I would like to call attention to a March 1 statement by two prominent South Korean democrats, Kim Dae Jung and Kim Young Sam. The constructive cooperation between these two very capable and experienced leaders of the democratic opposition is an encouraging development for the political future of Korea. Also encouraging were the strong showing of a new, truly independent opposition party in the February 1985 national assembly election and the Government's lifting of the political ban on 14 persons, including Kim Dae Jung and Kim Young Sam.

Nevertheless Kim Dae Jung and others are still prevented from exercising their civil and political rights because of prison sentences imposed on them on fabricated charges of sedition. The joint statement by Kim Dae Jung and Kim Young Sam indicates other steps which must be taken for South Korea to become a true democracy, including the restoration of freedom of speech and reform of the electoral system. Since Korean President Chun Doo Hwan is now visiting Washington, it is appropriate not only to recall the progress that has been made toward democracy in Korea but also to remember what still needs to be done. I request that the full text of the March 1 message from Kim Dae Jung and Kim Young Sam be inserted in the RECORD at this point.

The document follows:

THE MARCH 1 MESSAGE FROM KIM DAE JUNG AND KIM YOUNG SAM

The March 1 Declaration of Independence, six decades and six years ago, was an event that opened a new era in our people's history—an event of peaceful eruption of our people's longing for and will towards independence and liberation from the rules of others and fulfillment of a worthwhile life as a liberated independent nation.

The spirit of the March 1 Declaration—freedom, democracy, peace and independence—lives in our heart in spite of the fact that this spirit has been forced to bend and be contained by successive political powers since the 1945 liberation.

Our people's yearning for liberation and independence will be fulfilled only when freedom from the yoke of others is achieved and our people and land are reunified to permit them a dignified life as one nation without division.

We reiterate that reunification cannot be accomplished until and unless democracy

prevails so that everyone can participate in debate freely and without reservation.

Even under the undemocratic and irrational election system and the infinite unjustness of the ruling party, our people showed, through the recent National Assembly election, a clear resolution to reject dictatorship.

The election result is a lucid message, the most appropriate and firmest possible under the present election system, of protest against, and rejection of dictatorial rule. The administration and the ruling party have attempted, rather awkwardly, to interpret the election result as the people's desire for quiet reforms under stability. However, the claimed stability, which is a product of cunning manipulations of the undemocratic election rules, and that under unprecedented corruption and unfairness, is nothing but self-consolation to the present regime.

The New Korea Democratic Party and other opposition forces must be sincerely receptive to the will of the people, made apparent in the election result. We demand that the ruling party recognize the will of the people without distorting it and respond to it in humility.

The manner in which the present regime responds to the will of the people, expressed in the election results, and how well that is reflected in the regime's governing process will not only determine the regime's morality and its ability to survive, but will also become the criteria by which the people will judge whether or not the current regime has the capacity to achieve the national goals of democratization, peaceful transition of power, peace in the Korean Peninsula and reunification of our nation.

Together with the people, we will wait and watch the government's actions. However, to prevent possible calamities, we offer our sincere admonitions in the following:

If the present regime wishes to cleanse itself of its own trials and errors, self-righteousness, injustice and corruption, and, above all, of its historic crimes, and if it is prepared to accomplish its historic mission, then we urge the regime to restore, first of all, freedom of speech. The restoration of freedom of speech, not in words but in deeds, will guarantee vitality in diversity and self-determination of our society. We warn that the regime cannot avoid history's judgment, which will be more severe than the people's judgment by ballots, unless the regime humbly accepts criticisms from citizens, sheds its old self, and restores freedom of speech as a sign of awakening.

We strongly advise that the form and structure of political power be open, fair and just. The existence of shadowy power groups will not only entail behind-the-scenes politics of intrigues and conspiracies, corruptions and get-rich-quick deals, but will also increase the public's distrust and suspicion about official corruption.

In political, socio-economic, cultural and all other areas, the government must refrain from exaggerating its achievements and issuing irresponsible slogans and euphoric phrases.

Unless the election system is changed to make it democratic, the people cannot exercise their rights as the real masters of the government. Along with reforming the election laws, we urge that the autonomy of local governments be put into practice promptly. The establishment of local autonomy will be an important barometer to measure the present regime's commitment to establishing democracy.

Members of a societal unit must become the masters of the unit. Campuses must be returned to the students and workplaces must become the mutual ground for concil-

iation and cooperation by labor and management.

Students who are incarcerated because they expressed their opinions as democratic citizens must be released without delay. Instead of punishing these students, the government and the ruling party must repent for their enormous campaign corruptions. If the students are punished for the election-related charges, all the opposition parties and the people must band together to start a campaign to condemn the rigged elections.

The two of us would like to appeal to our countrymen.

We are well aware of the ongoing plots to divide and set us apart. As we had worked together for eight years under the Yushin rule and put an end to the Park Chung Hee regime, we will again work together now and in the future and dedicate ourselves to achieving the democratization of our country. It will be our greatest honor that we are remembered in our history and praised by our countrymen as two men who have fought together for democracy. Therefore, from this moment, we reject all divisive expression and distinctions.

Especially in matters pertaining to the economy, exaggerations giving a false sense of achievement will lead the national economy to disaster. Lies from the political power must be stopped immediately, because they corrupt the pure meaning of words and accelerate disillusionment among the people.

Democratic reform of the election system must be a precondition for restoring the people's faith in the possibility of democracy under the present regime.

The task left for us in the days ahead is to overcome all plots to divide and alienate us from one another, and to organize and magnify the great democratic capability of our people so that never again will dictatorships of any form stand in this land.

We will pour all our efforts into uniting the capabilities of opposition democratic forces and the democratic ideals of citizens, students, workers and farmers.

Finally, we would like to acknowledge our countrymen, at home and abroad, as well as friends of freedom and human rights all over the world for their concern for our safety and their support and encouragement in our struggle for democracy.

On this day commemorating the March 1 Declaration of Independence, let us commit ourselves to, and pray for, a great stride towards a bright future for our country and nation.●

THE PUCCIO REPORT ON WESTWAY

● Mr. HUMPHREY. Mr. President, yesterday I inserted in the RECORD the first half of the report by Thomas Puccio on the Westway Highway project in New York City. Today, I am inserting the second half.

This half of the report is particularly useful in exploring many of the major issues surrounding the Westway project—including environmental impacts, engineering questions associated with the project and the effect on New York's economy. In the end, Puccio rejects the "hang in there" attitude of New York officials who have persistently argued over the years that billions in Federal funds to build the project are just around the corner.

The Puccio report represents an important milestone in the years of wrestling over Westway, and it is impor-

Reports From Kwangju

デモ参加者に襲いかかる空挺部隊兵士（U.P.I・サン）

Army paratrooper approaching a demonstrator.

North American Coalition for Human Rights in Korea

0014

"Reports From Kwangju" is available for 50¢ per copy
(30¢ per copy for orders of ten or more) from:

North American Coalition
for Human Rights in   KOREA

110 Maryland Avenue NE, Washington, DC 20002

0015

2

Contents

Introduction   4
A Korean Journalist's Account   5
The Torn and Tattered Flag   7
Excerpts From Various Kwangju Reports   16
Chosun University Students' Statement   18
Chronology of Events in Kwangju   20
Poem -- "Kwangju, Cross of Our Nation"   22

22   한국 인권문제 제 사안 1

Introduction

Now that General Chon Too-hwan has seized the presidency of South Korea and has secured the de facto support, or at least the passive acquiescence, of the U.S. government, it is important to remember that the basis of his power is as narrow, and as two-edged, as a bayonet. Since the massacre in May, 1980, Kwangju has entered the political vocabulary of Korean history together with the Tonghak rebellion of the 1890s, the March First Independence Movement of 1919, and the Student Revolution of 1960. As long as the Korean people continue to hope and to struggle for the right to determine their own destiny, the sacrifices of those who died in Kwangju this summer will be remembered.

The eyewitness accounts published in this pamphlet are testimony to the horrors of the attack May 18-20 by special paratrooper commando forces against the unarmed civilians of Kwangju, and of the courage and discipline as well as the strength of their defense, which at least temporarily made Kwangju a "free" city -- until troops released from the U.S.-R.O.K. Combined Command attacked and conquered the city again on May 27. In the end, more than 1,000 were dead, and unknown thousands more were wounded, captured, or in hiding.

Even now, months later, the full account is unknown. No one speaks openly and no investigation is allowed, even by family members, of those killed or missing. Fear and isolation hold the Korean populace in their grip.

Yet the story of Kwangju is not finished. The bestiality of the military's action has left a residue of hatred and distrust which will undoubtedly erupt, sooner or later, shattering the fragile and tense quiet that now prevails. The Chon Too-hwan dictatorship will not long be able to hold silent a nation which so vividly and earnestly expressed its faith in democratic government during the six-month period after Park Chung-hee's death. Ultimately the people will prevail and find the only solace for those lost in Kwangju -- rule by law and by the willing participation of the people.

Now, as never before, we who have supported the struggle for human rights in Korea must remain constant, yielding neither to despair nor cynicism. The American people and government have deep responsibilities for the course of events in Korea and for the future of the Korean struggle for freedom. Our traditions have inspired them, just as our own government's actions in supporting their dictators have puzzled and sickened them. Unless we act strongly now in their defense, a 35-year legacy of trust and goodwill will swiftly dissipate, as will the very security in whose name these acts against the Korean people have been perpetrated by the Korean generals and excused by their American counterparts.

Let us persevere!

Peggy Billings, Chairperson
North American Coalition for
Human Rights in Korea

September, 1980

Lithographs by Tomiyama Taeko

0017

A Korean Journalist's Account

The following is an eyewitness account by an elder reporter who was in downtown Kwangju throughout the period covered. The reporter preceded this account by lamenting the fact that press censorship gives rise to rumors which then make it difficult to sift out fact from fiction. He emphasized that he would only relate things that he himself had seen and leave out things which he had only heard, even though they seemed credible.

. Students in Kwangju started demonstrating on May 14, following the lead of students in Seoul. Although Seoul students called off their demonstrations on May 15 (to await the government's response to their demands for democratization), Kwangju students continued on May 16.

That evening, students held torchlight processions from both Chonnam and Chosun Universities, meeting in front of the Provincial Administration Building. About 35,000 students and 15,000 citizens participated. The demonstration was peaceful and the police guided it rather than trying to suppress it. It broke up at about 10:30 pm, with participants promising to meet again on May 19 if the government had not responded to their demands, which were to lift martial law and hold elections within the year.

Instead, on May 17 the military (which had been controlling the government behind the scenes and resisting pressures for democratization) staged a coup d'etat. Complete martial law was declared and many people were immediately arrested.

Students began gathering at Chonnam University on the morning of May 18 until there were about 500. They started going downtown chanting "Lift Martial Law!" and "Don't Close the Schools!" The numbers grew. The riot police tried to stop them from entering Kum-nam Avenue with tear gas. The students turned over a tear gas truck and burned it. The riot police attacked again, but the students made a barricade across the street. The police continued to throw tear gas cannisters, and the students began throwing stones.

I heard from the police chief that paratroopers would come at 3:00 pm. They actually arrived at about 3:30. At first there were four truckloads of them with 20-30 in each truck. They formed five lines and started to advance on the students. Their faces were flushed. They plowed into the students, beating them with clubs, knocking them over, and trampling on them with their boots. There was much blood.

Students who were arrested were made to strip down to their underwear and to hold their clothes in a bundle behind their heads while they had their hands tied there. Then they were loaded into trucks. Many of them were still bleeding from their heads. It was really a frightening thing to see.

I saw one student who had been knocked unconscious dragged by the hair and thrown roughly onto a truck. Some of the women students were stripped completely. The paratroopers looked like they hadn't seen a woman for a long time. One man told his wife to go and give her underwear to one of the girl students, who were in plain sight of everybody (in downtown Kwangju). The paratroopers beat the woman for trying to give the girl underwear.

Later the students were taken out of the

5

trucks and made to lie on the road. Everyone could see them. The paratroopers made them roll over in one direction and then in the other. If they didn't do it right they were kicked or beaten. Onlookers were so shocked that they could hardly believe what was happening.

Later I had a chance to talk with a paratrooper who had been captured by students. I asked him why they had been so brutal. He told me that they hadn't been fed for three days, that immediately before being sent into Kwangju they had been fed "soju" (rice wine), and also that they had been told they were being sent in to put down a communist insurrection.

On those first two days many people with bullet wounds and other injuries were taken to hospitals, but soldiers came to the hospitals and took them away, saying, "We have our own doctors." Everybody assumed they would die.

On May 19 students were stripped, their hands tied behind their heads, and were made to sit on the road where everyone could see them with their heads between their legs for two to three hours. The paratroopers began shouting (in Kyungsang Province dialect) "Let's kill the Cholla Province bastards and then get out of here." Many, many were killed and injured. I counted 200 corpses. Other witnesses and rumors put the number much higher, but I myself counted 200 dead bodies.

On that afternoon the vice governor appealed to the martial law authorities that the situation was too severe and that the paratroopers should be withdrawn. They withdrew to the Provincial Adminstration Building at 1:30 pm. But the crowd's anger only continued to grow. They attacked and burned all cars that had Pusan license plates (because Pusan is in Kyungsang Province, and the paratroopers talked with Kyungsang accents). They also burned a Christian Broadcasting vehicle and a county office vehicle.

Even a group of middle-aged women gathered and threw stones at the Provincial Adminstration Building, shouting, "The army should stay out of politics!" Or that might have happened on May 20, I'm not sure. It's easy to get the days mixed up, and so some of the things may be on the wrong day.

On May 20 the soldiers did not appear, but stayed in the Provincial Building. Normal life downtown seemed to come to a stop and everybody came out into the streets. The Seoul newspapers reported the events of this day as a "violent riot," but that is not how I would describe them, and in any case what happened has to be seen in perspective. During the previous two days many, many people had been killed and there were many witnesses to the killings.

But the KBS and MBC radio networks were reporting that there had been only one death.

People couldn't stand this and so they burned and destroyed the broadcasting stations. But to call what happened a violent riot doesn't explain why the two buildings on either side of MBC were not even touched while MBC was completely destroyed. Taking this example, a group made up mostly of merchants went and burned the government tax office while shouting things about the tax system. Others went and burned the Provincial Building's garage while shouting anti-government slogans. But these acts of "violence" had concrete targets and could not be described as a riot.

May 21 was a holiday. Schools were closed, shops were closed, and it seemed like the entire city came to a stop as everybody came out into the streets. I'd say that 500,000 people gathered, although not all in the same place. At 12:56 pm the soldiers began shooting. The city became a "sea of blood."

Students went to the nearby town of Hwa-soon, came back with guns, and started fighting with the soldiers. But this is another thing which has been misrepresented by the Seoul newspapers. The students' taking of guns was very clearly a response to the slaughter which had already been started by the army. For example, a woman seven months pregnant went out looking for her husband because she was worried about him. Later he went looking for her, and found her dead with a bullet wound in the middle of her forehead.

On May 22 the army withdrew from the city. On that day a "citizens committee" was established to negotiate with the martial law authorities. But the students didn't recognize the committee because the people who set it up were self-appointed and there was no system of representation.

The people who occupied the Provincial Administration Building during this time weren't only students. There were also workers, shoeshine boys and some gangster-looking types. But the students were in command.

On the afternoon of May 25 there was a "Rally to Stand Firm" in front of the Provincial Building. There were about 100,000 people there. They burned Chon Too-hwan in effigy. There was no disorder during this time such as was reported in the Seoul newspapers.

On the morning of May 27 after the army retook the city, I went into the Provincial Administration Building. It was a "sea of blood." I myself saw 21 bodies. On the second floor there was one body that was completely burned, the person having committed suicide. At first I thought that maybe there really had been a spy among them, who had been trained to commit suicide like that. But when I went closer and looked, his name was still legible on the lapel of his shirt. Inside the pocket of his shirt were the cards of various foreign reporters,

6

0019

still intact.

He had been the spokesman, and had only talked with foreign reporters because he said that they were the only ones who would report what really happened. I had complained to him that it wasn't Korean reporters who didn't report things, but the government that didn't let them be printed. I felt very strange. We had talked just the day before. I respected his thinking and had felt that he was a very good person. But still things can't be reported. His body was listed in the newspaper as unidentifiable.

The Torn and Tattered Flag

This account was transcribed, edited, and translated from a tape-recorded description of events personally witnessed by the narrator from May 19 when he jumped off a highway bus which he had boarded to return to Seoul from Kwangju. He had arrived from Seoul that morning to check on his family's safety and was about to return again to Seoul when the above events occurred.

The account ends when he left Kwangju at 7 am on May 24, following railroad tracks to avoid the surveillance of the army. He went over the mountains and through a valley, trying to avoid using any roads. At one point he was checked by the army but was allowed to pass. He walked to the next town, took a taxi to the nearest train station, and boarded a train for Seoul.

He has reportedly since been arrested for making this account of events in Kwangju.

Beautiful City.

On May 19 of this year, Kwangju, a beautiful quiet pastoral city, the capital of South Cholla Province, and the birthplace of many heros of the struggle for independence and democracy, suddenly turned into a bloody hell.

It was on that day that I saw an intercity bus drive hurriedly into a public playground, quickly discharge its passengers, and zoom off in flight. Seeing this, I had my first direct gut-feeling of the seriousness of the situation.

I threw my exhausted body into a taxi and told the driver to go to the Provincial Administration Building. Before I had the words out of my mouth, he made a sign of death and said, "You'd better walk" as he slammed on the brakes and let me out again. There was nothing I could do but start walking toward Im-dong.

I came upon a burned-out police box, a charred fragment of a war-wasted city. Martial law forces, carrying rifles with bayonets, looked as if they were guarding captured enemy territory. They had control of all the streets.

I felt goosebumps all over my body. I gingerly made my way through their midst and, wiping the cold sweat which was already forming on my brow, approached the main street, Kum-nam Avenue, once a beautiful area with flowers blooming abundantly, a welcoming area for visitors.

Those carefully laid out streets with their atmosphere of simple warmth were turning into ruins which cried out the memories of better days. Overlooking Kwangju is Mudung-san, a beautiful mountain shaped like a mother's abundant breast, nurturing the city. There is also the river Kuk-rak with its scenes of Confucian gentlemen fishing on its banks in the spring. Now a cold wind blew across this beautiful pastoral city.

License to Kill.

The people of Kwangju are as gentle as sheep. However, they were being sacrificed on an altar of blood as offerings for the cause of democracy. The authorities were using their unlimited powers to block any changes in the present structure so as to preserve their power in the future. We all know that any action in poor countries which seeks to promote change or improvement is immediately interpreted by the authorities as a plot to overturn the system and becomes the object of cruel repression.

The recent events in this corner of Honam (south-western Korea) will go down in history as the ultimate in oppressive measures used against the people. The cries heard everywhere, the passionate sobs sounding as if hearts were breaking, the breathless whispers which seem to be annoucing death. It was as if the earth was dry and was gorging itself on the blood of those young spirits.

The heavens seemed ready to burst with the echoes of their sorrowful cries. The demonstrating students and the innocent bystanders who had come to observe them had been surrounded without the slightest warning by the dreaded paratroopers who had descended like a swarm of bees.

7

0020

"They wouldn't kill innocent townspeople!" I
had thought with simple and childish trust as I
came toward the central city. Only moments
later I was fleeing in desperation, urged on
only by the basic instinct for self-preservation.
Conscious of a bayonet brushing against my
shoulder, I managed to hide inside a building.
The people who had arrived after me had the good
sense to pull down the steel shutters. Thanks
to their quick action I was able to escape without having my head split open by an iron truncheon or having a bayonet thrust in my chest.

I was painfully aware for the first time in
my life of the presence of death like a black
cloud around us. Pressed in on all sides by the
others who had fled, I felt like an escaping rat
shivering in fear. I peered through the holes
in the shutter and was unable to take my eyes
from the drama taking place outside.

There was the deafening sound of gun fire,
the flash of sharp bayonets, the sound of flail-
ing truncheons. I heard the screams of someone
dying, the whole thing piercing through my consciousness like a scene from hell. Men and women, young and old, students and townspeople --
the paratroopers hit them all without discrimi-
nation.

I had a momentary flash that I was witnessing
firsthand the Nazis butchering the people of
Mozambique during World War II. But just as
quickly, my attention was re-directed to what
was happening in front of me.

I watched as the iron truncheon of one of the
paratroopers descended on the head of a man about
70 years old who was totally defenseless. Blood
spurted like a fountain from the old man's head
and mouth and he collapsed silently on the spot.
I stood in my shelter not knowing how to respond
to this. I felt icy pain shoot through me and
fell weakly to a sitting position on the stone
steps.

The youngish woman next to me stamped her
feet and shuttered before falling to the ground
herself. The collective sorrow and outrage of
the weak, defenseless people was rising. It was
a lonely, isolated sorrow lacking anywhere to
plead its cause or to establish roots. We were
witnessing outright murder. In the next hours,
we were to be direct witnesses to the most cruel
and merciless killings imaginable. But that
would not be the conclusion to this death drama.

The woman that the two paratroopers were
dragging like a dog was pregnant and close to
delivery. "What does this woman have in her
bag?" I didn't know what they were talking
about and I looked at the woman's hands but saw
no bag in them. "This woman! Doesn't she know?
Is it a boy or a girl?" The men seemed to be
very excited and it was at this moment that I
realized what they were saying.

I couldn't hear the woman's voice but it

Swinging his truncheon, a paratrooper pummels a detained demonstrator

seemed as if she didn't understand what was
happening either. "Well, then. Let's show her!"
At that instant, before the woman had a chance
to defend herself, he grabbed her dress and tore
it. You could see her body through the tear.
The soldier took his bayonet and plunged it into
her side. He must have twisted it when he
pushed it in for her entrails came out with it.
Once again he inserted the bayonet and drew a
line along her abdomen, pulled out the fetus
and tossed it to the woman writhing on the
ground.

All those who stood by helplessly witnessing
this unbelievable cruelty hung their heads and
gnashed their teeth, while actually shaking with
disgust. I closed my eyes and bit my tongue.
Spasms broke out throughout my frame.

When I opened my eyes again, both the corpses
and the soldiers were no longer visible. The man
next to me told how the bodies had been stuffed
into straw bags like so much rubbish and thrown
into a refuse truck. I unconsciously cried out,
"Oh Lord, what can be done?" What can we do to
atone for this innocent blood which had been
shed? What will happen to this country now?
Are these actually soldiers of the Republic of
Korea, selected to perform the sacred task of
defending this land?

I began to feel ashamed of myself for having
hid to save my own skin and then witnessing in
hiding these shocking happenings. I saw my own
baseness, unable to muster any resistance to
these happenings, and saw myself as I was -- a
truly shameful creature. At the same time, I
felt undescribable feelings of disillusionment.
Not because I had witnessed the death of this
woman whose abdomen had been torn open, but
rather because seeing my own baseness and lowli-
ness, I had experienced my first feelings of
self-hatred.

The people who had stood next to me were
gone, having escaped to some other place while
I was unaware. Outside, where the martial law
forces had been, there remained only blood-stains,
fragments, refuse, and rage. Seeking to escape
from the bayonets and truncheons, the crowd took

8

refuge in alleys, restaurants, shops, buildings -- anywhere they could find safety. Like blood suckers seeking more, the soldiers grabbed anyone in sight and stabbed, kicked -- sending people to their death on the spot. Men and women, young and old -- they had license to kill them all.

> Men and women, young and old -- they had license to kill them all.

"Quo vadis. Whither goest thou? I am going up to Rome to be crucified." Christ's words to his disciple Peter who was fleeing when he found that the early Christians were being slaughtered by the Roman soldiers.

Because they believed in God, the early Christians were trampled upon by the authorities. They, who were isolated from abundance, who suffered starvation and cold in the midst of isolation and alienation, who were the victims of power and military force, probably did not put much value on their own lives.

Peter and the other early Christians checked their steps toward refuge and made the decision, that historical turning point, to go to Rome and deliver themselves up to crucifixion. We all know that their action forms the very basis of modern Christianity. But where was I attempting to go now? Was I not fleeing the scene where my brothers, my compatriots gave their blood and went to their deaths? Was I not fleeing to Sandong on the outskirts of the city?

As reasons for my flight I thought of how I had to check on my wife's family and find out whether my brothers were still alive. But these were not sufficient reasons for my flight. I thought again. It would not do for me to die here. If I said that it was necessary for me to do God's work, would this stand as sufficient reason for my flight? I will probably never know, but let me put these matters aside for now and continue.

I tried as much as possible to use alleys as my escape route. Fortunately I had nothing in my hands to hinder me. Threading my way through an alley, I checked my steps at the entrance to the main street. Almost reflectively, I hid myself behind an empty box. I was about to be the witness to the unexpected cruelty and tragedy which has accompanied similar scenes since the beginning of history. Were these soldiers actually members of the same Korean race, speaking the same language and holding the same nationality as myself? Even if they had been guerrillas sent from North Korea by Kim Il-sung, I doubt that they could have equalled the cruelty of these men.

Paratroopers stopped three women who appeared to be university students and stripped them naked. They even took off their underclothes,

and the cruelest of their number started kicking the women with his boots. "Get the hell out of here, you bitches! What do you think you're doing starting demonstrations?!!" He sounded like some crazed wolf.

The women made no attempt to escape but instead held fast to each other and sat down on the ground. I wanted so much for them to take flight. Contrary to my wishes and as if my prayers had not been heard, they sat down on the ground and refused to budge.

One of the soldiers cried out at that moment, "These women don't deserve to live! There's nothing else we can do!" The soldiers with one movement thrust their bayonets into the backs of the women and blood spirted out like a fountain. When the women fell down, the soldiers made an X-mark across their chests with the bayonets and threw them into a refuse truck without even checking to see whether they were alive or not. I had no way of knowing whether they were going to bury these bodies en masse or cremate them.

> Even if they had been guerrillas sent from North Korea by Kim Il-sung, I doubt that they could have equalled the cruelty of these men.

Just at that time, the anguished cries of the people grew even more intense and the excitement reached a feverish pitch. I heard someone saying, "Citizens! Let's rise up in defense. All our sons are going to die. Grab a hoe, a chisel, anything you can get your hands on and fight back!" There was a unified cry in response and several people gathered together and took tools from a lumberyard.

The citizens who had been fleeing like a frightened mob had now reverted to a fighting stance and the massacre worsened. Not holding anything in my hands, I thought that I would not be able to fight in their midst. It seemed a useless waste of life to put up resistance against bayonets. Restraining my own excitement, I ran off as fast as I could.

It wasn't until past eleven that night that I was able to check on my brothers. The scene of the three girls being killed kept flashing before my eyes and I was unable to sleep at all.

Love Greater Than Words.

The sound of gunfire echoed through the night, the rat-tat of automatic weapons that you hear in war movies. First carbine rifles, then machine guns rattled on. In heaven's name, I thought, at whose hearts were all these guns being directed? The asphalt of the streets was stained with fresh blood as the indiscriminate

9

volleys of the martial law forces thunder-
ed on until dawn.

My younger brother, in his final year
at high school, escaped back to the house
after having spent the night throwing
Molotov cocktails at the army. According
to his report, over 500 demonstrators had
fallen in the melee. I said that it was
not right for them to go out and die like
dogs.

"Are you trying to say that I should
run away while my friends and brothers are
dying?" My brother was unable to check
his excitement and his words seemed directed at me. I could not make any reply.

Having seen the blood of their friends
and relatives, the students and citizens
had reached a peak of rage and frenzy.
All the taxi drivers in the city got into
their cars to carry demonstrators and form
a parade of cars. No matter where you
went, the streets were packed with people
greeting the demonstrators with applause
and cheers of approval. Young men surged
forward to get a place on the vehicles.

The vehicles were of all sizes and
shapes: highway buses, municipal buses,
bulldozers, captured armored cars, officer's personal cars, amounting in all to
several hundred vehicles. From the Asia
Motor Company came several hundred maintenance workers to do quick repairs on
damaged cars and send them off again.
They spared no pains in servicing the cars
which were forming a line for the demonstration. Gas station attendants were
giving out gas to any vehicle that needed
it.

On each car people hung placards written
in their own blood. The slogans, some of
which had run before the blood had dried,
tended to make the crowd even more excited.
"Kill the murderer Chon Too-hwan!" "Release Kim Dae-jung!" "Evict Pres. Choi
Kyu-ha from office!" The vehicles were de-
corated with Korean flags along with the
bloody placards. Many times I didn't know whether
to laugh or cry.

Ten or more students sitting on top of a
highway bus banged on the roof with various makeshift weapons they had gathered in place of
bayonets and raised hoarse cries as they called
out slogans. The collected energy of the mob was
a fearful thing indeed.

My younger brother had fixed a torch on a
small hauling vehicle and was off to the city
center to set up a loudspeaker to urge on the
people. I didn't want to stop him. In fact, I
felt grateful for his spirit of loyalty in want-
ing to risk his life to fight together with his
friends.

There was a rumor that the paratroopers had
withdrawn from the city. It was reported that
one military officer, enraged at the actions of
the soldiers who had indiscriminately slaughtered
townspeople, killed five soldiers by his side
before shooting himself. Disorder grew among
the ranks.

After the paratroopers retreated outside the
city, the regular martial law forces moved in on
the demonstrators with free license and opened
fire indiscriminately. The blood of the young
people still lay on the street. Could the townspeople, seeing the blood and the bodies of young
children in the gutters, just stand by and do
nothing?

10

0023

> Having seen the blood of their friends and relatives, the students and citizens reached a peak of rage. No matter where you went, the streets were packed with people greeting the demonstrators with applause and cheers of approval.

Kwangju had become a city of fear and terror. Pillars of fire rose up in every direction. It was an isolated island with all communication with the outside world cut off by the military. But the hearts of its people were burning with righteousness.

Unless you had been there and seen for yourself these people banded together in unity, you could not completely understand. In the faces of the youths who had thrown their lives into a struggle to preserve democracy you could see tears. Blood stained their chests. They wore headbands inscribed with slogans written in their own blood and raised hoarse cries to the sky. Love is on our side. Young innocent children.

Now even women and aunts vied for a place in the cars. Young children shouted out again and again until they were hoarse and could shout no more, whereupon they appealed with their tears. Seeing them, I could not help crying myself.

The citizens who were unable to gain places in the cars came forward with rice balls and drinks, sparing no pains to supply the others with refreshments. One woman in her 70s, the owner of a small store, gathered all the food on her shelves -- eggs, bread, cola, milk, juice. She wanted to give it all to the demonstrators. Having put all the items in the box, she was unable to lift it. I picked it up, stopped a passing car, and put it inside. On the faces of the riders, I could clearly see their determination to fight to the death.

Those women who were unable to supply food brought tubs of water to wipe the faces of the others and to give them to drink. With intent faces the citizens ran along with the speeding cars. It was a struggle of blood and love in which they were giving their lives along with the others. Some rubbed the backs of the others and urged them on. Drugstore owners brought out medicines and energy tonics. It was a wave of humanity showing their whole beings as they urged on the others with shouts and applause.

Blood Donors.

The tear gas fumes spread out over the area and I was unable to keep my eyes open. The city which had changed to one of heat and waste was like a scene out of hell. As the struggle of the demonstrators grew more intense, the martial law forces once more released indiscriminate volleys of gunfire. There was no way of count-

the innumerable young people who screamed and fell to the ground.

The people began to band together on Kum-nam Avenue, which had become something like a volcano. A great human wave of perhaps 300,000 people completely covered the street and formed snakelike columns.

I had heard about the terrible effects of riot gas but this was my first experience with it. I went into a fit of sneezing and tried desperately to clear my running eyes and nose. All the while I attempted to thread my way through the crowd.

The army had armored cars stationed in a zig-zag pattern in front of the Provincial Administration Building. They had built a barracade and their guns were pointed at the citizens. It seemed like the mouth of an active volcano which could belch fire at any time.

> Now even women and aunts vied for a place in the cars. Young children shouted out again and again until they were hoarse and could shout no more, whereupon they appealed with their tears.

Around three o'clock in the afternoon, there began to be a feeling in the air that there would be a fierce clash in the near future. For the unarmed students, the only possible weapons were crowbars and kerosene taken from gas stations. One group loaded five drums into a truck and filled them to the brim with kerosene. With the full drums they drove off in the direction of the martial law forces. They set fire to torches and tossed them at the drums. A hugh pillar of flame rose up in the sky.

As if this were a signal, one by one the martial law forces began to open fire. A student, perhaps in his last year of junior high school, stood on an armored car waving the Korean flag and shouted slogans. Suddenly, blood started pouring from his temples and abdomen and he fell to the ground.

The bullets rained down upon the crowd like hailstones. A youth who had been directing the crowd in front of me shouted out and fell to the ground. Here and there among the crowd people began to take the injured on their backs or put together makeshift stretchers out of their implements to carry the injured and dead from their midst. The youths fell like petals from a flower, nameless and innocent.

How will we record the name of that youth who was shot down by his fellow Koreans in senseless death while waving his country's flag? Will he go down as a delinquent, a suspected communist banded together with treasonable forces, a spy working against his country? An unknown flower

11

0024

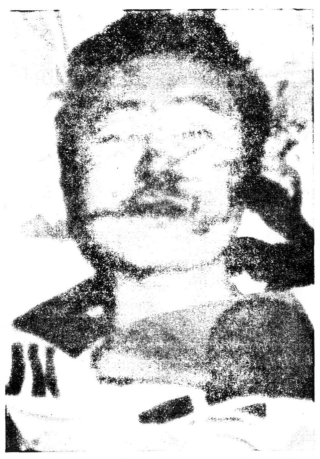

Body of a dead demonstrator wrapped in a flag

in the field cut down before it had a chance to bear fruit or give forth its perfume. What name shall we give to that young bloom now covered with frost?

There was the flag torn and tattered and stained with blood but still fluttering. In it were bullet holes as well as the contained hostility and resentment of the people.

What is it that today's intellectuals and religious people should do more than anything else? The people's resentment which has been collecting over many years with breast-beating the only outlet -- if we ignore it and join with the forces of power and immorality in order to achieve personal safety and prosperity, thus only increasing the government's oppression and power, what will happen to that accumulated rage in the future?

In our current crisis with the course of our history broken and the pulse of our people seemingly cut off, can we afford to hold on to a dream of a future heaven? Sa Ryuk Shin, who failed in their attempt to bring back Tan Jong, and Chung Mong-ju, who gave his blood to oppose the government of Yi Tae-jo -- these people have gone down in our history as heroes. Why then

will these young people falling for the same just cause be called rioting hooligans? What personal gain could they have pursued, going as they did to such cruel deaths?

The crowd retreated to escape the bullets and turned a street corner only to find another disaster awaiting them there. As several thousand people attempted to crowd into that narrow street only a few yards wide, many people were crushed and some 50 people were killed or wounded. In this melee I thought, "Well, I escaped bullets and bayonets only to meet my end here" and closed my eyes. Miraculously, however, I lived to tell about it.

"Citizens, donate your blood! We need blood. People are dying from blood loss." The students were using microphones to make appeals for blood donors. Several men and women came forth to donate blood. I boarded an ambulance on which the words "Blood Bank Car" had been written in real blood. The vehicle departed for the Red Cross Hospital.

The smell of blood and injury greeted me at the entry and I wanted to vomit. Surveying the rooms and halls of this large hospital, I found it to be already filled to overflowing with pa-

12

0025

> There was the flag torn and tattered
> and stained with blood but still flut-
> tering. In it were bullet holes as
> well as the contained hostility and
> resentment of the people.

tients. There was not even space to sit down and give blood. Not knowing what to do, we got into the car again and drove off to another hospital located by Yan-rim-dong Bridge.

Along the way a youth emerged from the crowd and threw a rock at a soldier trying to put down the crowd. The soldier fell down without a struggle. Two boys who looked like students removed his helmet and began pummeling him on the head. The crowd applauded. Looking at the faces of those people witnessing their first act of revenge, you had the feeling of a surging wave of victory. I myself had a pleasant feeling of excitement in seeing them retaliate against their oppressors.

Every hospital we went to was filled to the brim with patients. After finally giving blood, I had a few moments to reflect. When I thought of my blood mixing with that of some nameless youth, a selfless feeling of commiseration and pity rose up in me. "Live! Please live and fight bravely. May none of these young people spill their blood in vain!"

May 23 - Who Incited Them to Rebel?

All the martial law forces sent into Kwangju retreated to the outskirts of the city. The citizens were in control of the Provincial Adminis- tration Building. They had taken weapons and ammunition from Hwa-soon, Song-jong-ri, Kwang- san-gun, Ra-ju, and Han-pyon, arsenals in the area. There were 4000 guns, 50,000 rounds of ammunition, hand grenades, and dynamite, more than enough to do battle with the martial law forces.

Realizing that attempting to do battle with the heavily armed forces using only tools and implements would only lead to more wasted life, the citizens had decided to change their tactics. They discarded their crowbars and shovels and took up carbines, machine guns, and hand grenades. Rumors spread that some people were planning to blow up the Provincial Building and the City Hall with dynamite. I prayed that they were really just rumors.

The army, realizing that the students and towns people were now armed with real weapons, had retreated to the outskirts of town. Hearing this, the people began to display the first signs of a collapse in morale. They were warriors with weapons in their hands but with no enemy. The collapse of morale was a truly unfortunate sign. The citizenry, having lost their battle-

ground, also lost their will and started to roam the streets like a swarm of bees.

Junior high school students were now holding grenades. Elementary school students had car- bines in their hands. In giving weapons to un- trained hands which did not know how to use them, who knew what damage this could have on the towns- people themselves? Once again the city became a city of fear.

Throughout the night they shot off their rifles at the sky. Who had incited these basically good people to revolt? What had given birth to this tragic situation in which they were forced to steal arms? Their hands, unused to holding wea- pons, shot off volleys into the night, turning the night sky into a shower of sparks. The people, fearful that one of those bullets would hit them, closed their doors and held their breaths in their homes.

The next day, I urged my younger brother and my cousin to leave the city. In this South Cholla Province, where all vehicles had been confiscated, we could at least resort to walking, the method of travel of the Yi Dynasty. We re- verted back 300 years in the past. We had gone back to an age which brought back thoughts of straw sandals and bundles carried on the back.

The two of them left, but came back in the afternoon. They had returned in fright after seeing a pile of corpses lying on the railroad tracks. They were the bodies of people who had tried to escape from Kwangju only to be shot down by the army. This army had completely surrounded the city. Inside the city, the demonstrators continued to shoot off their guns day and night. These three days filled with frightening events seemed longer to me than three years.

> Realizing that attempting to do bat-
> tle with the heavily armed forces
> using only tools and implements would
> only lead to more wasted life, the
> citizens decided to change their
> tactics.

We heard the news that members of the new Cabinet (the old Cabinet had been forced to resign after the military coup d'etat on May 17) were planning to visit Kwangju, and the citizens re-assembled at the Provincial Building to meet the prime minister. Tens of thousands of people sat in front of the building for five hours in the hot sun.

They began to take the bodies of the dead from the basement of the building and bring them outside. They wanted to show the prime minister just how ridiculous and false the re- ports had been of how the army had acted with restraint and patience. Upon descending to the basement and seeing the 475 bodies there, some

13

0026

undergone many nights of suffering. Their actions were not hooliganism or misdirected rioting. Were they not following the completely natural and basic direction of history, like the movements of heavenly bodies seeking to return to their natural courses?

A youth was hit. The flesh seemed to be flying from his stomach. As if unaware of the pain, he took his own blood and wrote, "The tree called liberty is nurtured in blood." When such a tragedy is thrust upon our own town, our nation, our fellow countrymen, what possible hopes can we retain?

Seeing the rivers and mountains of our town dyed deep with the color of blood, who can close his or her mouth and say nothing? Will the cries of 800,000 citizens simply disappear without further echo into the empty sky? Will their pains and trials be in vain, going down in the records as nothing but a riot incited by "impure elements"?

with faces burned beyond recognition, people once again gnashed their teeth in anger and indignation. As it became five and then six o'clock, the citizens gradually began to lose spirit and disperse. The bodies were taken back to the basement.

The new prime minister, who had promised to meet with the people and work out a solution, instead broke that promise and, without setting a foot within the city, labeled the incident a riot. After receiving a report from the chief of the martial law forces, he did not bother to stay any longer and flew back to Seoul. This was how he carried out his first action after taking office.

He left with words in his mouth like "complete lawlessness" and "a city with hooligans in control." If that is the case, who are the ones who incited the people to hooliganism?

> I can still hear the heart-rending gasps of the townspeople striving to preserve their lives. Their struggle was just, a fight for the most basic of God-given rights.

I can still hear the heart-rending gasps of the townspeople striving to preserve their lives. Their struggle was just, a fight for the most basic of God-given rights. Was their struggle not an expression of their desire to gain a human existence? For the sake of their country's future they had judged that they had to stand up at this moment in history, and as a result had

The Emperor's New Clothes.

Throughout the Honam area, where communications had come to a total halt, seemingly endless lines of worried parents headed toward Kwangju to check on their sons and daughters. After witnessing the tragedy in the city, we now had to witness another tragedy in the reactions of these sorrowful parents, many of them old, who came from all surrounding areas.

Upon finding that their child was dead, they beat the ground and demanded to know who had killed him or her. Those who found their sons or daughters alive wept tears of joy. But it proved very difficult to rescue them. This was because the forces surrounding the city had now blocked off all escape routes.

The flyers which the military dropped from airplanes had the words "A Petition" written across the top, but the contents were pure intimidation, written with deceit. The announcements that people heard over the radio also only served to incite them further. "The government acted with restraint and patience, without opening fire, and several soldiers were the victims of rioters."

The entire citizenry was being described as hardened spies and criminals. "Please return to your homes at once and restore order." "Detach

14

0027

yourself from the rioters!" "The wounded are receiving good treatment." With these outright lies they sought to get the people on their side. Upon reading the flyers containing these lies, the citizens could not hold back their rage. "There are limits to how much you can deceive people. Can they really do something like this?"

The reports from the government were such that even if they had told the people that milk comes from cows probably no one would have believed them. In seeing the government officials relying on force to make their excuses, how could anyone of conscience hold back their indignation? In this city of death, a city which had become a sea of blood, the authorities labeled the cries of the people as those of hooligans. What kind of treachery is this?

Of course, no one denies the possibility that, in the midst of such great confusion, actual spies may have made their way into their midst. No one can deny the suggestion that "black guests" (North Korean spies) may have made use of arson and murder to create an atmosphere of fear as part of an attempt to overthrow the government. But the actions of the people were by no means the result of instigation by spies. Not even the most fervent anti-communist would have been able to sit down in his room and think of his own safety in the face of what was happening in Kwangju.

> My younger brother and my cousin left Kwangju, but returned in fright after seeing a pile of corpses lying on the railroad tracks. They were the bodies of people who had tried to escape the city only to be shot down by the army.

Mouths which are unable to speak the truth as it is. Pens which are unable to write the truth as it is. Radio and TV stations which are unable to report the truth as it is. This is South Korea today.

What is the fairy tale about the "Emperor's New Clothes"? The government officials are too afraid to tell the emperor that he is wearing nothing at all. In order to present themselves as the most spotless, the most true, the most patriotic, all the officials made believe they were feeling clothes that they couldn't even see and praised their wonderfulness.

Today, the army is like that emperor whose deceits and treacheries cannot be pointed out. A foolish emperor goes out with no clothes, and the officials are unable to tell him that he is naked in order to save their own shameful skins. They have become the very embodiment of false praise and deception.

But in the fairy tale a little child points

out the truth. He calls out in a loud voice that "The emperor is naked!" Is there not even one public servant in South Korea today who has the conscience of this child? Why do they refuse to point out the shame of that nakedness and allow themselves to become eunuchs of power? They think that if they continue to deceive the people with this trick or that ploy they will be able to stay in power. They are trying to deceive the people whom they should be serving. But the people cannot be fooled indefinitely.

> Mouths which are unable to speak the truth as it is. Pens which are unable to write the truth as it is. Radio and TV stations which are unable to report the truth as it is. This is South Korea today.

Today's politicians must awaken from the mistaken belief left over from the colonial period (when Korea was a colony of Japan) that you can overcome any opposition in governing simply by using force and killing. In front of people who lost their sons, their husbands, their daughters, in front of the corpses, some of them charred so black from flame throwers that they couldn't be identified, do you actually pretend not to hear the sorrowful cries of the surviving families?

History has taught us that those who conquer through injustice will definitely be crushed by the weight of the injustice they have committed. We must move with all haste away from this primitive system of government which throws people of conscience into dark prisons and attempts to hide the truth with arrest and torture, killing and oppression.

You may cite Amin in Uganda or Hitler, or Nero of Ancient Rome, but we who have no way of knowing those dictators firsthand are still left baffled by our own country's present system of governing. Looking at those people fleeing across the river attempting to escape from that city of fear, I could not find a whit of difference between them and refugees fleeing a war-wasted land. Even officers among the troops were shaking with rage and disgust at the terrible loss of life that this tragedy had brought about.

A certain university student who was leading a line of cars in the demonstations reported 1,200 as the number who were shot dead, in addition to another 800 or so who were killed either in traffic accidents or from bayonet wounds. But we will not be able to verify these numbers until a full body count is taken. Since many of the wounded who crowded into the hospitals probably died or will die because of the lack of available blood and drugs, the number of dead will no doubt rise even higher. One religious group has cited more than 20,000 for the number of dead and wounded.

15

0028

The Torn and Tattered Flag.

Look at the flag tattered by bullet, stained with the blood of its countrymen, laden with the collected resentment of its people. Who will be brave enough to find a solution to this collected anger?

When I close my eyes, I still see it. That torn and tattered flag. The hot tears flow over my cheeks without end.

Translation: Japanese Catholic Council for Justice and Peace. "These materials were received from reliable sources in the Korean Catholic Church who verified the validity of the contents before sending them to us. We take responsibility for the truth of the contents." -- Japanese Catholic Council for Justice and Peace, June 6, 1980.

Excerpts from Various Kwangju Reports

Many non-governmental accounts of the situation in Kwangju are now available -- some written diaries, some descriptions by reporters and other individuals, and some statements released by groups such as the Catholic Archdiocese of Kwangju. Perhaps the most remarkable aspect of these various accounts is their consistency with one another. The following are excerpts from some of these accounts.

A universally misunderstood idea about the Kwangju incident is that it just happened in that town of 800,000 and a few select towns around it. Nothing could be farther from the case. Direction and leadership came from the urban areas but the rural areas supplied the support. Before the road south was cut at the Nam-pyong Pass on the night of May 21 vehicles could travel the entire area to cheering crowds and people handing out supplies and riding in their vehicles.

The countryside contributed a sizeable portion of the support by keeping Kwangju as best supplied as it could with food stuffs and other essentials. Journalists never reported this as they never made it into the rural areas. The government can always blame it on unruly city dwellers -- but the thousands of subsistance farmers know better.

> --From the diary of a foreigner living in the countryside near Kwangju

(May 19) When youths attempted to flee into the houses, the soldiers went in and dragged them out, even pulling out any young people who happened to be living in the house. They beat them and used their bayonets on them. Paratroopers tied one university student to the back of a truck and dragged him around the streets. The youth died from his wounds.

The brutality of the paratroopers did not stop at this point. Arriving in the vicinity of Sang-mu Dae, I saw a girl student from Central High School wiping blood from a wound on her forehead and weeping. She seemed to be half out of her senses. It took about ten minutes for her to regain enough composure to talk.

"We had planned to leave class to join in the demonstration but troops were guarding the main gate. After class we attempted to leave but the soldiers flailed out at us with bayonets. About twenty of my friends died from bleeding. Even my teacher was stabbed to death." At this point, she began to tremble and weep.

> --From the testimony of a Christian who served on the citizen's committee established to negotiate with the military

(The situation in Kwangju following the take-over of the Provincial Adminstration Building): The students took it upon themselves to form a group to maintain order within the city. The Provincial Building became their temporary headquarters. The square in front of that building as well as Kum-nam Avenue were filled to over-flowing with people.

A committee was formed made up of religious leaders, student representatives, professors, lawyers, and journalists. It resolved that to

16

avoid further bloodshed, the martial law forces must not be allowed to come back into the city. Receiving this promise from the military, they began collecting the weapons. They decided on demands that President Choi acknowledge responsibility for the events in Kwangju, agree to compensate victims, and publicly promise that the government would take action against participants in the demonstrations.

While discussions of these matters were going on with the military, the leader of the martial law forces broke faith and gave orders to make an armed assault on the city. Fearing that the streets would become a blood bath if the military moved into the city, the citizens' committee decided to make a protest in non-violent death and marched to the front of the tanks. The forces gave way and the commander went into conference with the committee members.

At 2 am on May 27 in complete disregard for the efforts of the committee the army released flares and opened attack.

--From "The True Facts Relating
to the Incidents at Kwangju,"

prepared by the Archdiocese of Kwangju. As a result of this document and others, six Catholic priests were arrested by the martial law command.

The martial law authorities have promised that they would be of assistance and make reparations if people (in Kwangju) cooperated in reporting the missing and injured. A certain family did so, bringing along a picture of the person in question and giving details on his background. The authorities immediately sent out a bulletin to arrest that person.

Regarding the wounded, witnesses have been asked to supply information about what day, where, at what time, and by whom the victim was stabbed. If the witnesses say that they are unable to remember the face and name of the soldier, they are accused of spreading vicious rumors and are punished. As a result, family members are very troubled and do not feel free to report on missing or wounded persons.

--Information from Kwangju

Kwangju citizens meet after troops are forced to withdraw from the city.

17

Chosun University Students' Statement

O, this is a time of tragedy in our nation's history. God has forsaken us. The military, whose mandate is to defend the nation, has slaughtered its own people.

Our nation's heart is shattered, and this is a day of unbearable tragedy. On the night of May 17, the military under Chon Too-hwan's control extended martial law to cover the entire country. They arrested politicians and democratic leaders critical of the military's rule, crushing our hopes for democracy.

Their betrayal evoked the students of Chonnam University, Chosun University, junior colleges, high schools, and citizens to rise up in a peaceful demonstration in Kwangju. The martial law command sent 30,000 riot police into the city. They blocked the roads to isolate the demonstrators, and discharged tear gas into the crowds who were unable to escape.

Then nearly 3000 paratroopers from Seoul were sent in. These troops began indiscriminately killing people with their clubs and bayonets. Soon the streets were colored by blood. Bodies were thrown into army trucks.

They chased young people into houses, breaking doors and fences. Several girl students were dragged out of houses and were brutally killed by bayonets in front of others. Such brutal killing evoked the wrath of the citizens, causing them to rise up to resist. But their empty-handed protests were only an invitation for them, too, to be killed. A 70-year-old woman, protesting the killing of a girl student, was also killed on the spot by the paratroopers.

Another girl student was caught as she carried stones, and she was stabbed to death in plain sight of others. Eyewitnesses shouted at the soldiers, but they threatened to kill them as well, waving their blood-stained bayonets. Many girl students had their clothing torn, and others were stripped, and they were dumped into army trucks.

The military stopped buses and cars and arrested young people riding in them. Before dragging them away, the troops kicked and trampled on them. Their flesh was torn and bones were broken. Many bodies of young people were found in the waiting room of the bus terminal. Many other bodies were left on street corners until late at night.

The military forced the young people to lie down in the street in rows like sardines. They shouted to each other, "Kill any young person you see!"

Older people, seeing this brutal genocide, said that it was worse than the communists during the Korean War. Their sorrow and despair are hard to describe.

In the city of Kwangju just being young is a crime, and the young are condemned to be crippled for life or to be killed. "We can kill 70% of the people of Kwangju" and "How many dogs have you caught?" were the slogans of the military.

The military followed a wounded girl student into a hospital, beat up the nurses, and destroyed the instruments necessary for her treatment.

Alas, the genocide of unarmed people in Vietnam is being repeated upon our own people. The patriotic citizens of Kwangju rose up because of their anger at one of the most barbarous massacres in the history of the world. They confronted the well‑armed and well-trained paratroopers with their bare hands.

The people's anger was also directed at the mass media because they distorted the truth. They set fire to the Munhwa Broadcasting Company Building, several police boxes, army trucks, and tear gas launchers. All these were the spontaneous reactions to cruel attacks upon unarmed people. The martial law command has distorted the truth, claiming instead that citizens had planned such distructive actions.

By the night of May 20, all communication channels within South Cholla Province had been cut off, and the troops' genocidal operation moved into its last phase. Even high school students were beaten up and crippled. So far the number of victims is known to be more than 200, and more than 10,000 have been wounded.

The Korean mass media kept silent about these events, especially during the five-day nightmare between May 18 and May 21. They parroted the scripts handed out by Chon Too-hwan, saying that the incident was instigated by "impure elements." The sun refuses to shine on us, and we cannot describe our broken hearts in writing.

On May 21, Chon Too-hwan branded a number of facts as "groundless rumors," but we confirm the the following happened: on the first day, at least 40 people were killed in bright daylight by the bayonets of the paratroopers, and a girl student, stripped and tied to the fountain in front of Kwangju Railway Station, had her breasts cut off before being killed.

At the present, the paratroopers have been driven out of the city by the citizens. Many government buildings in the city are now burning,

18

and all the transportation and communication lines have been cut. Citizens destroyed a railway leading into Kwangju as well, in order to stop the military from moving into the city. The citizens are pledging to each other that "we will die together" and "let them kill us"...

During the Pusan-Masan uprising (October 1979) the military sent soldiers from the Cholla area to put down the people. Now in Kwangju they have deployed paratroopers from Kyongsang Province to exploit regionalism in manipulating the people. Chon Too-hwan is dividing the nation to remain in power, and this is a clear betrayal of our nation's dreams. We will not sit quietly and watch such things take place.

In order to pass on to our next generation a glorious history no longer tainted with oppression and exploitation, we have to drive Chon Too-hwan and his cohorts out of our society. With this task in our hearts, let us rise up together, fight together, and march together, singing our national anthem, as long as we can breathe.

Long live the Republic of Korea!

Long live democracy!

The 800,000 citizens of Kwangju are witnesses to the unbelievable situation described above. The citizens of Kwangju will fight until the very last one.

--Chosun University Committee for Democratic Struggle

Kwangju, Korea -- May 22, 1980

Note: Whoever has seen this leaflet, please duplicate it and pass it on. This is our only way to report the situation since the newspapers have been silenced.

Those professors at Chosun University who had signed statements for the liberalization of universities were beaten up in front of their families at noon on May 17. Many were vomiting blood before being taken away. Their whereabouts and whether they are still alive are unknown at this time.

The citizens are in charge of maintaining order throughout South Cholla Province, since we cannot leave this responsibility to the police and the military who are killing their own people.

19

0032

Chronology of Events in Kwangju

Oct 26
1979   President Park Chung-hee is assassinated by KCIA director Kim Jae-kyu in the
        midst of growing demonstrations for democracy; martial law is imposed
        throughout South Korea except for Cheju Island; Prime Minister Choi Kyu-ha
        becomes president.

Nov 24 140 leaders of the democratic movement are arrested at a meeting at the Seoul
        YWCA calling for rapid democratization. Of these, a number are taken to
        the Army Security Command, headed by Gen. Chon Too-hwan, where they are
        brutally tortured.

Dec 12 Gen. Chon Too-hwan leads a coup within the military in which Gen. Chung Seung-
        hwa, Army chief of staff and martial law commander, is arrested; troops
        guarding the DMZ are illegally moved; and Gen. Chon's son-in-law is
        appointed the new martial law commander. Gen. Chon is known to have been
        a strong supporter of Pres. Park.

Mar 11
1980   Gen. John Wickham, head of the U.S.-South Korea Joint Command, is quoted in
        the Asian Wall Street Journal as saying that the South Korean military's
        proper role includes "being watch-dogs on political activity that could
        be destabilizing, and in a way making judgements about the eligibility and
        reliability of political candidates that may have some adverse influence
        on stability."

Apr 14 Gen. Chon Too-hwan becomes acting director of the KCIA while continuing as
        head of the Army Security Command. Under South Korean law it is illegal
        for persons in the military to hold civilian positions.

Mid Apr Widespread campus demonstrations and labor strikes begin. Students call for
        campus reforms and reinstitution of student councils, which were banned
        during Park's presidency. Workers demand unpaid back wages and wage
        increases to help compensate for inflation, running at an annual rate of
        89.2% for the first three months of 1980.

Early May Demonstrations continue to grow. Students begin peaceful, disciplined
        demonstrations off-campus calling for the end of martial law, resignation
        of Gen. Chon Too-hwan, and the abolition of compulsory off-campus military
        training.

May 15 Over 50,000 students demonstrate in downtown Seoul. Prime Minister Shin
        Hyon-hwak announces that the government will make concessions and try to
        speed democratization.

May 16 Students in Seoul call off demonstrations to await government's response.
        Kim Dae-jung and Kim Young-sam, opposition political leaders, meet and
        urge students to exercise "maximum self-restraint." In Kwangju, 35,000
        students and citizens hold a peaceful torchlight procession and then call
        off further demonstrations.

May 17 Gen. Chon Too-hwan leads a coup d'etat. Nationwide martial law is declared,
        forbidding all political activity; universities are closed; National
        Assembly is banned from meeting (it was to have met on May 20, when a vote
        was expected to end the already-existing limited martial law); criticism
        of present and past national leaders is forbidden; hundreds of democratic
        leaders, politicians, students, and others are arrested, including promi-
        nent opposition leader Kim Dae-jung.

May 18 In Kwangju, approximately 500 students demonstrate, demanding the end of
        martial law and the resignation of Gen. Chon. Martial law troops re-in-
        forced by dreaded paratroopers surround demonstrators and spectators and
        indiscriminately beat and bayonet them. Several dozen people are killed.

May 19 Military in Kwangju harass townspeople, indiscriminately singling out people,
        particularly those who appear   to be students, and brutally beat or bayonet
        them. Citizens join the student demonstrations, shocked at the military

20

0033

brutality. Demonstrations are held in over 30 locations, and the main streets are filled with tens of thousands of people. Hundreds are killed, including children, pregnant women, and old people.

May 20   Word of paratrooper brutality spreads. Over 100,000 Kwangju citizens demonstrate; two radio stations are burned for broadcasting falsified news reports about the situation. Hospitals are completely filled. In Seoul, the military forces the Cabinet to resign.

May 21   About 200,000 people demonstrate in Kwangju; city is sealed off by government troops. Many army vehicles commandeered by demonstrators; citizens obtain arms from police stations and army stockpiles; army retreat from city; telephone service is cut. At about midnight demonstrators take over the Provincial Adminstration Building. In Seoul, new Cabinet is appointed, all with close ties with the military. Members of the Korean Journalists Association stop work to protest arrests of members following their decision to defy censorship.

May 22   Citizens control Kwangju. Military accuses opposition leader Kim Dae-jung of sedition for supposedly instigating student demonstrators and rebellion in Kwangju, even though he was under arrest when it began. 10,000 troops encircle Kwangju, where people form a citizens council, which begins negotiations with the military. Demonstrations spread to neighboring areas. U.S. Pentagon announces that it has released 4 battalions of Korean troops under its control for use in suppressing the Kwangju demonstrations. According to one report, 500 people are confirmed dead in Kwangju, 960 reported missing.

May 23   Hodding Carter, U.S. State Department spokesperson, announces to reporters that the Carter administration "has decided to support the restoration of security and order in South Korea while deferring pressure for political liberalization." Kwangju is orderly and quiet, and reportedly 85 - 95% of weapons have been returned to the citizens committee. In Seoul, the military execute Kim Jae-kyu and 4 others convicted of assassinating Pres. Park.

May 24   50,000 Kwangju residents demonstrate in the rain to protest martial law in spite of warnings from the martial law command. The army moves tanks into the edge of the city. Troops around the city stop anyone trying to enter or leave.

May 25   30,000 people assemble in front of the Provincial Administration Building. Citizens council meets to formulate demands.

May 26   Citizens in Kwangju appeal to the U.S. government to help negotiate a truce.

May 27   The U.S. State Department declines to mediate, saying "We recognize that a situation of total disorder and disruption in a major city cannot be allowed to go on indefinitely." One hour later thousands of martial law troops invade Kwangju. Many persons are killed, military regains control.

Afterward   Martial law troops search house-to-house for participants in the demonstrations. Thousands of people are detained, interrogated, and released or arrested. Military suppresses accurate accounts of the situation. Numerous publications in the Cholla Provinces (where Kwangju is) are banned. Kim Dae-jung and others are brought to trial on charges of sedition, with a possible death sentence.

'Kwangju, Cross of Our Nation'

O Kwangju, and Mudung Mountain.
Between death and more death,
City of our eternal youth, flowing
with blood and tears!

Our father: Where has he gone?
Mother: Where has she fallen?
Our sons:
Where were they killed and buried?
And our lovely daughters:
Where are they lying, mouths agape?
Where were our spirits
torn apart, ripped to shreds?

Kwangju, by the flocks of birds
and by God as well
abandoned: City of our bloody wounds,
where the truly human
beings still abide, dawn to dark
thrown down, beaten, and yet rising again.
In death refusing
and through death seeking life.
Province of Lamentation! Phoenix!

Though the sea winds tumble down headlong,
and all the other mountains of this age
tower up in a sham,
no one can rip,
no one can steal
this banner, Freedom's,
banner of humanity,
with flesh and bone given life
at the core.

City of ours!
Our songs, our dreams, our love
at times mount up like great waves,
at times like an ancient tomb
collapse, and yet

Kwangju! O, Kwangju!
Shouldering the cross of this nation,
He climbs over Mudung Mountain,
over Golgotha, the Son of Heaven,
on His body
the wounds,
the death.

Truly we have died.
We who cannot love this land,
who cannot love our children
have died.
Truly we have died.

From Chung-jang Road, and Kum-nam;
From Hwa-chong Block, from San-su and Yongbong,
Chi-san, Yang-dong, Kye-rim,
and on, and on...
O wind that has blown down upon us, swallowing
our blood and pieces of flesh!
Ceaseless futility of life!

*by Kim Chun-tae, poet
and teacher at Chon-nam
High School, Kwangju*

*translated by David R.
McCann*

22

0035

Thrown down again and again,
is weeping all that is left us?
To draw a breath: is that all
of terror and of life?

Those who have survived
hang their heads in guilt.
Those who have survived
have all lost their souls.
To face a bowl of rice
is too difficult, too frightening
to do.

I died, my love, waiting
for you, waiting outside the gate
for you...
Why was it my life they robbed?
It was our lot to live
in a rented room, but how much gladness we knew!
How I wanted to provide well for you!
O, my love!

And I, with this body bearing life
have now found death. My love,
forgive me. My love,
your child, yours...
O, my love, I have ended
by killing you.

O Kwangju! Mudung Mountain!
Piercing the very center of death
and emerging, city
of our eternal youth, vibrant
with the fluttering white cotton sleeves!
Phoenix
          that you are
                    Phoenix!
                         PHOENIX!

Bearing the cross of this land
returning over Golgotha,
Son of our nation's god:
Jesus who once died
and rose again:
Has He not lived until today,
and forever?
And we who have died by the hundreds,
our true love will return to life.
Our fire! Our glory! Our pain!
Even more surely, we shall survive.
Our strength increases, and even we
shall rise into the blue heavens
and touch our lips to the sun and moon.

O Kwangju! O Mudung Mountain!
Our eternal banner,
dream,
and cross.
Even as life flows on,
City of Youth
may you be ever younger.
For now we are sure,
gathering together. Hands joined
in sure affirmation,
we have risen.

23

North American Coalition
for Human Rights in KOREA

110 Maryland Avenue NE, Washington, DC 20002

FIRST CLASS MAIL

0037

North American Coalition
for Human Rights in

KOREA

110 Maryland Avenue, NE
Washington, DC 20002
(202) 546-4304
Telex: 292001 HR WASH

0038

Korea: A Peninsula Divided, A People Oppressed

The Korean War ended in 1953 but the governments of north and south Korea remain hostile, heavily armed enemies. For over thirty years the division of the country has kept apart families separated during the war. Each side uses the tension caused by the division to justify the curtailment of human rights and political freedom. The presence of nuclear weapons in south Korea and the resistance to negotiations increase the threat that hostilities on the peninsula could lead to a larger conflict involving the superpowers.

Under Kim Il Sung, north Korea has become a closed, regimented society. The United States has no diplomatic relations with north Korea. The lack of reliable information about north Korea makes a realistic assessment of their intentions impossible and the reduction of tension difficult.

Since 1948, democratic development in the south has been sidetracked by power hungry leaders. President Syngman Rhee was forced to step down in 1960 following massive student demonstrations against his government's corruption. The transition government that replaced Rhee was overthrown in 1961 by Gen. Park Chung Hee. Park ruled for 18 years, promising prosperity but relying heavily on foreign investment, low wages and the suppression of dissent. In 1979, Park was assassinated just as the democratic movement was gaining clarity and strength. Moving quickly to exploit the opening provided by Park's death, Gen. Chun Doo Whan consolidated his control of the military and in May, 1980, seized the government.

Jailed dissidents, torture, press censorship and the suppression of political, academic and labor activities are only the most visible signs of repression in south Korea today. An American missionary in Seoul said in late 1983 that since Chun took over, "the suppression of civil liberties and rejection of human rights has become subtly systematic."

US Korea Policy: Rhetoric vs. Reality

In principle, the United States has supported democracy in Korea since 1948. In reality, it has supported successive military-backed dictatorships. Billions of dollars of US aid has created the world's sixth largest army in south Korea, which faces the Soviet and Chinese supplied north Korean army, the world's fifth largest. 40,000 US troops and nuclear weapons stand guard to protect the current regime from attack. Korea's "economic miracle," fueled largely by US loans and investment, has brought huge profits for big Korean and foreign companies, but only by the repression and exploitation of Korean workers. For thirty years, US policy has sacrificed support for human rights to concern for national security, narrowly defined in military terms. The result has been continuing political instability and frustration of the Korean people's oft-expressed desire for democracy. Without the restoration of democracy there can be neither stability nor security.

Supporting the Democratic Movement

In 1973, shortly after President Park declared himself president-for-life under a revised constitution, the theological leaders of Korea drafted what was to become the founding declaration of the present movement for democracy in Korea. In part, that statement said: "We as Christians must struggle to destroy this system of extreme dehumanization and injustice; for we are witness to the ongoing movement of the Messianic Kingdom in history, in which the poor will be enriched, the oppressed vindicated, and peace will be enjoyed by all the people."

In 1975, in response to those concerns and other appeals for solidarity and support, church groups in the United States and Canada made a commitment to support the struggle for human rights and democracy in Korea. The North American Coalition for Human Rights in Korea (NACHRK) was founded to provide information and analysis about the situation in Korea to the people of the United States and Canada.

"NACHRK is the most important organization and channel through which we can transmit our struggle to the world in general and to our friends in the United States in particular."

Kim Dae Jung
democratic opposition leader

NACHRK mobilizes people in North America to advocate for policies by our governments that enhance and protect the human and political rights of the Korean people so as to enable them to shape their own political and economic systems free from suppression by domestic authorities or interference from other countries. Our activity is rooted in the biblical tradition of *shalom* and the precepts of international law enshrined in the Universal Declaration of Human Rights.

NACHRK gathers and distributes news from and about Korea and translations of important documents from the democratic movement. We work with policymaking bodies within the government and churches and occasionally testify before Congressional committees.

Among the approximately 40 organizations that support and work with NACHRK are:

The National Council of Churches in the USA
The Anglican Church of Canada
The United Methodist Church
The Presbyterian Church, USA
The United Church of Canada
Maryknoll Fathers and Brothers
The United Church of Christ
The Christian Church (Disciples of Christ)
The US Catholic Conference
The Columban Fathers
Church Women United
and various local and regional human rights organizations.

North American Coalition
for Human Rights in Korea

Honorary Chairperson	Kim Chai Choon
Chairperson	Peggy Billings
Vice Chairperson	Lee Sang Chul
Secretary	Edwin Luidens
Treasurer	Pang Sook-ja
Executive Director	Pharis J. Harvey

**North American Coalition
for Human Rights in Korea**
110 Maryland Avenue, NE
Washington, DC 20002
(202) 546-4304

NACHRK publications include the *Human Rights Data Packet,* a collection of translated documents, news clippings and brief analysis of current developments in Korea with policy and action suggestions, and *Korea Update*, a summary of current political and economic developments in Korea. The *Human Rights Data Packet,* formerly *Key Contact,* is published 10-14 times a year and costs $20. *Korea Update* is published four times a year and costs $5. NACHRK also offers a *Perspectives on Korea* series on topics relevant to the human rights situation in Korea. The series includes essays by Korean specialists, journalists and activists. *Call or write NACHRK for a complete resource list.* For a weekly update of news from Korea, call *Korea-phone* (202) 546-NEWS.

□ I would like to help support the work of NACHRK. Enclosed is a tax-deductible donation of $ _____.

□ Please send me the following publications:

_____

_____

□ Bill me   □ Payment enclosed _____

Name _____

Address _____

City, State, Zip _____

*Tax-deductible donations should be made payable to: United Methodist Board of Global Ministries project #006827-1 R-A.

0040

PREPARED STATEMENT BY

PHARIS J. HARVEY

EXECUTIVE DIRECTOR

NORTH AMERICAN COALITION FOR HUMAN RIGHTS IN KOREA

WASHINGTON, D.C.

PROSPECTS FOR DEMOCRACY IN SOUTH KOREA

JOINT HEARING OF THE FOREIGN AFFAIRS COMMITTEE

SUBCOMMITTEES ON ASIAN AND PACIFIC AFFAIRS

AND HUMAN RIGHTS AND INTERNATIONAL ORGANIZATIONS

UNITED STATES HOUSE OF REPRESENTATIVES

MARCH 5, 1985

0041

PROSPECTS FOR DEMOCRACY IN KOREA

Thank you, Mr. Chairman. My name is Pharis J. Harvey. I am the Executive
Director of the North American Coalition for Human Rights in Korea, an endeavor
supported by both Catholic and Protestant churches in the United States and Canada.
Formed in 1975 at the request of Christians in South Korea who were under
persecution for their adherence to democratic freedom, the North American Coalition
works to provide to the churches, to the press and to governmental and non-
governmental organizations information and analysis of the current human rights
situation in Korea, both north and south, and to advocate policies that enhance
protection of those rights.

Earlier this month, I was privileged to be part of a delegation of persons from
the U.S., Canada and the Philippines who accompanied the Korean opposition leader
Kim Dae Jung back to Seoul as an expression of concern about his freedom and safety.
This visit to Korea was important not only in terms of its objective, which I
believe was fully realized, but also as a source of insight into a critically
important transition period which South Korea has entered in its political
development.

In many ways, the attitudes shown by the United States Government will be the
key external factor in influencing the direction of that transformation. I am
greatly encouraged that you have scheduled today's hearing as part of a
Congressional effort to assess that role.

I. Security and Democracy in Korea

I would like to preface my response to your questions with a brief comment
about the presuppositions that have prevailed in the U.S. in the debate over human
rights and security in recent years. U.S. Korea policy is perhaps the most extreme
instance of zero-sum thinking about these matters, and it is increasingly evident

1

0042

that such thinking is blinding us to the very serious security threats that inhere in politically repressed but unstable situations.

Section 502(b) of the Foreign Assistance Act requires that "no security assistance may be provided to any country the government of which engages in a consistent pattern of gross violation of internationally recognized human rights exist warranting provision of such assistance." Successive administrations, both Democrat and Republican, have alternated between attempts to demonstrate that the Republic of Korea was not a <u>consistent</u> violator of human rights and efforts to show that special security risks warranted the provision of aid in spite of such violations. The public debate conducted within these narrow parameters has consequently come to pit security needs against human rights concerns, seeing efforts to enhance respect for human rights as expendable if a country faced a serious security threat. Since South Korea has faced a genuine threat to its security from a hostile and heavily armed regime to its north, a consistent pattern of excusing human rights violations has characterized U.S. policy.

It is our opinion that this formulation is fundamentally wrong and not in keeping with the intent of the law. We believe that <u>the protection of human rights is an essential ingredient in national security,</u> for deprivation of rights creates a corrosive social environment that undermines the unity of will necessary for a nation to defend itself against or negotiate with any serious adversary. The <u>strongest, and most essential element of national security is the commonness of will between government and people.</u> As our experience in Vietnam showed, where this is missing, no amount of security assistance from outside can safeguard a government from defeat.

Nowhere is this truer than in the Republic of Korea today, where a well-educated and increasingly sophisticated people have in the name of national security been prevented by draconian laws and overwhelming police force from active

2   0043

participation in the political decisions that affect them. Furthermore, a younger generation of alienated students and workers, with no memory of the atrocities of the 1950-53 war, has come into adulthood questioning the national security ideology that is used to justify continued suppression of human rights and to prolong the division of their country. By this group, the United States is viewed as a supporter of repression at home rather than as a protector against foreign invasion. This generation, increasingly restive in the past couple years, is capable of a level of social and political unrest that could seriously undermine the economic and social fabric of the country. It goes without saying that major American economic and military interests would be affected by such a disruption.

In a situation in which north and south Korea have reached approximate parity in military strength, and where the cost of all-out war by invasion is beyond rational consideration to either government for a broad range of reasons, internal dissension and unrest are a necessary condition for any provocative behavior. Where the objective conditions for unrest already exist, the danger of subversion and external manipulation is far greater.

The issue of whether South Korea is a democracy is, therefore, important not only from the perspective of our nation's stated policy of strengthening democracies around the world, but also from the viewpoint of our national security interests. It is with both interests in mind that I will attempt to assess the present state of democracy in South Korea and to make some policy recommendations.

II. Establishment of the Fifth Republic and its Character

There have been several recent changes in the political situation of South Korea, but in order to place them in their proper perspective, it is useful to recall the context and the structural continuity of the political system in which these changes have occurred. At the risk of repeating a ritual chant of complaints, let me summarize the process by which the current regime took and holds power.

3

0044

The group of military figures led by Maj. Gen. Chun Doo Hwan, commander of military intelligence, took over the Korean government by a series of power seizures in 1979-80, first by a coup within the ROK Army on December 12, 1979, then by taking over the Central Intelligence Agency in March, 1980, and finally through the extension of martial law and rule by military council from May 17, 1980 until late January, 1981. During the period of martial law, the national assembly was closed, all political parties were banned, and Kim Dae Jung and several hundred politicians and political activists were arrested. Kim was sentenced to death in a military tribunal on charges the State Department characterized as "far-fetched." Thousands of government officials were purged, 551 prominent persons were banned from politics until 1988, 300 labor union officials were fired, 700 journalists were forced to resign from their news organizations, all electronic media was taken over by the government directly (except the Christian Broadcasting Service, which was forbidden to broadcast news), 132 publications were banned, 86 university professors were driven from their teaching posts., With these changes in place, a new constitution was written by the military (and adopted by a referendum without debate in October, 1980).

When people in Kwangju,the capital of Kim Dae Jung's home province, protested the beginning of these measures by demonstrations on May 18, 1980, paratroopers were sent into the city and left hundreds, perhaps as many as two thousand, dead in a siege that lasted nine days. To this day, the final death toll is not known as it cannot be investigated by any impartial organization.

Under martial law, a series of special restrictive laws were enacted that were given special protection in the new constitution, i.e. they cannot be amended by the National Assembly but only by the Constitution Committee, a body appointed by the president. These laws, still in force today, include: the Law on Assemblies and Demonstrations, which severely restricts the freedom to assemble or demonstrate

4

0045

peaceably; the Basic Press Law that undermines the autonomy or freedom of the press; the National Assembly Election law, with severely restricted campaign and political financing rules that hamper all opposition parties; several laws regulating and restricting trade unions; and the social protection law, which enables the government to keep under special detention for periods of 7 to 10 years any prisoners determined by a special panel, to which the prisoner has no access or appeal, insufficiently repentant at the end of their prison term. More than 2,000 persons are known to be currently incarcerated under this law, for political or criminal offenses.

The new constitution provided for a proportional representation system that on the surface appears similar to parliamentary devices used in other countries to protect under-represented minorities. However, in this case, it is designed to grant a permanent majority to the party in power, by making it virtually impossible for an opposition to reach sufficient strength to challenge it.

The terms of the new basic law called for what the State Department Human Rights report has referred to as a concentration of power in the executive, which is elected indirectly. The legislature has little influence, but even that is concentrated in the government party through the system of proportional election. One hundred eighty four members of the 276-member unicameral National Assembly were to be elected directly, including the top two candidates from each of 92 districts, and 92 were to be appointed on a proportional basis, with the party having the plurality of elected members automatically receiving 62 proportional members. Thus, the government could, by placing either first or second in at least 76 of 92 districts, be guaranteed a majority in the assembly, despite its receiving less than 1/3 of the popular vote. To lose the absolute majority, it would be necessary for the government party to place third in at least 16 districts.

Government control of the new system, of course, depended on the opposition being split into several competing parties. Thus, having banned all existing

0046

5

parties, the government created a variety of new parties in January, 1981, including the ruling Democratic Justice Party, the Korea National Party, the Democratic Korea Party, and the New Socialist Party. Membership of all these parties was chosen by the government, since most politicians of any stature had been banned from political life.

With these "reforms" in place, martial law was lifted in late January, 1981, shortly before Chun Doo Hwan made a state visit to Washington to meet newly inaugurated President Reagan. A few weeks later a national assembly election took place which, to no one's surprise, elected a 55% majority for the government (on a 36% popular vote). Following this, a newly-created 5,000 member electoral college elected Chun Doo Hwan, the only candidate, president by a 99.9% vote. On March 3, 1981, the Fifth Republic was launched.

From its inception, the Chun Doo Hwan government has insisted it will respect the provision in the constitution that forbids the president to serve more than one seven-year term. The promise of "a peaceful transfer of power" has become the government's response to all criticism of its undemocratic character. It hardly bears mentioning that, due to the pattern of action by which this group of generals seized power in 1979-80, that promise is widely believed to be fraudulent or without democratic substance.

From the beginning of the Chun regime, extraordinary political power has rested in the hands of a group of the president's military cronies and followers, primarily graduates of the Korean Military Academy. Every ministry has military people at either the top or second position, with the exception of those ministries responsible for economic affairs. The Blue House is staffed by military advisors in most sensitive posts, particularly those concerned with political affairs. The penetration of a politicized military into civilian politics is thorough.

0047

6

III. The reforms of 1984 and continuing problems

After three years with almost no significant easing of repression, during 1984 a series of steps were taken by the Chun government to accommodate its critics, especially among students and intellectuals. About 220 students imprisoned for political involvement were released and some 1400 students expelled from universities since 1980 were allowed to return to their studies. The 86 professors barred from teaching in 1980 were finally allowed back onto their own campuses, and the government announced that the 700 journalists banned in 1980 could be re-hired by newspapers. (Almost none have been re-hired, as a matter of fact, because of quiet interventions by government agents to prevent it.) Finally, on November 30, all but fifteen of the persons banned from politics were removed from the ban. (Many of them remain unable to participate in politics, however, due to their civil rights having been deprived as part of the political trials in 1980.) The country's two leading dissidents, Kim Dae Jung and Kim Young Sam, and several of their key followers, are among those fifteen.

Human rights monitors such as the Korean National Council of Churches Human Rights Committee, however, have insisted that while this apparent relaxation was taking place, the use of police violence was becoming much more commonplace. In the past two years, the national police forces have been vastly augmented by the creation of two new units: (1) the "Combat Police", reported to number 66,000 men in full battle array who are now positioned daily in buses throughout Seoul, prepared to stop any demonstrations with massive use of "pepper-fog" tear gas; and (2) the so-called "Third Force", plain-clothed police who infiltrate college campuses in large numbers and congregate on streets and in front of Churches and other Christian buildings to intimidate anyone trying to attend meetings related to human rights. It is reported that the "Third Force" personnel are recruited from prisons or from the street gangs that were subjected to "Purification Camp"

7

treatment in 1980.

Whatever the exact nature of the new police, it is undeniable that their numbers have vastly increased and that direct conflict between police and human rights activists has become much more frequent in recent months, as has the number of serious injuries caused by police violence.

While this violence by combat police has most publicly been directed toward students, whose protest demonstrations have been kept from spreading off-campus this past year by the use of unprecedented amounts of tear gas, the unofficial but tolerated violence directed by non-uniformed personnel against human rights organizations, labor unions and churches is perhaps more destructive of the social and political order.

The most glaring instance of this is the 18-month-long campaign being conducted by unknown persons against the Rev. Park Hyung Kyu, pastor of Cheil Presbyterian Church in Seoul, and the past chairperson of the NCC's Human Rights committee, who has been repeatedly beaten by gangs of assailants who refuse to allow the pastor or the congregation to worship in their church building. Appeals to the police for assistance and security have been fruitless. It is reliably reported that some of the gang of men occupying the church are from military intelligence. The Presbyterian Church of the ROK, parent body of Cheil Church, in its General Assembly in September, 1984, directly placed the blame for the violence on the government and called for an end to it. Yet, as late as last week the violence was unabated. I have appended to this testimony a statement about the Cheil Church situation dated February 1, 1985.

Also, it should be added that, while in 1984, student arrests were kept to a minimum, and large numbers of political prisoners were released, beginning in January 1985, there has been a return to an older policy of charging students under the Law on Assembly and Demonstration. Since January 1, as many as 200 students have been arrested and are awaiting trial on these more serious charges.

8

0049

Thus, despite the reforms enacted in 1984, no basic change has yet been made in the Chun government's attitudes toward democracy or dissent. No genuine reform has yet taken place.

The results of the recent elections, however, suggest that the government may soon be forced to take more serious the popular demands for basic change. It may be useful to discuss the election in some length.

IV. The Recent National Assembly Elections

On February 12, 1985, the National Assembly elections were again held, to choose two-thirds of the members of that body. These are the only persons elected at any level of government in Korea; all others, from the lowliest village clerk to the Chief Justice of the Supreme Court, are appointed directly by the President or by presidential appointees, in a system of centralized control which has been in place since 1972. (Prior to that time, regional and local autonomy was practiced, and the President and all the members of the National Assembly were elected directly.)

This election was notable for three developments:

(1) First was the formation of a new political party, inaugurated on January 18, 1985. This party, named the New Korea Democratic Party, was formed by formerly banned politicians, mostly of the old New Democratic Party, and was backed by the two most prominent banned politicians, Kim Dae Jung and Kim Young Sam. With only two weeks to raise campaign funds and locate candidates amidst much government harassment, the new party was able to field a full slate and, even more surprising, received 29% of the popular vote to become the major opposition party. Its campaign was conducted almost solely on the slogan of ending military dictatorship and restoring genuine democratic rule.

(2) Even more significant was the result of the election in all the cities of Korea. In Seoul, the new party won 42% of the vote, to the government's 27%. Other

9

0050

cities had similar if not quite so dramatic results. Only in rural districts was the government able to gain a plurality. (As is well known, rural Korea is tightly organized and controlled by the government credit union and the Semaul (New Village) Movement headed by President Chun's brother. Under these conditions, a government majority in most rural districts was expected.)*

(3) The third striking development in this election was the role played directly or indirectly by Kim Dae Jung, who arrived home only four days before the election and, together with his wife, Lee Hee Ho, was placed under tight house arrest. Virtually every opposition politician, not only of the new party, but of the "official opposition" Korea Democratic Party as well, campaigned on the basis of his or her closeness, real or presumed, to Kim Dae Jung. Government party candidates maintained a discreet silence about Kim. Even though Kim's name was not allowed to be printed in newspapers (except on tightly controlled terms), the election in many ways turned into a popularity contest between Kim and the government.

The election was a stinging defeat for the government, even though it was of course able to retain almost the same number of seats in the National Assembly as before, 148 as against 152 in 1981.

This election has been hailed by some as a demonstration of the vitality of democracy in that country. There is some truth to this claim, for in comparison to the last elections, there was at least a vigorous 10-day period of campaigning allowed and an opposition that offered a genuinely alternative vision. Insofar as is known, vote counting by government officials was honest. News coverage of campaign issues mentioned, although indirectly, the hard challenge to military

----

*For a full discussion of the structure of political control of rural Korea, the USAID publication, Korean Agricultural Services: The Invisible Hand in the Iron Glove by David Steinberg, 1984, is highly recommended.

10

0051

domination of politics, a subject which before, and after, the election, was proscribed.

However, it would in my judgment be premature to declare that democracy has come to Korea on the basis of this election alone. It should be borne in mind that none of the institutional restraints on popular expression of political will have been lifted. All of the laws that restrain the freedom of assembly, the press, or the right of association are firmly in place and being used. Furthermore, in terms of the election itself, a government party with a plurality of 35% has been given 54% of the seats in the national assembly, while the party that came in second, with 29%, ends up with only 24% of the votes. This is a severely compromised democracy.

Nevertheless, this election has demonstrated that major sectors of the populace of Korea are discontent with the present level of suppression and are demanding an opportunity for political participation. Furthermore they are insisting that the military retire from politics and return to their rightful task of defending the nation's borders. If this participation should continue to be denied by the government, or if in the name of a "peaceful transfer of power", the government attempts to bypass any democratic process by choosing Chun Doo Hwan's successor from among his military colleagues, it is fairly certain that a major upheaval would result.

An important factor in the victory of the new opposition party was the mobilization of thousands of youths and students in its support. Rather than boycott the election, the dissident forces turned it into an occasion for expression of political opinion. And with great success, even to the point of electing a student dissident to the National Assembly. In Kangnam District of Seoul, a new high-rise apartment area south of the Han River populated by the new middle-class elite -- government officials, business executives, journalists and teachers -- the election was won by a 37-year old student activist, Lee Chol, who had been

0052

repeatedly imprisoned for political reasons during the past 12 years. The DKP candidate placed second, and the government ran a distant third.

The February 12 election then, was a two-edged sword. As an expression of popular will, it was a limited success--limited by the unfair election laws, restrictions on the press, and the overwhelming use by the government of its institutions to support the ruling party. However, since despite these limitations, the election returns greatly challenge the government's policies, the election has raised expectations of democratic reform that must be met. Failure by the government to respond adequately to these demands with genuine reforms will be sharply challenged by an opposition that feels a new sense of momentum and popular support.

The major question all Koreans are asking today is whether the government will respond positively to the election results, taking the lead in instituting democratic reform, or whether hardliners within the military will react with fear and repression and endanger a new level of confrontation and social unrest.

There are many strong incentives to a course of democratic reform. Some are international in character. Later this year, South Korea will host the International Monetary Fund and World Bank; next year the Asian Games and in 1988 the Olympic Games will be played in Seoul. For the success of these events, in which the Chun government has invested a great deal of prestige, a peaceful social climate is essential. Disruptive demonstrations of popular discontent at the level of this past year would be embarrassing to a government that is seeking international approval of itself as a modern industrial democracy, and, if they broke out before the games began, could cause the games to be moved or, at least, lead to failure due to lack of participants and tourists.

Another important external incentive to reform is the current attitude of North Korea. For complex reasons, both governments appear to desire some sort of

12

0053

negotiation leading to at least a temporary detente. North Korean prestige has been severely hurt by the Rangoon incident of October, 1983. It also appears that the plans for the "peaceful transfer of power" from Kim Il Sung to his son, Chong Il, have not been received with univeral accolades in the socialist world, and may well be the source of some political uncertainty at home, although this can only be guessed from this distance. At any rate, North Korea appears moderately anxious to open negotiations with the South, and has been prepared to forget its earlier convictions that it could never deal with Chun Doo Hwan. South Korea also needs these negotiations, as a hedge against North Korean efforts to disrupt or sabotage the 1988 Olympics. This mutual need has provided a "window of opportunity" which may last for some time. But as ample past experience shows, civil unrest in South Korea will seriously weaken its bargaining position vis-a-vis the North.

There are domestic pressures also that should motivate moderation and political reform, as the Chun Doo Hwan government begins to prepare for the peaceful transfer of power it has promised. If, as one would expect, the Democratic Justice Party wishes to remain in power after Chun Doo Hwan resigns in 1988, it must either justify its bid to continue on a record of democratization or be prepared to force its way by another military intervention. The latter course would surely cause major social unrest just at a time when, for international reasons, the government needs domestic tranquility.

Prior to my recent visit to Seoul, I would have said that these incentives were sufficient to ensure a rational and moderating response. However, after having experienced the violence at Kimpo Airport, I am not so confident. Whatever else that incident revealed, it showed that there is within the South Korean Government a continuing capacity to over-react, to substitute brute force for persuasion and to rely on military answers for civilian problems.

In your questions you asked if I believed further actions by Congress in response to the Kimpo Airport incident are needed. Actually, although there are

13

0054

many questions unanswered regarding that incident, such as why the U.S. Embassy was caught so completely off-guard and who in the Korean Government betrayed an agreement between the Foreign Ministry and the U.S. Embassy, I believe it will be more fruitful if we turn instead to considering the structural problems in the way of Korean democratization and exerting American pressure on these basic points, keeping the airport incident firmly in mind as a vivid example of the havoc which a militarized government can wreak.

V. Democratic Reforms Needed

In response to your question about what reforms are needed to ensure democracy in Korea, apart from reaffirming that democracy cannot be said to exist without freedom of expression, assembly and association, it is not appropriate for me to make proposals for concrete reforms. Those proposals can rightly be made only by the people directly involved in the Korean polity. However, from long and deep contacts with the movement for democracy and human rights in Korea, I can outline what I believe to be the basic demands that are being made by them.

Freedom of communication is basic. As the Christian Broadcasting Service said in its annual report in January this year:

> Most of the Korean people desire an open, democratic society rather
> than the rigid, controlled society that they experience under the
> present repressive political situation. ... Communication--among people,
> opinion groups and social classes--must be guaranteed for the growth of a
> healthy democratic society. The process of communication itself
> naturally acts to enhance political democratization, expand economic
> justice, instill the capacity for social self-control (rather than
> control from the top), and encourage cultural diversity. The function
> of the mass media is in fact a basic pre-condition for social develop-
> ment.

Free communication can only be assured if the following reforms are made.

1. Revoking the current Basic Press Law, and allowing the free expression--of ideas in print and electronic media. This includes allowing the religious broadcasting service the freedom to set its own programs and to broadcast news and

OC55

social commentary, which are currently prohibited.

2. Freedom of assembly and association--which requires revoking the Law on Assembly and Demonstrations, and amending the labor laws to allow workers the right to organize freely and to build industry-wide or city-wide labor alliances, as well as the right to participate in politics collectively.

3. The end of military intervention in politics.

4. Revoking the special law banning certain individuals from politics and the restoration of rights of all those remaining under the ban.

5. Release of political prisoners and restoration of the civil and political rights of all persons who are now deprived of those rights as the result of past convictions.

6. An end to the use of illegal measures such as the current house arrest of Kim Dae Jung and his wife.

7. Restoration of the rights of students to elect their own student councils, respect for academic freedom and university autonomy.

8. An end to the use of military conscription to punish students for political activity.

There are many other areas needing reform before Korea can be considered a democratic state. Constitutional change is undoubtedly required, as is a measure of local autonomy. But if the basic freedoms of press, assembly and association can be protected, the will of the public regarding these other more basic changes can find expression.

VI. U.S. Policy Implications

What can the United States do to encourage greater progress toward democracy in Korea?

U.S. interest in Korea demands that appropriate steps be taken to encourage this increasingly important ally and trading partner to move in a positive direction

15

0056

toward a more democratic government. To be sure, our leverage is in fact limited and if exercised in the wrong way can easily trigger defensive reactions that exacerbate the problems and make progress more difficult. While bearing this in mind, I believe that there are four areas of influence and leverage that might be strengthened in the period ahead.

A. Moral encouragement of democratic forces.

The U.S. Embassy in Seoul, breaking precedent with earlier patterns, has opted to hold at arm's length the democratic opposition in Korea, apparently on the grounds that they are not elected officials. The current ambassador, for example, has never visited with Kim Young Sam or Kim Dae Jung, unlike all his predecessors.

In the wake of the February election, it should now be official policy to relate as broadly as possible with the full spectrum of political leadership in Korea, including specifically those who remain banned under the special law. We should no longer give the appearance of accepting that law at face value nor should we allow it to restrict our official and unofficial access to important opinion makers in Korea.

Also, whenever appropriate American political leaders should be openly encouraging those who strive in Korea to bring about democratic reforms. Having observed the warm reception Members of Congress provided to Mr. Kim Dae Jung before his departure for Korea last month, I can assure you that your efforts have greatly strengthened this man, have aided his cause of moderate reform, and have influenced the government of Korea to respond somewhat rationally to his return. I certainly hope your efforts in this vein will continue and that you will extend the same kind of supportive interaction to other democratic leaders in Korea.

Third, greater use should be made of cultural and educational exchange programs to enable persons such as dismissed journalists, fired labor leaders, student leaders and others in the democratic movement to get better acquainted with this country and its political and cultural leadership. These are our natural allies.

16

0057

Fourth, Congress should periodically express itself in resolution form about the concern for the growth of democracy in Korea. Despite the press censorship, news of such a resolution does get known eventually in Korea and counters the official line that the United States backs the present government's every move.

The period ahead, prior to the visit to Washington of President Chun Doo Hwan, is an ideal time for such a resolution. It should state clearly that continued support for Chun's government by the the United States is contingent on genuine progress toward democracy, including: full civil and political rights for Kim Dae Jung and all remaining banned politicians, full assurances that the military will refrain from political involvement, restoration of freedom of the press and freedom of assembly, and the establishment of a definite timetable for the peaceable and democratic transfer of power and for constitutional reform.

B. Pressure on the Military

It is universally believed in Korea that the military hold the key to political progress, and almost as universally, that they will not allow any genuine democratization. Yet there are strong hints that within this quite hermetically sealed sector of Korean society there are persons who would like to see the military return to its proper role of providing national defense, and leave politics to the politicians.

These forces need to be strengthened, and their opposites restrained. U.S. leverage is stronger, personal and institutional ties more permanent, and direct command relationships clearer in the military area than any other aspect of Korea-American relations. I would suggest that some of the following steps might be helpful in strengthening the hand of elements in the ROK military opposed to the political gamesmanship that have characterized the Chun Doo Hwan group:

1. The Commander of the U.S.-ROK Joint Command Structure should make it known down through the chain of command that he expects all his officers to observe

17

0058

political neutrality, and that any breach of discipline for political purposes such as occurred on December 12, 1979 would be met by the strongest sanctions available.

2. On the occasion of Chun Doo Hwan's visit to the United States, the President and Members of Congress should in their meetings with him underscore-- preferably while on Korean television cameras--the expectation that political development in Korea will mean the full restoration of civilian initiative in politics without fear of military interference.

3. In the authorization of FY 1986 foreign assistance, language should be included that conditions the transmittal of any funds or credits thereunder on the continued restraint of the ROK military from political interference, and the development of a definite timetable for political reform leading to the 1988 elections.

4. IMET funds for FY1986 should be withheld until full assurances have been given by the ROK Joint Chiefs of Staff that the military will abstain from interfering in the political process. It should be made clear that if military interference occurs, the program will be suspended and all current trainees sent home. When the program is resumed, there must be a much stronger emphasis on training Korean officers to respect democracy. (It ought not to be forgotten that Maj. Chun Doo Hwan became a specialist in psychological warfare in a training program at Ft. Bragg financed by IMET, a specialty he as turned against the Korean people in devastating ways.)

These suggestions are based on a recognition that the military assistance the U.S. provides Korea is more important symbolically as a sign of our ongoing relationship than substantially in terms of meeting military needs that could not b met otherwise. But because the symbolism is important, it should be expanded in significance to symbolize our growing concern at the reluctance of the present government to make genuine moves toward democracy.

0053

18

C. <u>Full use of our own press freedom to encourage the Korean press</u>

If the essential problem is one of communication, as I have suggested, the United States has several instruments at its disposal that can be used to prod the Korean media into more honest and comprehensive reporting. These instruments include the Voice of America, Armed Forces Korea Network, and the semi-official "Stars and Stripes newspaper." All of these media should be encouraged to give much fuller coverage to Korean news, including but not limited to news of U.S. positions and attitudes toward developments in Korea.

At the time of Kim Dae Jung's return in February, the American networks played a very important role in communicating what had really happened at the airport. The Korean press reported only that Kim Dae Jung had arrived at Kimpo, had been taken by government vehicle to his home, and was resting comfortably. Only after the American networks broadcast fuller coverage to the U.S. forces via ABC's "Night Line" or NBC's "Today Show" did it become necessary for the Korean press to amend their coverage to discuss the conflict and violence at the airport. That is a small example of a positive action which should be encouraged.

D. <u>Invoke the labor rights provisions of the new Generalized System of Preferences</u>

Effective January 5, 1985, the U.S. Trade Act restricts participation in the Generalized System of Preferences to nations that respect the internationally recognized rights of workers, including the right to organize, to bargain collectively, freedom from forced labor, child labor or work under unsatisfactory health conditions. The Administration has apparently taken the interpretation that all countries eligible under the previous program are automatically eligible under the new program.

Because of the massive suppression of labor rights in Korea, we believe it should be excluded from this program immediately. Furthermore, the U.S. Trade

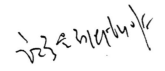

19

0060

Representative's Office should establish clear guidelines for certifying countries on labor rights grounds. If necessary, Congress should direct it to refrain from including any country in the new program if eligibility is challenged, until a process for adjudicating the complaint can be carried out.

While I realize that the Trade Law is not within the purview of this current hearing, it is important in considering the instruments available to influence human rights improvements in Korea to recognize that this additional pressure point exists and can be utilized if the political will to do so can be exerted.

VII. Chun Doo Hwan's Planned Visit to Washington

You have asked for my opinion regarding President Chun's planned visit to Washington in April. You will not be surprised that I do not favor such a trip; his last visit here was used in Korea to signify that his regime and all its actions were fully supported by the United States. That greatly contributed to fostering an atmosphere of anti-Americanism in Korea. Four years have passed since Chun was here, and the political reforms promised by him then have almost without exception not been enacted.

The call for the cancellation of Chun's April visit was made because of the treatment given Kim Dae Jung and the delegation accompanying him at Kimpo Airport. While I understand that the ROKG has apologized to the U.S. for the treatment of American citizens at the airport (although as one of those citizens I have received no direct word of this from either government) Kim Dae Jung has received no such apology. In fact, he is being held prisoner at his home under conditions that if they were in South Africa would be called "banning", but which in South Korea do not even have the sanction of a bad law in their defense. His house is surrounded by somewhere close to two thousand police and agents. Neither he nor his wife, who has never been convicted of any crime and whose political rights were specifically restored last November, can leave their home. They have received no mail since

0061

20

arriving February 8, and are unable to have any visitors except immediate family members. Their only contact with others, either in Korea or outside, is by way of a monitored telephone line. Kim Dae Jung continues to be a non-person in the press in Korea, and in the last few days a new, massive propaganda campaign has been launched by the government to convince people that Kim is a pro-Communist demagogue. Millions of leaflets have been distributed with this claim throughout the country.

In the face of these facts, to continue to welcome Chun Doo Hwan to Washington is in my opinion unjustified. To express American distress at the way his government treats its critics, however, it might be preferable to allow the man to continue his plans and, while here, be subjected to the full force of American public and political opinion. If we could be assured that our president would take up forcefully the questions of human rights and democratization in Korea when he meets Chun, such a visit might be useful. Pending this assurance, it will be up to the Members of this body to meet with Mr. Chun and his staff and press these matters strongly. Were such exchanges to take place, a visit here may not be without merit.

I sincerely hope that the Members of this Committee will take the lead in this dialogue.

VIII. Prospects for North-South Talks

I do not follow North Korean diplomatic affairs with any precision, and so cannot presume to understand its policies well. However, as I mentioned earlier, I have the impression that both the ROK and the DPRK want some negotiations, and that the current hiatus in the talks is only temporary, due not as much to "Team Spirit" as to the North's desire not to enhance the prestige of the government in the South just before the National Assembly election. I assume that, unless something intervenes to prevent it, both sides will attempt to return to the bargaining table later this spring.

Having said that, however, let me add that "Team Spirit" is obviously a serious

21   0062

point of contention to the DPRK. As the largest and longest annual war-game played anywhere in the world by the United States and its allies, "Team Spirit" by its very size and length suggests a bellicose attitude, especially to a country like North Korea which is already given to paranoia about all its neighbors. While the U.S. has repeatedly invited the North Koreans to observe these exercises (in the hope of securing a return invitation to witness the DPRK's military games) it is not surprising that in the absence of any other signs of civility in our relationship, the North is hesitant to exchange these observer missions. Would it be too much to suggest that the U.S. consider scaling down Team Spirit next year, as a conciliatory gesture?

Other steps that could be taken at the same time, I believe, include: a return to the pre-Rangoon practice of allowing casual diplomatic contact between U.S. and DPRK officials; the granting of visas to North Korean academic specialists for legitimate research or lecturing purposes; a phased relaxation of restrictions on North Korean diplomats at the UN, etc. Each of these individual steps might in fact be unwise; the specific action is not as important as finding those steps that signal an openness and a willing to move toward a normalized relationship without at the same time undermining our ties to the Republic of Korea.

For me to make serious detailed proposals in this area is presumptive, for I am not privy to information the variety of third-country contacts or negotiations that may be underway. Nor would I want to make proposals that remove pressure from North Korea to deal directly with the government of South Korea on matters between them. All I can urge is that our policy be one of openness to dialogue, rather than being intimidated by either the north or the south into frozen hostility.

IX. Summary

The Korean peninsula is in considerable flux, with a positive potential for democratic change in the south and some sort of detente and negotiations with the

22

north. International pressures can play an influential if not determinative role in shaping these transitions. The United States is the key external actor in both the issue of democratic reform in the ROK and in lessening tension between north and south.

Now is a time for careful but firm actions by the U.S. Congress, to support forces of moderation and progress, to restrain elements of reaction, and to assure all parties of our abiding alliance in the pursuit of peace and freedom in Northeast Asia. I am hopeful that some of the suggestions I have made above will contribute to this goal.

23

결 번

넘버링 오류

Rally - 2.

The Moderator, Vice Moderator and General Secretary went in to the Police Station and met with the 2nd Bureau Chief of Seoul City Police and the Choongbu Police Chief. The General Assembly officers claimed that since the Church was trying to hold a General Assembly event in one of its own churches, and was being prevented from doing so by the unlawful blocking of the entrance, this was a clear instance of violence, and asked if it was not the responsibility of the police to do something about it. While not denying that the church was being unlawfully possessed, they refused to do anything about it, insisting that police could not go inside a church.

For some two and a half hours the church leaders stood outside the Police Station in the bitter cold shouting slogans such as "Down with this violent regime!", and "Lets fight for the protection of the Church and of Democracy!" Upon receiving the report that no solution had been reached, they agreed to go temporarily to Hyangnin Church to hold the program. Carrying in front of them a banner reading "We denounce a government which upholds violence", the four hundred or so church leaders appealed to citizens on the street. The people they met as they walked along the road were very much in sympathy with their protest.

At Hyangnin Church the Vice Moderator, Rev. HAN Sang Myun, conducted the opening worship of the rally, and the Moderator, Rev. RHEE Young Chan, preached the sermon. Prof. CHANG Bul Byung then delivered a lecture on "The General Election, Democracy and The Role of the Church". The meeting ended at 10:30 p.m. with the decision to gather at Cheil Church again next morning.

At Cheil Church January 29

The Moderator, Vice Moderator, Chairperson of the Church and Society Committee, and the General Secretary arrived in front of Cheil Church at ten o'clock. This time the metal gate was closed and locked, with the hoodlums inside the gate standing around a fire they had lit to keep them warm. They had clubs, lead pipes, a fire hose with a nozzle, sand bags and such all laid out, clearly ready to commit violence against the church leaders. Three or four of them were on top of the wall with cameras, taking pictures of the church leaders, and spouting abuse over the loud-speaker. Someone announced, "The Moderator is about to speak, so if you people are good church members, you will keep quiet and listen," at which the abusive language became louder and more forceful than ever.

At around 10:30 someone shouted, "Let's cut the cord of the speaker," at which those inside the fence suddenly began throwing sand, and then turned the hose fully on the church leaders. They took up the clubs and lead pipes, and brandished them, shouting even worse insults. The church leaders soaked with cold water propelled at them from the fire hose in the freezing cold, while also being showered with intolerable abuse, protested. This went on for some time, but the police simply stood looking on.

Here were young 20 year-olds brandishing lead pipes and taunting, "Come on over the fence you s.o.b. ministers, and we'll kill you!" daring them to do so with taunts that they "were afraid to come over". Unable to stand any more, Rev. MOON Dae Kol (Seoul Presbytery) who had been at the very front and got the full force of the water, at hearing this climbed up the gate. The youth with the lead pipe struck him on the head, knocking him to the ground, from the top of the gate onto the other side. Then the whole group of hoodlums trampled and kicked him as well as beating him with pipes and clubs. Unable to bear this excess, Mr. PARK Moon Ki, ordinand, (Chun Buk Presbytery) and Mr. PYUN Jei Ok, Kangjin Eup Church steward (Chunnam Presbytery) climbed up the gate and suffered the same treatment. The hoodlums then turned the hose on the three lying unconscious on the ground in the freezing cold until

0066

Appendix I

THE PRESBYTERIAN CHURCH IN THE REPUBLIC OF KOREA
NATIONWIDE RALLY OF CHURCH LEADERS FOR THE ERADICATION OF VIOLENCE
Sponsored by the General Assembly
January 28-29, 1985

The episode described below is the most recent in the continuing series of incidents threatening the existence of Seoul Cheil Church (PROK).

When it became evident to Church leaders that the violence at Seoul Cheil Church would drag on indefinitely, a Nationwide Church Leaders Rally was planned to be held at Seoul Cheil Church on January 28-29, in accordance with the decision of the 69th General Assembly of September 1984.

After notices of the Rally had been sent out, the General Assembly received the following notice, dated January 26, "From all the pioneer members of Seoul Cheil Church": "...We, the pioneer members of Seoul Cheil Church are planning a Prayer Meeting for the Normalization of the Church from January 27. Since the General Assembly Church Leaders Rally will conflict with our church's prayer meeting, we ask you to make alternate arrangements."

The Rally

From the morning of January 28, the day of the rally, several of those who had been disrupting worship and committing acts of violence against the minister and church people, had built a fire in front of the gate, where they stood guarding it. They had plastered various slogans and notices on the walls of the church. At the 1st floor entrance was a two-column makeshift sign reading: "The Office of The Counter-Measures Committee for the Protection of Cheil Church, Choong Ku Branch of the Anti-Communist Youth Association". A few hours later, the second half of the sign had been blacked out to form an arrow.

At around 12:40 p.m. that day, Rev. KIM Ho Shik, Chairperson of Seoul Presbytery, along with several Presbytery officials, went to the church and quietly urged those who were illegally occupying it to come out, but were met with refusal. Shortly after this, Rev. RHEE Young Chan, Moderator, Rev. HAN Sang Myun, Vice Moderator and Rev. KIM Sang Keun, General Secretary, approached and asked the occupiers to vacate the church since the rally was about to begin. They were likewise met with high-handed abuse and refusal.

Around 2:00 p.m., in spite of falling snow and chilling cold, the church leaders began to gather a few at a time. As they approached the entrance of the church they were met by the brandished fists of several persons who had no former connection whatever with Cheil Church. Furthermore, over a loud-speaker in unimaginably abusive language, the church leaders were told that the rally was a plot by Park Hyung Kyu, and that they should leave before they suffered worse humiliation. The number of church leaders increased to some 450, and they began pressing on those illegally holding the church. The atmosphere changed when around 2:30 p.m., on the excuse that they had come to prevent violence, riot police came and blocked the gate, holding the church leaders back from approaching it. It was only the church leaders they held back, however. When the perpetrators of violence attacked the church leaders, the police stood by as spectators. Finally, judging that the police were there to protect the doers of violence who were illegally holding the church, the Moderator and officers of General Assembly and all the leaders agreed they should go to the Choongbu Police Station and lodge a protest.

At the Choongbu Police Station

In the bone-chilling cold of over -10°C, the church leaders gathered in front of the Choongbu Police Station. Police blocked the entrance to the Station and surrounded the church leaders.

0067

it seemed they must freeze to death. At this exhibition of cruelty, Rev. LIM Heung Ki began to climb up the gate only to be struck a fierce blow with a club which knocked him to the ground outside the gate with a great gash on his head.

At this point the hoodlums inside the gate dashed inside the church building, leaving the three men lying unconscious. The church leaders outside the gate were covered with icicles from the water from the fire hose, and many of them had blood on their faces from being strick by gravel thrown at them. They were about to go over the gate en masse, but the police who, up to now, had stood quietly as spectators, moved to block the gate to prevent the church leaders going inside. The police pushed the leaders back, so they agreed, "Fine! We won't go in, but please get those men to a hospital!" The police let on they didn't hear, and continued pushing the church leaders until they were some distance from the gate.

At last the police got the help of those inside to open the gate and they brought out the three unconscious church leaders and one woman from inside who had been injured by flying gravel. Then they re-locked the gate.

The Moderator, Vice Moderator, General Secretary and Chairperson of the Church and Society Committee again went to the Choongbu Police Chief and the Intelligence Department Chief and asked, "What more are you waiting for? Arrest these hoodlums!" Appearing flustered, the officers then promised they would arrest them, and went off to the scene of violence.

Police agents arrived at the church in a riot police vehicle. They went up to the gate and called out, "Hey! Some of you guys come out here. Come out, I say!" but just stood there waiting.

After what seemed a very long time, CHUNG In Suh came out from the church and said, "We're having worship just now, so please just wait quietly," and the so-called agents continued to wait.

At a general outcry from the church leaders, the agents warned those inside, "If you haven't come out by 1:00 o'clock, we're going in after you," but at 1:15 CHUNG In Suh came out again and said, "We're discussing the matter now. Wait a bit longer," and the agents continued to just stand there.

At around 1:40 CHUNG again came out and said, "There are 55 of us Christians inside, and since we were all together in the violence, you'll have to take all of us." (There could not have been more than 20 of them.)

The church leaders standing near protested, asking, "When did you ever use such methods when you arrest people? Can't you take all of them in, investigate them according to the law, and release any who are not guilty?" But the agents replied, "Just wait a bit longer. They're going to come out." Finally, three of the agents climbed over the gate and went in to where the hoodlums were gathered. Thirty minutes later they had still not come back. The waiting church leaders were wondering what in the world was going on, when they finally got their answer. The three returned and reported, "They insist we will have to take all of them, so it's impossible to take them at all."

In this way the incident dragged on until 3:00 p.m. Finally at 3:30, the General Secretary and the Chairperson of the Church and Society Committee suggested meeting formally with the Choongbu Police Chief. They announced "We have now ascertained that the government has no intention of detaining even persons who commit crimes of violence. Their claim that it is impossible

0068

Rally - 4.

to detain the whole group confirms that it is official policy to allow the
continued illegal possession of the church by violence. From now on we will
wage our struggle against the government on our own." With this the church
leaders left the street in front of Cheil Church and made their way to the
Christian Building.

On the way to the Christian Building eight persons, including CHUNG Kwang
Suh, assistant minister of Cheil Church, who were shouting slogans and distributing material to people on the street, were dragged off by police, who
severely beat them inside the police vehicle on the way to the Police Station.

At the Christian Building

In the 2nd floor Auditorium of the Christian Building those who gathered—
fifty to sixty were stopped at the entrance to the building, and though they
struggled with the police there, they were prevented from entering—discussed
what measures should be taken. They issued a Statement (see attached), and
the rally ended around midnight. The leaders of the rally lodged a strong
protest at the detention of the eight persons, who were finally released six
hours after they had been detained.

0069

The General Assembly of The Presbyterian Church in the Republic of Korea

S T A T E M E N T issued January 30, 1985

· In the name of "All the participants of the Nationwide Church Leaders' Rally
for the Eradication of Violence" · ·.

The 69th General Assembly of The Presbyterian Church in the Republic of
Korea on September 20, 1984 received the Church and Society Committee's
report on the Seoul Cheil Church Incident, identifying it clearly as a case
of government authorities violating human rights and invading the authority
of the Church. The General Assembly issued a Statement by which the whole
Church demanded that strong steps be taken to deal with the situation.

Nevertheless, on September 23, only a few days after General Assembly
ended, following Sunday worship, Rev. PARK Hyung Kyu (minister of Cheil Church)
and a number of the church people under his leadership were physically attacked
by hoodlums inside Cheil Church. We see this as a clear instance of a direct
challenge to the denomination, and we warned that should such incidents continue,
we would see it as being totally the responsibility of the government. But even
after that, in spite of the sincere efforts of Seoul Presbytery to normalize
the dignity of worship, there continued to be a series of incidents of violence,
to which, by abandoning their plain responsibility and simply acting as spectators, the authorities gave tacit assistance.

General Assembly believed that Seoul Presbytery would succeed in working
out a solution to the Cheil Church problem, and in the meantime prayed for a
solution to the problem, and waited for results. Finally, judging that the
violence was not stopping, and that there was no change in the National
Police's attitude of spectators to the situation, in accordance with the
decision of the 69th General Assembly, it was decided to hold a nationwide
Church Leaders' Rally January 28-29 in Seoul Cheil Church, under the theme:
"A Nationwide Church Leaders' Rally for the Eradication of Violence".

But when the Church leaders, who had been praying for, and worrying about
the situation at Cheil Church, arrived and tried to enter the church, they
could not contain their bewilderment and shock at what they found there.
Those who had been perpetrating violence and preventing worship at Cheil Church
were blocking the entrance to the church where the Rally was to be held, and
poured unbelievable abuse upon the Moderator and officers under him, and on
all the Church leaders who gathered for the Rally.

We do not recognize as members of our Church persons who defy the
authority of Presbytery and General Assembly, and who treat with violence the
Moderator and officers of the General Assembly and the leaders of the Church.
We made it very clear, moreover, that if the police were fulfilling their
proper responsibilities, they would arrest these perpetrators of violence,
who have taken over Cheil Church as if it were their own possession, and who
are guarding it by violence.

Nevertheless, the Church leaders were treated abusively and with
violence by a group of people who refuse to recognize the authority of
the highest body of the Church, the General Assembly, while the police were
protecting those perpetrators of violence. We saw this terrible reality
with our own eyes.

Large numbers of persons sustained moderate to serious injuries—eight
persons needed medical treatment, several had to be sutured, while many others
were less seriously injured—through violence, while the police authorities,
who were on the spot, far from arresting those committing the violence, made
no move to help the Church leaders who were knocked unconscious by lead pipes,

0070

wooden clubs or water from a fire hose, but on the contrary, unbelievably pushed back the Church leaders who tried to help those who had fallen to the ground.

The police have admitted that those who have taken possession of the church have done so illegally, and issued an ultimatum for them to vacate it. However, we saw that they had no intention of arresting the culprits, since they extended the deadline again and again. We heard those who are illegally in possession of the church invite police to take all of them, and heard the police decline, suggesting that a few of them come out, making it clear that the authorities have no intention of ending the illegal possession. Thus they clearly announced that the root cause of the whole Seoul Cheil Church incident, including the illegalities and violence, rests in the police force itself.

If this is not a total challenge by the authorities to our denomination, what else can it be? It is unchangingly a matter of oppression by government authorities of human rights, and an invasion of the Church's authority and of the freedom of mission.

We are well aware that the present government has already brandished violence over the whole society. We have been vividly shown that from beginning to end this regime has been one of violence. Recently there have been incidents of violence to labourers, violence to displaced slum dwellers, shaming of women students. The recent attempted kidnapping of the younger brother of Elder KIM Young Chin at Kangjin Eup Church shows that this government will use any method at all for the purpose of extending its rule, and that its true character is violence.

All of these things have strengthened our resolve as a Church to stand firmly to protect the honour of the leaders of The Presbyterian Church in the Republic of Korea against the evil powers which have tried to destroy and bring to an end the true authority of the Church. We pledge with all our strength to finally sweep away from this land all kinds of violence and bring in God's kingdom of peace. To this end we make the following resolutions:

1. Since we can certainly not recognize as members of our denomination persons who defy and violate the Church's authority, we strongly urge Seoul Cheil Church and Seoul Presbytery to take measures to severely punish such persons and to restore to its proper image Seoul Cheil Church.

2. We strongly urge all members of our denomination to severely judge this violent regime which would control and destroy the Church, through their vote in the up-coming 12th general elections of the Republic.

3. We request the Church and Society Committee of General Assembly to urge each Presbytery to hold a Rally for the Eradication of Violence.

4. We propose to General Assembly that in the event that the incidents of violence at Seoul Cheil Church are not resolved, that there continue to be Rallies called of the nationwide Church leaders.

5. We demand the resignation of CHU Young-Bok, Minister of Home Affairs, who has overall responsibility for the Incident of Violence at Seoul Cheil Church.

0071

DEMOCRACY IN KOREA AND AMERICA'S ROLE
FOR A NEW KOREA-US RELATION: A REVIEW

KIM SANG HYUN

I

I am grateful to the United States of America for the friendship and noble political ideals of freedom and democracy that the U.S. have shared with my country for the last four decades. I am extending also my personal appreciation to the American people who have shown a continued interest in political realities in the Korean peninsula.

Korea had observed the hundredth year of opening the diplomatic relation with the United States a few years ago. The nationwide celebration was marked by the enthusiastic participation of citizen groups, and reaffirmed the close ties between the two countries. President Chun Doo-Whan, after meeting with President Reagan in February 1981, expressed his satisfaction that Korea was no longer a recipient of American aid, but she had become an equal partner in the international scene.

On surface, the realationship between the two looks friendlier and firmer than ever before. Even I cannot deny the friendly relationship. Both Korean and American administrations may even have an illusion that they are honeymooning and nothing can go wrong.

However, I have to point out that there are serious political problems hiding behind this seemingly amorous relationship. The undercurrent crisis may be parapharsed as a nuclear bomb to be exploded any moment. When it explodes, all the mutual trust and friendship that we have built over a century will be wiped out momentarily.

In order to build a genuiene partnership based on friendship and mutual trust, we have to examine explosive problems that are buried deep underneath deceiving protocol gestures of feigned smiles and handshakes. I am here today to unearth those problems and discuss them freely and without any reservation.

II

Let us go back to August 15, 1945. It was the day when the World War II came to an end. It was the day that Korea was liberated from the Japanese colonial rule.

On that day Koreans took to the street to greet American soldiers as their liberators. Everybody was overcome with joy, and placards of 'Welcome Americans.' could be found everywhere. A genuine friendship between Korea and the U.S. began on that very day.

Koreans adopted democracy as the political ideal like most other nations in Asia and Africa which gained independence after the World War II. Democracy was the tide of the time that no one could go against. With the fall of fascists who challenged democracy, democracy was appealing to everybody. The word 'democracy' was so attractive that even communists exploited the word.

0072

Unfortunately, however, before democracy took its root, dictatorship and authoritarianism emerged in those new independent nations which were not quite ready for the democratic system and practice.

The most frequently quoted definition of democracy is the famous phrase from the Abraham Lincoln's Gettysburg address "...a government of the people, by the people, and for the people...". But the government "of the people and for the people" is not necessarily a democratic government. We have witnessed many times that dictatorial or fascist regimes claimed the government of the people and for the people, and yet relentlessly repressed their people.

The democracy is a political institution "by the people." What this means is that the people be allowed to decide freely what is best "for the people." If the political system of a democratic nation is not "by the people", but "of the people and for the people", then the system will deteriorate.

Korea was no exception. Democracy in Korea had soured more rapidly than any of those new independent nations. Korea also became a victim of the ideological showdown between the US and Soviet Union. The tragic Korean War of 1950 made the partition of the Korean peninsula permanent.

The political problems that are now ticking to explode to blow up the century-old friendship may have started brewing since August 15, 1945. Unlike other new independent nations, the US Military Government was imposed upon Korea immediately after the liberation. Korea had to endure another three years of the foreign rule before she was granted a government of her own in 1948.

Political scientists of both countries have been studying the merits and demerits of the Military Government. Their studies have already produced some results that are critical of the Military Government. Any criticisms, however, must be viewed as attempts to improve and maintain ties between the two countries.

The immediate outcome from the World War II for the Korean people was merely to replace the colonial rule by the Japanese imperialist with the partition of the Korean peneisula by the US and Soviet Union. Therefore how the US Military Government influenced the future of this new republic must be reviewed before examining the characteristics of internal politics and foreign affairs of Korea in the last forty years.

We will review three aspects of what the Military Government achieved.

First we have to review the free democratic system introduced into Korea during the three-year rule by the US Military Government. Second we will review the impact of the cold war between the two super powers on the Korean peninsula. Finally we have to reveal how the Military Government ignored the realities of Korea and disregarded nationalistic pride of Koreans.

Before criticizing the US Military Government, I must admit our inability to cope with the liberation from the Japanese rule not won by our own hands but handed over to us by others.

Let us review the substance of democracy introduced into Korea by the Military Government. One Korean political scientist once dubbed it as "Yankee Democracy." According to the "Yankee Democracy" theory, democracy introduced into Korea does not conform to the classical ideals of European democracy. It is commercialistic and resides on the strength of grass-roots.

0073

Democracy in Europe is the ideal and system that the middle class won in order to participate in the industrial activities and decision-making process on social policies. Democracy was not given to them. They won after fiercely fighting absolute monarchs and feudalistic aristocrats. Following the Industrial Revolution, the rapidly rising working class was absorbed into this political ideal and system, from which parliamentary democracy spun off, and achieved the welfare state of popular democracy called 'The Rose of Democracy.'

Industrialization in Korea created the class of haves and the class of workers. Yankee democracy, however, failed to resolve the conflict between the two classes. Rather it created confrontation by forcing one side to compromise. Yankee democracy imposed tyranny by plurality. After trial and errors, Yankee democracy proved to be unsuitable as a political system for the Korean people.

This hastily transplanted Yankee democracy entailed only unending political unrest in Korea. The authority amended, at will, the Constitution as many times as necessary to hang on to the power, and always ended up with the tragic end. The Rhee Syng Man's regime had to be brought down by the student revolution in 1960. The Park Chung Hee's 18 year rule was collpased with his assasination. The Park's military dictatorship has been suceeded by yet another military regime after the back-to-back military coup d'etats. It is deplorable and may be attributable to the generic characteristics of Yankee democracy that we have yet to experience a peaceful transfer of power.

The US Military Government cannot avoid the responsibility of the partition policy in the Korean peninsula, because it was predisposed to partition the country and govern a part of the partitioned. The Military Government made a number of attempts to prevent a permanent partition through the US-Soviet Joint Committee and the United Nations. It also tried to have the left and right reconcile. Such efforts, however, were made not for the sake of Korea but as a part of the overall US foreign policy toward the Fareastern Asia to protect the interest of the US.

The insensitive treatment by the Military Government damaged our national prestige and pride so deeply that its after-effects have not completely dissipated yet.

The 24th US Army Corps advanced into Korea from Okinawa. Its commander General Hodge did treat the Korean people not as the liberated but as a part of the defeated Japanese people. The first leaflet was dropped from airplanes on September 2, 1945. Without a single word of congratulation or consolation for the Korean people, General Hodge warned Koreans that any violent acts against Japanese or the US landing force were banned. The first proclamation was too cold and hostile for the liberated people.

In his second proclamation a week later, General Hodge went even to say that any indiscreet resistance to the landing force would be dealt with loss of lives and destruction of our 'beautiful land.'

Soon after the second proclamation, the US forces landed in Inchon, a port city about twenty miles west of Seoul, fully armed and under the air cover as if they were about to launch an all-out assault before the enemy. Japanese army and police force were mobilized to keep Koreans out of the streets. Some Koreans, apparently unaware of the proclamations, took to the streets to

0074

"Welcome American Liberators" only to be shot indiscriminately by Japanese
soldiers for intrusion of security zones, leaving heavy casualties. In an
announcement in reply to a protest against the incident, the US Army authoritis
sided with the Japanese who only carried out what they had been ordered to do.

Korea's liberation was not won by our own hands. However, the Korean people
staged bloody fierce resistance and campaigned for independence. After the
Japanese occupation of Korea in 1910, hundreds and thousands of Koreans exiled
to Manchuria, Shanghai, Hawawii, and America. The Independence Army was organized
in Manchuria, and a provisional government in exile was established in Shanghai.
Rhee Syng Man was the first president of the provisional government, before he
exiled to the United States.

The Declaration of Independence was declared on March 1, 1919, and anti-
Japanese demonstrations spread all over the country like a wildfire. Japanese
soldiers had to be brought in to control the uprising. Holocaust took place
everywhere, in cities, small villages, and even at church buildings. Some six
thousand were massacred, fourteen thousand wounded, and fiftytwo thousand thrown
into jails. The March 1, 1919 Declaration of Indepencence is equivalent to the
beginning of the American Revolution in 1776.

The US Military Government authorities ignored our proud history of national
resistance. They committede mistakes of authorizing the Japanese Government-
General, a governing body of Japanese imperialists in Korea, to govern in the
interim. They ignored the Provisional Government in exile. Members of the
Provisional Government were only allowed to return to Korea as a private citizen.

The Japanese Government-General continued to function as it had been before,
and its Korean officials were later appointed to prominent advisory positions in
the Military Government. Those Korean traitors who had collaborated with the
Japanese exploiters and pro-Japanese intellects found their way in the Military
Government. Nationalists' organizations, left or right, were not recognized.
Members of the Provisional Government in exile were denied participation in the
transition process.

National mood at the time was to clean up immediately remnants of Japanese
imperialism and restoration of national spirits, and to start fresh as a new
independent nation. But the Military Government appointed to the police
leadership Korean high police officials under the Japanese rule who arrested,
tortured, and even murdered the patriots struggling for independence. All the
Japanese collaborators and traitors occupied high positions in the US Military
Government.

I would like to remind you that many French were executed for their
collaboration with Nazi right after the World War II. But not a single soul was
executed in Korea for their crime against their own people. Can you imagine
British collaborators occupy high positions in the American Revolutionary
Government? You can imagine how the Korean people were hurt when they witnessed
Japanese collaborators and traitors were appointed to the higherups in the
Military Government.

Growing anti-Military Government mood eventually led to a nationwide anti-
American demonstrations in October 1947. One of the fiercest riots in our
history that we call "October Riot" started in the City of Taegu, the third
largest city in Korea. After the riot, the Military Government commissioned
an US-Korea Joint Investigation Committee, and dispatched a fact-finding team

0075

to Taegu. There was an American news reporters, Mr. Bark, who witnessed the riot.

After reviewing the report by the Committee, Mr. Bark pointed out five major causes that triggered the riot: 1. police brutality; 2. hiring of Korean traitors by the Military Government; 3. abuse by interpretors working for the Military Government; 4. corruption of officials; and 5. agitation by communist elements. Mr. Bark further pointed out that the most serious mistake that the Military Government had made was treating the Korean people not as a liberated people but as inhabitants of an occupied territory.

The Military Government committed mistakes of introducing democracy in forms only without any substance before cleaning up the vestige of the Japanese imperialistic elements. The Military Government's inept handling of post-liberation Korea had become the toxic element that ruined the democratic development in Korea.

I have summarized the demerits of the Military Government and their after-effects. You may wonder why I am digging up the olde skeleton. You have to understand that the fallacies and follies that the Military Government had committed are still with us, influencing our political realities.

Democracy has not yet taken its root in our country. Never before in our history have we had a peaceful transfer of power nor a government "by the people." The confrontation between South and North Koreas, a byproduct of the cold war of the two super powers, is still the source of tremendous waste of national energy and resources. We are living under constant threats of another aggression by the North.

Those traitors and Japanese collaborators who had enjoyed high positions in the Military Government still flourish in every corner of Korean politics, economical enterprises, social organizations, and cultural fields. Their anti-nationalistic and anti-democratic attitudes such as self-centeredness, political manipulation, power-cure-all attitude, collusion with foreign powers, etc have had adverse impacts on all aspects of our life in Korea. Our nationalistic spirit and pride are all but replaced by defeatist's decadence, and democracy in Korea is nothing but a dead word.

III

The May 17, 1980 coup d'etat is a very important event in the history of the Korea-US relation.

The United States had poured tremendous amount of military and economic aid into Korea for the last forty years. Up until recently, the United States has been perceived by the Korean people as a Godfather figure that protected our country from the communist's aggression, a true friend that would help safeguard democracy in Korea. Our countrymen, government officials and civilians alike, did not hesitate to call the United States a country of blood-alliance, because 50,000 US soldiers died to defend Korea from the communist's takeover during the Korean conflict.

The assassination of President Park Chung Hee on October 26, 1979, put an end to his Yushin regime overnight. It looked like that we finally had an opportunity to establish a democratic government. Politicians, religious leaders, intellects, workers and students were together to clean up the vestige of the Yushin dictatorial rule. Everybody expected that the United States would

0076

lend helping hands for realization of democracy. They betrayed our expectation,
and gave us a total despair and helplessness.

In 1980, General Chun Doo-Hwan emerged as a military power and crushed
our cherished hope of democracy by brutal force. The army paratroopers were
sent to massacre thousands of innocent Kwangju citizens and students who were
protesting the military takeover of power and crying for democracy. The
bloodbath in Kwangju was one of the most tragic events in our history.

I have to point out that the United States bears more than moral
responsibilities for what happened in Kwangju. It is everybody's knowledge
in Korea that the Korea-US Military agreement specifies Korean troop movements
are authorized only after the US Military Commander in Korea concurs.

The Kwangju event made the Korean people rethink the Korea-US relation.
Here is a story. Kwangju citizens who were completely surrounded by the Korean
Army paratroopers believed that they were fighting for a rightful cause, and
hoped, in the fear of massive bloodshed, that the United States would come to
their aid. But the US action was completely the opposite.

When it was learned that the US sided with the dictatorial military force
that committed the Kwangju atrocity against their own people crying for democracy
in Korea, the US was no longer a friend and ally tied by blood. The US was
instantly branded as a collaborator of the murderour dictatorship, and became
a target of hatred and hostility.

In fierce student protests against the so-called Fifth Republic of General
Chun, anti-American slogans which had been unheard of before began to surface.
Students set fire on the United States Information Service buildings in Pusan and
Kwangju. It is a serious development that the Korean people now regard the US
policy makers as the equal of the present Korean rulers whose regime is by no
means 'by the people.'

In other words, the Korean people now have a new logic that punishment of
the US Government means punishment of the present regime and vice versa. This
new logical equation is threatening to undermine the century-old US-Korea
relationship.

I would not dismiss those incidents targeted against the US merely as acts
motivated by anti-American sentiment. This pain must be viewed as a pain
accompanying the growth of the infantile Korea-US relation into a more mature
one based on mutual respects.

I would like to quote Mr. Moon Bu-Shik who was tried on the charge of arson
of the USIS building in Pusan and sentenced to death. His death sentence was
commuted to life in prison by a special presidential clemency. This is his
final testimony before the Supreme Court.

" I am an university man and Christian. It is the civil right and duty to
indict and criticize an illegitimate political power. I would like you
to understand, Your Honor, the determination for our conscience-seeking
group of students to live a conscientious and truthful life. We do not
totally deny the value of our school education of ten years. We, a group
of students in theology, medicine and engineering, have endeavored to
make contributions to our society in our respective professional field.

0077

A democratic society calls for participation and contribution by not only professionals but also intellects and democratic citizens. Without constructive criticisms and participation through criticisms, a democratic society cannot advance.

Today's education tends emphasize only production of highly specialized professionals. It does not teach us to devote ourselves to the true democratic cause. Our student group was organized to study democracy and devotion to democracy.

Your honor, I ask you not to be prejudiced by my statement.

I wish to tell you more. When a prominent politician respected by the people had been arrested on a false charge of sedition and sentenced to death, I said to a friend of mine, "How many more conscientious people must be sacrificed before democracy is realized in this country?" He said, "Unless you and I are determined to risk our live for democracy in our country, we shall never have democracy." What he said was wedged into my passive sentimentalistic mind.

I had to repeat askng myself many times what force is behind to keep this unjust regime in power. It is not their euphoric slogans or propaganda that keep the regime in power. Our people are too mature to fall for the government's slogans and propaganda. The economic growth that they have boasted about does not keep this regime in power, nor the military power.

After eliminating other possibilities, I came to a conclusion that there were two factors responsible for this regime to exist. One is the fallacious Korea-US relationship and the other is our people's relinquishing the dream of democracy.

I have risked everything that I have including my life for this arson. I am willing to sacrifice myself for my people and the whole world. ... I only hope that my death will become a new milestone in the relationship between Korea and the United States and that my death will create a momentum for the Korean people to come to the nationalistic self-consciousness. I also hope that the United States Government will be motivated by this incidence to abandon its policy of forcing the cold war ideology to minor nations and to become a true friend nation to held us realize democracy and achieve reunification of our divided country.

Relationship between friendly nations should be based on true friendship, not on a master-servant relation. There is another growing sign that Japan is replacing the United States as a dominating power in Asia and following the suit of the US attitude toward Asia. What I did must become a warning toward Japan too. Your Honor, all I did was to trigger the alram bell at the risk of my life."

Ladies and Gentlemen, I would not add anything to this testimony by Mr. Moon. Mr. Moon risked his life to bring a new awareness to the Korea-US relationship. It is a pity that officials of both governments treated the arson incidence simply as an expression of anti-American mood.

0078

IIII

The Korea-US relation has never encountered more difficuylt challenge than we face now. But both Administrations seem to have been absorbed into deceptive honeymooning mood. There are very serious problems that can explode to unknown consquences. We must not pretend that there are no problems.

Errors committed during the three years of the US Military Government have not yet been corrected, but rather have been multiplying for the last forty years.

We have misgivings about the America's true intention with regard to its Korea policy. It has been supporting a government which is definitely not "by the people." We are worried about the possible emergence of new economic colonialization by American economic tyranny. We are concerned about the new development in the US-China relation which would have enormous geopolitical impacts on the already subtle relationship between Korea and China.

Korea is now evaluating where it stands as a member of the international society. Studies have been undertaken to answer questions on the role of Korea in the international society.

In the meantime, repression against democratic force is still rampant in Korea. In some areas of our society, repressive measures of the present regime are a lot harshier than those of the previous regime. Workers are shut out from their workplace, and labor unions are being dismantled. A number of dismissed university professors, journalists and students have not been able to find any place to go.

All these not only will make democracy in Korea even harder to achieve but also will do irreversible damages to the Korea-US relation. The present cozy relation between the dictatorial regime in Korea and US Administration makes us cast immediate doubt on the committment of the US on democracy in Korea. This doubt will certainly make the US-Korea relation sour.

Regardless of what I have said, I am optimistic about our future relationship. My optimism is based on the following three reasons: 1. your deep and unusual interest in an unknown politicians like myself; 2. my confidence in those American friends who are more enthusiatic for the democratization in Korea than some of our fellow countrymen; and 3. eagerness of the Korean people seeking qualitative sublimation of the Korea-US relation through a government by the people.

To make our dream come true, I ask for your unspared friendly affections and unreserved cooperation. Thank you.

0079

85.6.6. 잭슨목사 기자회견시 배포된 아국 인권관계 자료

1. Reports From Kwangju　　　　(한국인권을 위한

　　　　　　　　　　　　　　　　　　　　북미연맹 작성)

○ 서언 (상기 연맹회장 P. Billings 명의)

- '광주사태를 동학혁명, 3.1운동, 4.19와 동일시

- 사망자는 1,000이상으로 추정

- 미국정부 책임을 주장하고, 지금 광주사태
  희생자를 옹호하지 않으면 35년간의 상호 신뢰와
  호의가 사라지고 안보도 위태로와 진다고 주장

○ 아국 언론인의 목격담 (85.5.14~27)

- 자신이 확인한 시체 200구

○ 아국 카톨릭 단체가 제작한 사태증언 (목격자들의
  진술을 재구성 한것)

- 잔혹 행위 기록 (임신부 살해, 여학생 살해등)

- 사망자는 1,000이상으로 추정

○ 각종 증언, 일기등 기록 발췌

- 광주 카톨릭 단체 기록

　· 행방불명자 신원을 당국에 신고하면 동 신원
　　기록을 토태로 지명수배를 하여 신고를 꺼림.

공람	북미과	85년 6월 19일	담당	과장	심의관	국장
			위	權	辰	全

0080

- 당시 조선대학생 성명
- 사태일지
- 시

2. 미상원 의사록중 케네디의원 발언 부분

○ 양김씨의 85.3.1 성명 평가, 의사록에 수록 요구

○ 근래 한국 정치에 있어 하기사항이 고무적
   - 양김씨의 협력
   - 새롭고 독립적인 야당의 득세
   - 정부의 해금조치

○ 김대중 복권 촉구

○ 전대통령 방미관련 기 진행된 민주화를 평가하고 앞으로
  이루어져야할것을 기억하여야 한다고 촉구

3. 미하원 외교위 아.태지역 소위 및 인권소위 합동 청문회에서
   "북미연맹" Executive Director, Pharis Harvey 의 발언
   (아국 민주주의 전망에 관하여)

   가. 한국 안보와 민주화
      ○ 국가안보의 핵심적 요소는 정부의 국민간의 의견일치
        이므로 인권보호가 안보에 중요하다고 주장

0081

○ 6.25를 겪지않은 세대에게 미국은 억압적 정부의
    지지자로 인식

나. 5공화국 성립과 그 성격

  ○ 5공화국 성립과정、정치제도、각종 개혁 입법등
     비판
  ○ 권력의 과도한 집중、군의 정치간여등 비판

다. 1984년 개혁과,지속되는 문제
  ○ 형식적 개혁으로 보고 진정한 개선이 이루어지지
     않았다고 평가

라. 최근 국회의원 선거
  ○ 선거시 특기할 사항
    - 신민당의 괄목할 진출
    - 도시에서 야당의 결정적 우세
      · 농촌지역은 농협과 새마을로 철저히 조직화
    - 김대중의 영향력 부각
      · 대부분 야당 후보가 김대중과 유관성 주장
      · 선거는 김대중과 정부간의 인기투표 양상

  ○ 선거 민의를 외면하고 현대통령 측근에서 후계자를
     선택하려하면 major upheaval   이 발생할
     것임.

                                        0082

o 종래,한국이 당면한 국제행사(IMF / IBRD,
아시안게임、올림픽)、남북대화、국민여론 등으로
보아 민주화를 낙관하였으나 김대중 귀국시 폭력을
보고 비관적이 되었음•

o 집권세력내에 언제나 과잉반응을 보이는 과격파가
있음•

마• 미국이 취해야할 정책방향

o 민주세력을 정신적으로 고무 격려
- 워커대사는 전임자와 달리 양김씨를 방문하지
않았음•
- 주한미대사관의 야권인사 수시 접촉
- 의회가 결의안 형태로 한국 민주화에 수시 관심
표명
- 야권인사를 교육、문화 프로그램으로 초청

o 군부에 대한 압력
- 군부내에 정치 불간여를 주장하는 세력 지원
- 한•미 연합사체제 이용 군의 정치적 중립 압력
• 12•12과 같은 사태 재발시 엄격한 징계 표명
- 전대통령 방미시,군부 간여 없는 민간정부의
중요성 강조•

0083

- 86 대외원조시 군의정치 불간여, 민주화 일정
  확정등을 조건화

- 한국군 간부 미국내고육 혜택 축소 검토

○ 미국 언론을 이용한 한국언론 고무
  - VOA, AFKN, 성조지등을 활용, 한국내 반정부
    활동 상세 보도

○ GSP 에 노동자 권익보호 조항 포함
  - 노동자 권익 침해시 GSP 수혜 박탈

바. 전대통령 방미

○ 전대통령 방미가 과거처럼 국내 탄압에 대한 미국의
  지지로 이해되지 않도록 레이건이 인권, 민주화
  문제를 강력히 제기해야함.

사. 남·북 대화 전망

○ 남·북 양측이 어느선까지 대화를 원하는 듯
○ 남북한 직접대화 지지
○ 대화를 고무키 위해 하기 개방정책 검토 제의
  - 팀스피리트 작전 규모 축소 가능성 검토
  - 미·북한간 Casual Contact 재개
    • 학자교류
    • UN 에서 북한외고관에 대한 규제 완화

0084

4. 한국의 민주주의와 새로운 한.미 관계를 위한 미국의 역할

(김상현의 연설문)

○ 양국 정부 관계자들이 밀월관계라는 환상에 젖어 있는동안
   언제 폭발할지 모르는 잠재적 위험이 커가고 있다고 주장

○ 해방직후 미군정으로 부터 한.미관계를 개관

○ 우리손으로 독립을 쟁취하지 못한점이 문제의 시초임을
   인정

○ 연이나 하기 미군정의 실책을 비판하고 한국정치의 부정적
   측면이 이와 관련있다고 주장
   - 한국을 해방지로서가 아니라 정복지로 취급
   - 임정등 민족세력 불인정, 친일파등 식민 잔재세력 등용,
     옹호
   - 민족 자존심 손상 행위

○ 광주 사태시 미국이 민주 열망을 배신함으로서 한.미 관계를
   재고토록 하였다고 주장
   - 미국은 살인적 독재의 협력자로 낙인찍힘.

○ 상기에도 불구 자신은 진정한 민주주의를 신봉하는 미국
   친구와 민주적인 한.미 관계를 추구하는 한국민의 열정
   때문에 한.미 관계 장래를 낙관

0085

2. Int'l Human Rights Law Group 사무국장 방한, 1986. 1. 21 - 31

0086

외 무 부 착신전보

번 호 : USW-0073   일 시 : 601071805   종 별 :

수 신 : 장 관 (미북)

발 신 : 주 미 대사

제 목 : 인권단체 대사 면담 요청

1. 당지 INT'L HUMAN RIGHTS LAW GROUP (회장: DAVID GARLINER, 국제적 인권 의 보호를 위한 민간 비영리 단체로 78 년 설립)은 아국내 인권상황 특히 서준식, 서승 형제문제와 관련, 본직 면담을 신청하여 왔음.

2. 동 단체의 사무총장 AMY YOUNG 은 가까운 시일내에 아국 방문계획을 가지고 있다함.

3. 한편 서 형제 문제에 대해서는 RUDY BOSCHWITZ 상원의원 (민주, 미네소타) 이 자신의 선거구민이 동 의원 앞으로 보낸 서한을 당관으로 송부하여온바 있음 (동 서한은 파편 송부)

4. 상기 단체에서 발간한 아국관계 인권보고서 (83 년)를 검토한 결과 사실과 상 위하고 아국내 인권상황에 대해 잘못 인식된 부분이 많아, 본직은 상기단체의 면담요 청을 수락, 실상을 설명코자함.

5. 동 면담과관련 서형제 사건의 사실 및 참고자료를 회시바람.

(대사 김경원)

예고 : 1986.6.30. 까지

(handwritten: again?)

(handwritten: 지술득된?)

(handwritten: 6 6 20)

✓ 미주국   차관실   1 차보   정문국   청와대   안 기

외 무 부   착신전보

번 호 : USW-0096   일 시 : 601081632   종 별 :

수 신 : 장 관 (영사,법무부,미복)

발 신 : 주 미 대사

제 목 : 사증발급

연 : USW-0073

당관은 금 1.8. 자로 연호 INTERNATIONAL HUMAN RIGHTS LAW GROUP   사무총장

AMY YOUNG (86.1.25-31 간 방한, 목적 : 국내 종교계, 학계 및 인권운동 관계자와 접

촉) 에 대해 입국사증을 발급하였음을 보고함.

(총영사 문동석)

예고 : 1986.3.31. 까지

영고국   미주국   안 기   법무부   차관실 1차번   김문록   령아대

0088

외 무 부 착신전보

번 호 : USW-0127   일 시 : 601091825   종 별 :

수 신 : 장 관(미북)

발 신 : 주 미 대사

제 목 : 인권단체 인사면담

연 : USW-73

본직은 연호 INT'L HUMAN RIGHTS LAW GROUP 간부진 (회장 DAVID CARLINER,

부회장 ROBERT KAPP, 사무총장 AMY YOUNG) 과 1.18.(목) 15:00 본직 사무실에

서 면담키르 하였음.

(대사 김경원)

예고문: 1986.6.30 까지

발 신 전 보

번 호 : WU4-0168 일 시 : 60114 1P20   전보종별 : 지급

수 신 : 주   미   대사·총영사

발 신 : 장   관 (미북)

제 목 : 인권단체 대표 면담

　　　　대 : USW-0073, 0127

　　　대호 Int'l Human Rights Law Group 　간부진 면담과
관련 서준식·서승 형제에 관한 사건개요 는 아래와 같으니 동
면담시 참고 바람.

　　1. 서승

　　　가. 인적사항

　　　　ㅇ 생년월일 : ███████████

　　　　ㅇ 본 적 : ███████████

　　　　ㅇ 직 업 : 서울대 대학원 2년

　　　나. 범죄개요

　　　　ㅇ 64.6 조총련 유학생 동맹에 가입 활동

　　　　ㅇ 67.4 재일 북괴지도원인 형 서선웅의 권유로
　　　　　　　노동당 입당

　　　　ㅇ 67.8및 70. 8 2차 입북, 학생포섭 및 북괴의
　　　　　　　평화통일 정책 선전등 간첩교육

<table>
<tr><td rowspan="3">앙
고
재</td><td rowspan="3">76
년
1
월
13
일</td><td rowspan="3">북
미
과</td><td>기안자</td><td>과 장</td><td>심의관</td><td>국 장</td><td>제1차관보</td><td>차 관</td><td>장 관</td></tr>
<tr><td></td><td></td><td></td><td></td><td>전결</td><td></td><td></td></tr>
<tr><td></td><td></td><td></td><td></td><td></td><td></td><td></td></tr>
</table>

발신시간 :

<table>
<tr><td rowspan="2">외
신
과</td><td>접수자</td><td>과 장</td></tr>
<tr><td></td><td></td></tr>
</table>

0090

○ 68·4 서울 대 유학생으로 잠입, 학원내 지하망
구축 및 각대학 연합전선 형성을 통해 결정적
시기에 봉기기도등 암약

다· 검거일 : 71 · 3 · 7 ·

라· 공판상황

○ 72·10·22 1심 사형

○ 72·12·7   2심 무기징역

○ 73·3·13   3심 무기징역 확정

마· 선고죄명

○ 간첩죄

바· 근황

○ 면회, 차입, 편지수발등이 다른 재소자와 같이
항상 잘 시행되고 있고, 건강상태도 양호함·

~~사· 수용장소 · 보안관계상 공개불가~~

2· 서준식

가· 인적사항

○ 생년월일 :

○ 본   적 : 서승과 동일

○ 직   업 : 서울법대 4년 (당시)

나· 범죄개요

○ 64·5 조총련 산하단체인 조선문화연구회 가입활동

○ 70·8 입북, 간첩교육 받고 귀일

○ 71·3 모국 유학 가장 잠입, 학생포섭등 암약

0091

다. 검거일 : 1971.3.7.

라. 공판상황

    ° 71.10.22   1심에서 징역 15년

    ° 72.2.14   2심에서 징역 7년

    ° 72.5.23   3심에서 징역 7년 확정

    ° 78.5.27   보안 감호 처분

    ° 84.5.24   3차 보안감호 처분 기간갱신 결정

    ° 85.11.26   대법원 보안 감호 기간 갱신처분 무효

                 확인 청구 소송에 대한 상고 기각

  * 보안 감호 처분 사유

    - "혁명을 위해서 피를 보는 것은 어쩔수 없다"

    - "민족주의적 입장에서 후진국에서는 사회주의가

      필수불가결하다."

    - "자본가와 노동자는 영원히 융화할수 없다."는

      등 공산주의사상 고수 고집

마. 선고죄명

    ° 간첩죄

바. 근 황

    ° 면회、차입、편지수발등이 다른 재소자와같이 항상

      잘 시행되고 있고、건강상태도 양호함.   (차22)

~~사. 수용장소 : 보안관계상 공개불가~~

외 무 부 착신전보

번 호 : USW-0254　　일 시 : 601162200　　종 별 : 지급

수 신 : 장관 (미북)

발 신 : 주미대사

제 목 : 인권단체 대표 면담

대: WUS-0168

연: USW-73,127

1. 본직은 금 1.16.15:00 예정대로 INT'L HUMAN RIGHTS LAW GROUP 간부진 3명의
방문 받고 1시간여에 걸친 면담을 가졌음. (김상훈 참사관 및 김원수 서기관배석)

-회장: DAVID CARLINER

-사무국장: AMY YOUNG (1.27-1.31 방한예정)

-부작관: KAREN LOW

2. 상기인들은 본직과의 면담과정에서 김근태 사건, 서형제사건등을 제기하였으며, 본
직은 이에 대한 설명과함께 IHRLG 에서 과거 발간한 아국관계 브고서의 잘못된
점과 미국인권 단체가 아국 인권상황을 관찰할때 범하고 있는 오류를 지적하였음.

3. 김근태 사건

가. IHRLG 측은 조사과정에서 고문행위가 있었으며, 가족 및 외부인사의 재판방청이
금지되고 있다고 주장함.

나. 이에대해 본직은 동 사건의 구체적 내용은 이미 아국의 사직당국에서 밝힌바 있
고 본인이 알고 있는바에 의하면 김근태가족의 고문주장은 전혀 사실과 다르며, 아국
의 재판은 궁개되고있음.

4. 서승, 서준식 형제사건

가. IHRLG 측은 서 형제의 간첩죄 적용에 대해 가족, 친지들로부터 다른이야기를
듣고 있다는 주장과 함께, 서준식의 경우 7년 징역형후에도 왜 상금 석방이 안되고 있
는지 문의함.

√ 미주국　차관실　1 차보　정문국　청와대　안 기

PAGE 1

86.01.17 15:20
의신 2과 통제관

0093

나.이에 대해 본직은 서 형제 사건의 개요,적용된 사법절차 및 현재 상황을 대호 등 보내용에 따라 상세히 설명한후,서준식은 7년 징역형후에도 본인의 공산주의 사상 고수로인해 소정의 사법절차에 따라 보안감호 처분중이며,아국이 처한 안보현실상 간첩 죄는 특별히 다루어질수밖에 없음을 강조함.

5. AMY YOUNG   사무총장 방한관련 협조요청 사항.

(가.) AMY YOUNG   은 1.27-1.31간 방한예정이며,실제 활동기간이 1.28-30 의 3일간 이라고하면서,아래사항 협조를 요청하였음(주한 미대사관측에서 일정 협조할것으로 시사하였음)

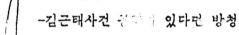

-김근태사건 있다면 방청

-김근태 인터

-서승 면회

나. 이에 대해,본직은 아국 사법절차상 외국인에 대하여 국내 재판방청 및 형사피고 에 대한 면회가 허가되는지 알수없다고 답함.

다. IHRLG   측은 상기 일정 주선이 어렵더라도 자신들의 의사를 본국정부에 전달해 달라고 재차 요청함.

6.상기 면담 과정에서 본직은 아래와같은 논지로 미국인권단체가 아국 인권상황을 관찰할때 범하고 있는 오류를 설명하면서, IHRLG 에서 과거에 작성한 아국관계 보고서의 잘못된점을 지적함.

가.외국인이 타국의 인권문제를 관찰할때 가장 범하기 쉬운 오류는 단순한 접근방법(SIMPLISTIC APPROACH) 인바 특히 변호사들의 경우 외국의 상이한 역사 또는 법전등 을 구시한채 자국의 법률적 척도로써 바라보는 잘못을 범하기 쉬움.

나.미국의 인권단체들이 아국의 인권상황을 올바로 보려면,아국의 역사적,사회적 전 등 및 아국이 처하고 있는 득수상황(즉 안보위협)에 대한 이해가 전제되어야함.

다. 그렇지 않은경우 근거없는 비판은 아국인이나 아국을 이해하는 많은 사람들이 볼때에 웃을수 밖에 없는 부분을 많이 포함하게되며,그예의 하나가 등 단체에서 작성한 보고서임.

7. 관찰

PAGE   2

0094

가. IHRLG 측은 면담초기, 구체적 사건을 제기하면서 상당히 강경한 태도를 보였으나, 면담이 진행되면서 아국의 특수상황 및 6항에 언급된 본직의 일반적인 설명에 다소 이해를 표시하였으며, 동 단체에서 작성한 보고서에 잘못된 부분이 있을수 있음을 인정하였음.

나. 그러나, 김근태사건 및 서형제 사건등 구체적 사안에 대해서는 범죄사실 자체와 범죄인 취급문제는 구별되어야하며, 조사과정에서의 가혹행위는 어떠한 경우에드 정당화될수 없다는 당초의 주장을 굽히려하지 않았음.

다. 이와관련, 등인들은 미국의 경우에도 경찰에 의한 가혹행위가 때로는 발생하기드 하나 이에 대한 철저한 조사가 이행되며, 관련자는 필히 처벌된다고 하면서 아국에도 이러한 선례가 있는지 문의하였음

(대사 김경원)

예그: 1986.12.31일반

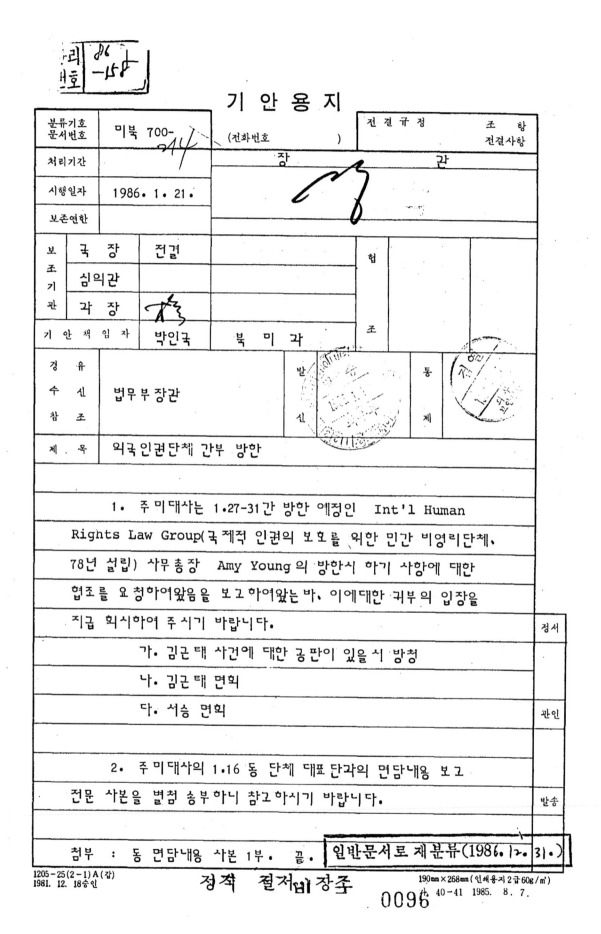

기 안 용 지

분류기호 문서번호	미북 700-	(전화번호)

전결규정 　조 항
전결사항

처리기간		
시행일자	1986. 1. 21.	
보존연한		

장 　　관

보 조 기 관	국 장	전결		협 조		
	심의관					
	과 장					

기 안 책 임 자	박인국	북 미 과

경 유	
수 신	법무부장관
참 조	

발
신　　통
제

제 목　외국인권단체 간부 방한

　　1. 주미대사는 1.27-31간 방한 예정인 Int'l Human

Rights Law Group(국제적 인권의 보호를 위한 민간 비영리단체,

78년 설립) 사무총장 Amy Young 의 방한시 하기 사항에 대한

협조를 요청하여왔음을 보고하여왔는 바, 이에대한 귀부의 입장을

지급 회시하여 주시기 바랍니다.

정서

　　　가. 김근태 사건에 대한 공판이 있을시 방청

　　　나. 김근태 면회

　　　다. 서승 면회

관인

　　2. 주미대사의 1.16 동 단체 대표 단과의 면담내용 보고

전문 사본을 별첨 송부하니 참고하시기 바랍니다.

발송

　　첨부 : 동 면담내용 사본 1부. 끝.　<u>일반문서로 재분류(1986.12.31.)</u>

1205-25(2-1)A(갑)
1981. 12. 18승인

정작 절저 장종

190mm×268mm (인쇄용지 2급 60g/㎡)
40-41 1985. 8. 7.

0096

발 신 전 보

번 호 : WUS-0369 일 시 : 601ㄴ7 1420   전보종별 : 지급

수 신 : 주 미 대사·총영사

발 신 : 장 관 (미북)

제 목 : 외국 인권단체 간부 방한에 대한 의견회신

　　　　대 : USW-0254

　　　대호 Amy Young 사무총장 방한시 협조요청 사항 관련 법무부의 입장은 다음과 같음을 참고 바람.

　　　1. 김근태 사건 공판 방청

　　　　ㅇ 제 6차 공판은 1·30 개정 예정이며, 공개재판의 원칙에 의하여 재판이 공개되나 법정질서의 유지를 위하여 재판장이 방청인을 제한할수 있음.

　　　　ㅇ 제 5차 공판까지는 재판장의 결정에 의하여 외국인은 방청이 금지된바 있었음.

　　　2. 김근태, 서승 면회

　　　　ㅇ 재소자와 무관한 외국인사의 면회는 불가함.

　　　예고 : 86·12·31·일반·

인권문서로 재분류(198 6.12.?)

양고재	86년 월 일	북미과	기안자	과장	국장	차관	장관
			이기철				

발신시간 :

외신과	접수자	과장

0097

법 무 부

검삽 700-3   503-7056   1986. 1. 24.

수신 외무부장관

참조 미주국장

제목 외국인권단체 간부 방한에 따른 의견 회신

귀부 미북 700-214(86. 1. 21.)와 관련, 아래와 같이 회신합니다.

                    아   래

1. 김근태 사건 공판 방청에 대하여

    동종사건 공판시 전례로 보아 외국인사가 방청하는 경우
피고인이나 방청객등이 법정에서 반정부 구호를 제창하는둥 소란이
예상되므로 외국인사의 방청은 바람직스럽지 못함.

2. 김근태, 서승에 대한 면회요청에 대하여

    재소자와 무관한 외국인사의 면회는 불가함. 끝.

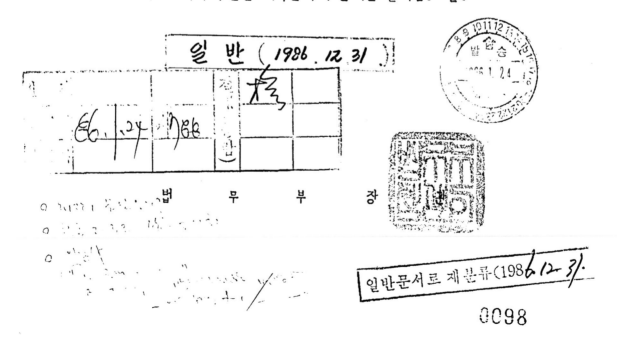

일 반 (1986. 12 31)

66. 1. 24   )66

법   무   부   장

일반문서로 재분류(1986 12 31.

0098

통 화 요 록

○ 통 화 일 시 : 1986.1.28(화) 18:00

○ 송 화 자 : Arvizu 2등 서기관

○ 수 화 자 : 박인국 사무관

○ 통 화 내 용 :

Arvizu : 본인은 내일 USIS 가 주관하는 세미나에 참석하기
위해 Dunlop 참사관과 함께 부여로 떠날 예정임.
2박 3일간 열리는 세미나에는 대학 신문에 관계된
학생들이 참석할 예정이며, 정기적으로 개최되는
모임임.

오늘은 한가지 요청할 일이 있음. 이미
알고 계시겠지만 Int'l Human Rights Group
의 사무국장인 Amy Young 이 방한하였음.

동인은 체한중 법무부나 검찰청의 관계자를
만나 김근태사건에 관한 정부측의 법적입장과 사건
배경등에 관한 설명을 듣고 아울러 한국의 사법제도
일반에 관해서도 의견교환을 희망하고 있음.
Amy Young 은 매우 신중하고 합리적인 사람인것
같았음.

0099

지난번 본인이 만났던 Lynn Packard
도 변호사였지만 완전히 개인적인 자격으로 방한을
하였기 때문에 대사관으로서도 어떤 판단을 내릴수
없었지만 이번 Amy Young 의 경우는 동기구의
성격등으로 보아 대사관으로서는 한국측 입장을
설명할수 있는 검사와의 면담이 유익할것으로 사료됨.

박사무관   :   IHRG 에 대한 귀관의 평가는 어떤지 ?

Arvizu   :   미국내 권위있는 인권단체중에 하나임. 동 단체가
                발행한 일부 간행물을 보면 한국의 일부 법적 절차에
                대해 비판적이긴 하지만, 다른 단체에 비해 합리적
                이며, 균형있는 입장을 취하고 있음.

박사무관   :   잘 알겠음. 관계부처와 협의하여 결과를 통보하겠음.

                                                        끝.

조치사항
1. 29 오전 북미2과장, 김경호 검찰3과장에 상기내용 통보
   오후 김경호 검찰3과장, 1. 30 15:00 면담가능 회신
   외무 방교국 사무관, Doming 2등서기관에게 면담가능 통보

   " 1. 30 15:00 법무부 검찰3과장 김경호 와 검찰부
     과의 면담이 확인 되었음 "

                                                    0100

미 주 국

1 9 8 6 . 2 . 3 .

북미담당관실	담 당	과 장	심의관	국 장	차관보	차 관	장 관

제 목   Amy Young, Int'l Human Rights Law Group
        사무국장 법무부 방문

요 약

1. 면담일시 : 86.1.30. 15:00-16:30

2. 면담대상 : 법무부 검찰국 검찰 3과장

3. 면담경위 : 주한미대사관을 통한 요청으로 당부에서
               주관

4. 주요 면담 내용

  o 김근태에 대한 고문등 가혹 행위 주장에 관한 법무부
     견해 청취

  o 주요 질문사항
     - 고문등 가혹 행위의 사실 여부
     - 변호인 및 가족의 접견 금지 여부
     - 외부 의사의 진찰 가능성
     - 김근태 처와 대한변호사 협회의 치안관계자 고소
       사건 처리 전망
     - 공판기록 열람 가능 여부

조치사항

0101

1986. 1. 30.

법 무 부 검 찰 국

0102

I. 개 요

o 일 시 : 86.1. 30. 15:00 - 16:30

o 장 소 : 법무부 검찰국 검찰제 3과장실

o 방 문 자

   . 에이미 영 (Amy Young Esq.)

     국제인권법협회 사무총장 (International
     Human Rights Law Group)

     * 동 단체는 1978년 포드재단등의 지원을 받아
       설립된 법률가 중심의 인권단체로 본부는
       워싱톤에 있음.

o 면담자

   . 법무부 검찰국 검찰제 3과장   김 경 한

o 배 석

   . 법무부 검찰국 검찰제3과 검사   김 승 년
                   "   이 상 형

o 통 역

   . 주한 미국대사관 직원   박 범 식

- 1 -

0103

Ⅱ. 면담내용

1. 방문자 인사

   o 면담에 응해 준데 대하여 감사하며, 김근태의
     인권문제에 관하여 몇가지 알아보러 왔으니
     협조해 주기 바람.

2. 검찰제3과장 인사

   o 국제인권법협회가 세계 각국의 인권상황에 관심을
     가지고 그 개선을 위해 노력하고 있는 점에 경의를
     표하고 당부를 방문한 것을 환영함.

   o 또한 Amy Young 여사가 일본에서 재일동포의
     법적지위 향상을 위하여 활동해 준데 대하여
     고맙게 생각함.

   o 우리 정부는 평소 인권상황의 개선과 향상을 위해
     부단한 노력을 경주하고 있음.

o 다만 어느 국가나 국민의 인권문제는 그 나라의
  시대적, 역사적 배경과 현실적 상황에 따라
  그 보장방법과 정도가 반드시 같다고는 할 수
  없다고 생각함.

o 우리나라의 긴박한 안보현실을 설명하고
  그러한 현실속에서 국가의 존립과 국민의 생존을
  위협하는 반국가사범에 대하여는 엄중히 대처하지
  않을 수 없음을 강조한 후,

o 김근태도 그러한 중대 안보사범의 1인임을
  설명.

- 3 -   0105

3. 구체적 대화내용

김근태가 경찰 수사기간중 고문등 가혹행위를

당하였다는 보고를 접하였는데 진실은 어떠한가.

고문이 사실이라면 관계자를 처벌해야 하지 않는가.

---

o 김근태는 민청련 이라는 불법단체의 의장으로서,

   1985. 2.경부터 불법시위를 주동한 혐의로 제적된

   학생들을 다수 모아놓고 북괴의 대남전술전략과

   일치되는 용공.폭력혁명 이념을 전파하고

   이를 위한 단체를 구성한 혐의로 1985. 9. 7.

   구속되어 현재 재판중에 있는 자임.

o 동인이 경찰 수사과정에서 가혹행위를 당하였다고

   주장하는 사람이 있으나, 검찰에서 다각도로 확인

   하여 본 결과, 고문등 가혹행위를 하였다고 인정

   할만한 사실이나 흔적을 발견할 수 없었음.

- 4 -   0106

o 김근례에 대한 고문시비는 그가 검찰에

송치되는 날 검찰청사에서 대기중이던 처를

보고 갑자기 복도에 주저앉아 이를 목격한

처가 아무런 근거도 없이 남편의 구명운동에

이용하려고 심한 고문을 당하였다고 재야

운동권 단체등에 악의적으로 외곡·과장전파

한데서 비롯된 것으로 밝혀졌음.

- 5 -

0107

김근태가 공산주의자는 아니라고 들었는데 어떠한가

o 김근태의 용공적 범죄사실은 수사과정에서

   여러가지 증거에 의해 이미 밝혀진 것이고

   또 앞으로의 재판과정에서도 사실관계가 명백히

   드러날 것이라 믿음.

- 6 -   0108

> 김근태가 경찰에 구속중일 때 변호인이나 가족과
> 면회한 사실이 있는가, 그 기간중 동인에 대하여
> 접견금지조치가 되어 있었다는데 사실인가.

o 우리 법률상 변호인은 형사절차의 모든 단계에서
  의뢰인을 접견할 수 있으나, 수사단계에서
  김근태는 변호인을 선임하지 않았으며 따라서
  그 기간중 변호인 접견은 없었음.

o 변호인을 제외한 다른 일반인에 대하여는 수사
  기간중 법에 따라 접견금지조치가 되었는데
  (형사소송법상 접견권과 그 제한규정 설명)
  동 사건은 관련자가 다수이고, 그들 상호간에
  통모를 하여 사실을 외곡하려는 움직임이 있으며,
  아직도 검거되지 아니한 관련자들이 수시로

- 7 -

0109

구속자들과 연락을 기도할 가능성이
농후하여 증거인멸의 우려가 있다고
판단되었으므로 변호인을 제외한 일반인의
접견을 금지한 것임.

- 8 -

0110

김근태에 대하여 의사가 진찰을 한 사실이 있는가.
또 외부의사에 의한 진찰도 가능한가.

o 구치소 의사가 김근태의 신체에 이상이 있는 가의
   여부를 확인한 결과, 이상이 없고 건강하다는
   보고를 받았음.

o 또 의료기술상의 이유로 구치소 의사만으로는
   충분한 진료를 할 수 없는 경우에는 외부의사의
   진료도 얼마든지 가능하나, 김근태의 경우는
   방금 언급한 바와 같이 건강에 이상이 없었으므로
   외부의사를 초빙할 필요성이 없었음.

- 9 -   0111

본인이 듣기로 김근태는 1회공판시부터 5회공판시
까지 법정에서 계속 고문을 당하였다고 주장하고
있는데 이에 대하여 재판부가 아무런 조치를 취하지
않고 있는 이유는 무엇인가.

o 우리나라도 미국과 마찬가지로 사법권이 완전히
   독립되어 있으므로 재판부의 조치에 대하여
   본인이 왈가왈부할 성질은 못됨.

o 그러나 우리 법률상 고문에 의한 자백은 유죄의
   증거로 할 수 없도록 규정되어 있으므로,
   재판부로서도 피고인의 그러한 주장에 깊은
   관심을 가지고 그 진위를 예의 판별할 것이라고
   믿음.

김근레의 처와 대한변호사협회에서 김근레의
그문사실에 관하여 내무부장관등 치안관게자를
고소한 사건은 어떻게 처리되고 있는가.
그 처리결과를 공표할 것인가.

o 김근래의 처가 어제 치안관게자등을 서울지검에
   고소하였으며, 이는 며칠전 변호사회에서
   고소한 사건과 동일한 내용이므로 앞으로 관할
   서울지검에서 함께 처리할 것임.

o 동 사건의 조사에는 어느정도 기간이 필요할
   것이며, 조사를 완료하는 대로 그 결과를
   고소인과 피고소인등에게 통보할 것임.

- 11 -

동 사건 고소 이전에 이미 정부에서 김근태를 고문한
사실이 없다고 표명하고 있으니 동 사건 고소는
아무런 실익이 없는 것이 아닌가.

○ 동 사건 고소 이전에 일부에서 김근태에 대한
  고문주장이 있어 검찰에서 다각도로 확인한 결과,
  고문사실을 인정할만한 증거나 흔적이 없었음은
  앞에서 언급한 바와 같음.

○ 그러나 고소인등이 새로운 증거를 제시하는
  등의 일도 있을 수 있으므로 검찰은 앞으로
  모든 상황을 거듭 정밀히 조사하게 될 것이라
  생각함.

- 12 -   0114

김근태사건 공판기록을 변호인이 열람할 수
있는가

o 변호인은 모든 사건의 공판기록을 열람할 수
   있음.

o 김근태사건 역시 변호인이 모든 사건기록을
   열람하고 있음.

- 13 -   0115

> 조금전에 설명하신 한국의 안보현실을 이해하나
> 그렇다 하더라도 고문은 금지되어야 한다고 보는데
> 이에 대한 견해는.

o 전적으로 동감하며 우리 법도 고문을 범죄행위로
  규정하여 고문행위자를 처벌하고 있으며,
  그문으로 인한 자백은 증거자료로 사용할 수
  없도록 하는등 고문방지를 위한 여러가지 장치들을
  마련하고 있고,

o 또 검찰은 사법경찰관리에 대한 지휘감독권을
  통하여 만에 일이라도 있을지 모르는 부당행위에
  대하여 세심한 관찰과 주의를 기울이고 있음.

0116

- 14 -

4. 맺는 말

(1) 검찰제 3과장

o 시간의 제약으로 좀 더 충분한 대화를 나누지
  못함을 섭섭하게 생각함.

o 북괴의 호전성 (특히 버마 아웅산 암살폭발사건),
  월남 공산화후의 월남국민 인권상황등을 강조 하고,
  북괴에서의 국제인권단체 활동 봉쇄사실등을
  상기시킴.

o 이와 같이 어려운 상황하에서도 정부는 인권개선을
  위하여 여러모로 노력해 왔고, 앞으로도 계속
  노력을 아끼지 않을 것이니 계속 관심을 기울여
  주기 바람.

- 15 -

0117

(2) 방문자

　° 검찰제 3과장의 설명으로 한국의 긴박한

　　현실을 이해하는데 큰 도움이 되었으나,

　　고문은 지구상에서 사라쳐야 할 악덕이므로

　　그 방지에 매견의 노력이 필요할 것이라

　　생각함.

　° 많은 시간을 내어 면담에 응해 준데 사의

　　표명.

0118

- 16 -

3. California 주 Berkeley 시, 광주의 날 선포문제, 1986. 4-5

외 무 부   착 신 전 문

번 호 : SFW-0208   일 시 : 604241100   종 별 :

수 신 : 장관 (영재, 정문)

발 신 : 주 상항 총영사

제 목 : 광주의날 선포

연: SFW-802(85.8.9)

   주상항정 700-354(85.8.23)

1. 주 라성총영사관(파견관)제보에 따라 당관이 확인 한바에 의하면 당지   BERKELEY
   시는 5.10을 광주의날 로 선포한다고 4.16   EUGENE GUS NEWPORT   시장이   PROCL
   AMATION   에 서명을 하였다고함(동 선포는 시의회의 의결을 거치지 않은 시장의 단
   독조치임)

2. 동 성명서는   YOUNG KOREANS UNITED   소속 최양일의 요청에 의한 것으로 광주가
   한국의 민주화와 문화발전에 선도적 역할을 하였다는 것과 광주사태시 3,000여명이
   사망 하였다는 것으로 되어 있다함

3. 동 성명서는 다소 배포가되어 회수는 어려울것으로 생각되나 더이상 유포되지 않
   도록 노력중에 있으며, 본직은 동시장을 면담코 광주사태의 진상을 설명, 동 선포가 그
   릇된 사실에 근거하고 있음을 인식시킬 예정임
   (시장 현재 출타중임)

4. 최양일(30세)영주권을 소지하고 있는 당지   HASTING LAW SCHOOL   학생으로 국회
   최치환 의원의 차남으로 알려지고 있는 자로서 지난 85.8.9 당관앞에서 데모를 한바
   있는   YOUNG KOREANS UNITED   핵심 인물임

5. 당지   BERKELEY   시 및 시의회 인사들은 전통적으로   RADICAL   한 성향을 강
   하게 띄고 있는바, 최근에는 동시를 불법 이민자들의   SANCTUARY   로 선프, 동 시내
   에서의 불법이민자들의 체포를 금하고 있고 동 시의회는   UNIVERSITY OF CALIFORNIA,
   BERKELEY   학생 데모에도 경찰의 투입을 반대한다는 결의안을 통과 시킨바 있음.

- (총영사 문기열-국장)   예고: 86.12.31 일반   86.(43)에 예고문에
의거 일반문서로 재분류됨

√ 영교국   차관실   1차보   2차보   정문국   미주국   청와대   안 기   총리실

PAGE   1   86.04.25   14:09
                                             외신 2과   통제관
                                             0120

발 신 전 보

번 호 : WSF-0183 일 시 : 6043061 0 전보종별 : 지급

수 신 : 주   상항   /뗴씨/ 총영사

발 신 : 장   관 (미북)

제 목 : 광주의 날 선포

대 ： SFW-0208

1. 광주 시장은 버클리 시장에게 표제건에 대해 광주
사태의 진상을 설명하는 내용의 서한을 발송할 것을 검토중에
있으니 참고 바람.

2. 이와는 별도로, 귀하는 동 시장을 조속 면담, 광주
사태 진상, 설명하고 결과 보고 바람. (미주국장)

예 고 ： 1987.12.31. 일반

검토필 (198 . . .)

보안
통제

영사교민국장:

앙 고 재	86 년 4 월 3 일	북 미 과	기안자		과 장	심의관	국 장		차 관	장 관	외 신 과	접수자	동 재
			이기철										

0121

발신 : ○○○○○○
수신 : 전미라(○○○)

6 ○○가 회하 주변이 불순한 정치적 목적을 가진 일부 인물들이
○○이 계속 되고 있음을 뒤늦게 알고 우려를 금치
못하며, 귀하에게 진실을 알려드리기 바라오니
우리 양국이 더 좋은 유대를 갖게되기 ○○는
마음에서 이 서신을 보내는 바입니다

친애하는 시장님

본인은 귀하께서 5월 10일은 광주 시민의 난을 결정, 선포
했다는 상심을 ○○과 우연인지 인지마저 무엇이라 표현할 수 없는
착잡한 심정으로 몇가지 유감스럽게 생각하는 사항에 대하여
밝히고도 되고 이의 시정을 촉구하고자 합니다.

먼저 귀하가 광주시민의 난을 선포함에 있어 광주시민에 대해 깊은
관심을 표명해 주신데 대하여 일면 감사를 드리는 바이나, 그 간은
조치를 강구함에 있어 광주시민을 대표하는 본인과는 한마디
합의도 없이 일방적으로 결정, 선포한데 대하여 유감의 뜻을
전하고자 합니다. 하여 다음과 같은 ○○○을 ○에○○에서
귀하의 이해를 촉구하려고 합니다.

다음 그 같은 조치가 이뤄지기 까지에는 필시 좋은 사되는 정치적
음모가 내재되어 있음을 본인은 지적하지 않을 수 없습니다.
즉, 광주 시민의 난 제정은 비정치적 순수한 동기에서 출발하지
않고 광주사태를 악용하려는 불순세력에 의해서 조직된 흔적이
너무 명확하다고 하는 것입니다.

그곳은 다음과 같은 사실도 입증됩니다.

첫째, 광주사태는 귀서의 선언문에 명시된것 같이 광주시민들의
민주주의에 대한 열망에서 비롯된 것이 아닙니다.

0122

6-1

1979년 10월 26일 박대통령이 급서하자 각종 정치세력들이 극단적인 정권경쟁을 벌여 국가의 안정질서가 무너지고 경제가 급속으로 냉각되는 와중에서 학생들은 과도정부 에게 조속히 정치를 정상화하도록 요구하며 계속적인 시위를 벌였읍니다.

동사태는 학생들의 시위와 이를 진압하는 과정에서 일부 불순세력의 선동과 유언비어 유포, 그리고 군경의 과격한 진압태도등 복합적인 요인에 의해 발생된 것입니다.

사태가 확대되자 학생들은 당황하여 모두 달아났고 일부 불순세력과 지부식간에 이들의 조종을 받은 폭력배들에 의해 난동으로 변했던 것입니다.

정부가 무한히 인내하였음 에도 불구하고 자기들의 재산과 다름 없는 수많은 정부 및 민간인 재산을 파괴, 방화하였으며 총 5,000정에 달하는 무기를 탈취, 많은 인명피해를 냈고 특히 고등고소를 습격한 행위를 민주적 시민의 행동이라고는 볼 수 없다는 ....
주광대 시장님께서도 동의하시리라고 봅니다.

동재, 귀시의 선언문에 "근 3,000명의 인명을 앗아간 시민의거" 다고 기술하고 있는데 아연실색하지 않을 수 없으며, 이점이 바로 불순세력들의 정치적 농간이라는 점을 인식해주시기 바랍니다.

0123

6 - 2

만일 "근 3,000명" 이라는 것이 사실이라면 그같이 주장하는
사람들은 비슷하게나마 그 근거를 제시해야 할 것입니다.
근거를 제시하지 못하는 한 그같은 주장은 극히 경계해야 할
불순한 주장으로 단정지을 수 있읍니다.

우 미식는 1980. 5. 27. 사태후 즉시 사망자 신고를 접수 했고,
민간인, 목사, 의사, 변호사등 49명으로 구성된 합동조사반역게
사망자수를 확인케 한 결과 총 191명이었으며, 이는 민간인 164명,
군인 23명, 경찰 4명으로 판명되었읍니다. 그리고 부상자는
122명의 중상자를 비롯, 극히 경미한자 까지를 포함, 총 852명
이었읍니다.

몸돈 조사는 연고자와 각종 증명을 확언하고 의학적, 법적 및
행정적 절차를 기쳐 실시되었읍니다. 심지어는 상해부위 및
중상위치를 확인키 위한 시체부검까지 실시하여 결본에 도달
했으며 이와 관련된 모든 서류가 완전무결하게 보관되어 있읍니다.

그리고 정부는 모든 상해자에 대한 보상금을 알선하는 한편
부상자들과 유족들 에게 무료 의료 혜택부여, 학비면제, 취업알선
등의 각종 시혜를 배풀고 있읍니다.

그럼에도 불구하고 일부 불순세력들은 특히 해외에서 3,000여명
운운하며 저항활동을 계속 행하여 왔읍니다.

0124

6- 3

이에 따라 아국의 국방장관은 85년 6월 7일, 125회 국회회기서 민간인 사망자가 164명외 더 있다면 언제든지 국회, 정당, 언론 기관, 종교 및 사회단체등 어떤 경로를 통해서라도 신고하도록 요망한 바 있읍니다.

이 공고후 85.6.7-9.7 (3개월)간 8명의 친적가 신고를 하였읍니다. 정부는 광주시를 관장하는 전남도지사를 위원장으로 심사위원회를 구성, 조사를 실시, 8명중 2명은 사태와 관련되어 사망한 것으로 인정하였고 잔여 6명은 사태기간중 행불사실이 인정되기는 하나 사태와 관련되어 사망했다고 입증할 자료가 전무하여 단순 행불자로 처리하였읍니다.

2명이 최초통지에 누락된것은 유족이 사태당시 신고를 기피단데 연유합니다. 그 이유는 사태직후에는 보상문제가 거론된바 없어 신고 필요성이 절실하지 않았고 또 무엇보다도 유족들이 사망과 동시에 독자적으로 시체를 매장 처리했는데 신고를 위해 시체를 다시파서 제시해야 하는 절차를 극히 꺼렸기 때문입니다.
(한국에는 매장된 시체를 다시파서 부검등 재조사하는 행위를 사람을 두번 죽이는 짓이다 하여 극히 꺼리합)

그러나 금번에는 유족들이 보상금을 수령키위해 신고를 했고 또 조사위는 묘소확인과 목격자 증언, 병원 관계서류등 만으로 사태와

0125

6-6

곧 던 사망한 사실을 인정하였읍니다.

물론 2명의 유가족에 대해서도 여타 유가족에게 한것과 같이 1인당 1,430만원의 위로금을 추가로 지급하였읍니다.

심사는 검사 지휘하에 가족과 친지 및 목격자의 증언청위, 호적부, 주민등록관계 공부조사, 그리고 병원기록조사등 합법적 절차와 모든 자료를 활용하여 실시되었음을 말씀드리며 아울러 이같은 자료들이 완전이 보존되어 있음을 전하고자 합니다.

따라서 동 사택와 관련 사망한 민간인은 166명으로 되어 있음을 강조해 말씀드리고자 합니다.

(그리고 동 민간인의 사망경위에 대하여 지면관계상 자세히 말씀 드릴 수 없음을 유감스럽게 생각하나) 사태와 관련된 보다 자세한 사항은 동봉하는 귀국의 *The Heritage Foundation*에서 85.9.16. 발간한 연구보고서를 필히 참고하여 주실것을 당부하고자 합니다.

친애하는 시장님

본인은 오도된 사실에 기초하여 어떤 행위가 이루어질 때 얼마나 큰 불행이 초래되는 것인가를 이번 기회에 절감하었읍니다.

0126

귀나가 일방적으로 광주시의 날을 제정, 선포한 사실과 그
배경을 인지한 많은 광주시 시민들은 침몰한 가운데 귀아의 판단을
~~더격 한 일부 불순세력에 대한 증오와 울분을 감추지 못하고 있~~
~~위처에 대한 연민 포만 자극합니다.~~ 서로 다른 조직 구성원간의
우정과 친선은 상호 이해와 협력, 그리고 사실에 그 근거를 두어야
한다고 생각하기 때문입니다.

따라서 오도된 사실에 근거하여 일방적으로 선포된 광주의 날
선포는 취소되어 마땅하다고 생각합니다.

본 광주시는 귀국의 텍사스주 산 안토니오시와 자매결연을
맺고 상호 우정어린 협력을 해오고 있다는 사실을 참고하시기
바랍니다여, 광주 시민들 기산들의 강렬함은 상처도 있고 긍지적으로
건강하고 있은 뜻도 합니다.

친애하는 시장님

국적적인 협력과 이해의 정신으로 광주시민에 대한 확고한
지원을 계속 확대하겠다는 귀하의 말씀에 다시한번 사의를 표하면서
진심에 기초하여 광주 시민에 대한 보다 깊은 이해와 사랑을 간직해
주실것을 바라는 바입니다.

0127

6-6

발 신 전 보

WLA-0596

번 호 : WSH-0185   일 시 : 6043018:00   전보종별 : ____

수 신 : 주 라성 //(?)// 총영사 (사본 : 주상항 총영사)

발 신 : 장   관 (미북)

제 목 : 광주의 날 선포

　　　1. 주상항 총영사 보고에 의하면 캘리포니아주 버클리시가 5.10을 광주의 날로 선포하는 성명서에 동 시장이 서명을 하였다 하는 바, 동 성명서는 광주가 한국의 민주화와 문화발전에 선도적인 역할을 하였다는 것과 광주 사태시 3,000여명이 사망하였다는 내용으로 되어있음 (연락처 : (?)937-9814)

　　　2. 동 성명서(선포)는 현재 귀지 체재중인 최치환 의원 (국민당)의 차남 최양일 (30세, 영주권 소지)의 요청에 의한 것이라고 하는 바, 동 의원에게 최양일과 연락, 동 성명서가 그릇된 사실을 기초로 하고 있으므로 동시의 광주의 날 선포가 취소되도록 설득할 것을 종용하고 결과 보고바람. (미주국장)

　　　예 고 : 1987.12.31. 일반

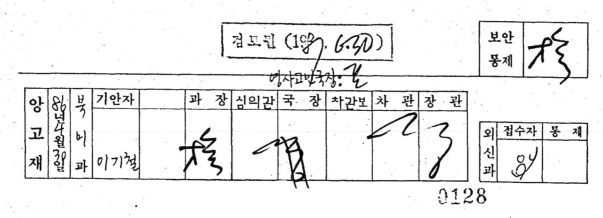

앙고재	86년4월30일	북미과	기안자		과 장	심의관	국 장	차관보	차 관	장 관
			이기철							

접수된 (1987. 6.30)
영사교민국장:

보안
통제

외신과 접수자 통제

0128

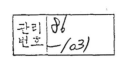

외 무 부

번 호 : SFW-0224　　　일 시 : 605011700　　　종 별 :

수 신 : 장 관 (미북,영재,정문)

발 신 : 주 상항 총영사

제 목 : 광주의날 선포

대 : WSF-0183

연 : SFW-0208

1. 대호 4.29 출장에서 귀임한　NEWPORT　버크리시장을 면담코자 연 3일간 노력하였음에도 상금 면담약속을 하지 못하고있는바 동 시장은 의도적으로 면담을 회피하고 있는것으로 판단되나 계속 접촉을 시도 하겠음.

2. 또한 광주의날 선프 관련, 주라성총영사관 통보에 의하면 라성을 방문중인 최치환의원은 동 의원의 차남 최양일의 연호 관련설을 <u>부인하</u>고있다 하는바, 당관은　BERKELEY 시 인접　OAKLAND　거주 변호사　MR.BRUCE QUAN,JR.　를 통해　BERKELEY 시　CITY ATTORNEY　를 접촉, "KWANGJU PEOPLE'S DAY" 라는 제목의 성명서를 입수하였고 동　CITY ATTORNEY　에게 동 선프경위를 문의한바 최양일이 배후에서 요청하였다고 알렸으며 최의 전화번호까지 가지고 있었음.

3. 상기와 같은 점과 85.8.9 당관앞 데모에 동인이 포함되었던 점등으로 보아 동 선포가 최양일의 요청에 의한것이라는 점은 신빙성이 있는것으로 판단됨.

(총영사 분기열-국장)

예 고 : 36.12.31. 일반

미주국　차관실　1 차브　2 차브　영교국　정문국　청와대　안 기

PAGE　1　　　　　　　　　　　　　　　86.05.02　14:20
　　　　　　　　　　　　　　　　　　　　의신 2과 통제관

0129

외 무 부   착신전보

번 호 : LAW-0721   일 시 : 605011730   종 별 : 지급

수 신 : 장 관 (미북,정이,기정등문)

발 신 : 주 라성 총영사

제 목 : 광주의 날 선포

대: WLA-0596

1.대호 관련,박부총 영사가 4.30.당지 체류중인 최치환 의원과 접촉한바를 아래 브고함

가. 최의원은 출국전에 이미 자기의 차남 최양일이 버클리시의 광주의 날 선포에 선도적인 역할을 하였다는 이야기를 듣고 최양일에게 이를 확인한바,최양일은 이에 전연 관여한바 없으며 자기는 전연 모르는 일로서 제3자가 자기를 악용하고 있는것이라고 단언하였다함

나.최의원은 또한 자기 아들에 의하면 동 주동 역할은 이경복과 최00(성명미상) 양인이 하고있는데 자기와 혼동하고 있는것인지 모른다는 의견을 개진하였다하며 최양일은 법과대학에 10위내에 들어있는 우수한 학생으로 5.19.까지 시험기간으로 현재 시험준비에 매진하고있어 그러한 일에 관여할 시간적 여유가 없고 또한 대한민국 정부에 대하여 건전한 생각을 갖고있다함

다.최의원은 워싱톤 방문후 시험 기간이 지난후 상항을 방문,더욱 정확한 상황을 알아브겠다 하였음

2.상기 최의원 발언 관련, 주상항 총영사관과 협의한바 주상항총영사관에서는 믿을만한 인사를 통하여 확인한 것으로 최양일의 선도적 역할은 확실한것으로 판단되고 있다하였음.

(총영사 김기수-국장)

예고:86.12.31.일반

19 86.12.27 에 예고문에 의거 일반문서로 재분류됨

외 무 부 착신전문

번 호 : LAW-0735   일 시 : 60504 1120   종 별 :

수 신 : 장 관(미북,영재,정문) 기정등문

발 신 : 주 라성 총영사

제 목 : 광주의 날 선프

연: LAW-0721

연호관련, 5.3(토) 최치환 의원과 재접측, 최양일의 버클리시 광주의날 선포에 선도적 역활에 관하여 아들과 접촉한바 있는지 여부와 아버지로서의 설득을 재 강조 한바 이를 아래 브고함.

1. 최의원은 연호 브고한 최양일의 무관여 입장에서 어느정도 후퇴한 입장으로 아니 땐 굴뚝에 연기날수 없다는 입장을 취하면서 일부 악질적인 자들에 의해 이용 당하고 있는것으로 브고있다 하였음.

2. 현재로서는 아들의 무죄를 단정할수 없지만 5.19.이후 상항을 방문, 아들의 관여 여부를 조사해서 사실인 경우 아버지로서 오해 소지가 없도록 조치할 것이며 그결과를 공관에 알려주겠다 하면서 이해해 줄것을 요청하였음. 끝.

(총영사 김기수-국장)

예고: 86.12.31. 일반

1986.12.31.에 예고문예
인반문서로 재분류됨

미주국   차관실   1 차보   영고국   정문국   청와대   안 기

4] 미 남가주 교회협의회 인권조사단 방한, 1986.6.20-

외 무 부   착 신 전 보

번 호 : LAW-0993   일 시 : 606181700   종 별 : 지급

수 신 : 장 관 (영재,미북,정일,해공,기정동문)

발 신 : 주 라성 총영사

제 목 : 미국 교회 인권관계 인사 방한 (자료응신 제 5호)

1. 금 6.18 (수) 오후 당지 김용성 (김상돈 사위,김대중 서울 귀환시 주치의로 수행)은 남가주 교회협의체인 SOUTHERN CALIFORNIA ECUMENICAL COUNCIL 내 소위 한국 인권문제 특별반 (TASK FORCE FOR HUMAN RIGHT IN KOREA) 조사단 (6명)이 방한 예정 (NW-23편, 6.20(금) 18:50 서울도착 약 1주일 체류)임을 통보하여옴과 동시 또한 미 국무성은 6.23(월) 10:00 주한 미대사관으로 하여금 이들에게 브리핑토록 조치하였다고 알려왔음.

2. 동 방문단 인적사항은 아래와 같음.

가. REV.DR.LESTER KIM(단장,한국인 3세)

나. REV.SPENCER GIBB(SYNOD OF SOUTHERN CALIFORNIA AND HAWAII, PRESBYTERIAN CHURCH)

다. DOUGLAS FITCH (METHODIST CHURCH OF SOUTHERN CALIFORNIA)

라. DIANNE KENNY (여, UNIV.OF SOUTHERN CALIFORNIA CHAPLAIN,UNITED CHURCH OF CHRIST)

마. LEE CABLE(QUAKER)

바. JAMES LEE(한국인 2세)

3. 동 김용성은 평소 국내 인권문제 운운하면서 동 교회협의체를 이용해온 인물로서 금번 교회 방문단 방한도 동인이 적극 추진하여온것으로 사료됨을 참고바람. 끝

(총영사 김기수-국장)

예 고 : 86.12.31. 까지

영교국   차관실   1차보   2차보   미주국   정문국   청와대   안 기   문공부

PAGE 1   86.06.19 11:29
외신 2과 통제관
0133

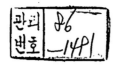

통 화 요 · 록
----

1. 일   시 : 86.6.20, 10:30

2. 송 화 자 : 김원수 북미과 사무관

3. 수 화 자 : Alexander Arvizu   주한미대사관 정무과 서기관

4. 제   목 : 남가주교회 협의회 인권 조사단 방한

김원수 : 남가주교회 협의회에서 인권조사단이 방한 예정

이라고 들었는 바, 이들의 체류 일정등에 관해 알고

있는지?

Arvizu : 처음 듣는 이야기임. 관내의 다른 직원이 담당하고

있는지 알아 보겠음.

(수분후 Arvizu 서기관 재차 통화)

관내에 확인한 결과, 대사관이 동 조사단을 위해

준비하고 있는 것은 6.23 오전의 브리핑(Lambertson

공사 실시 예정) 뿐임. 동 조사단은 브리핑외에

일정주선등 다른 요청을 하지 않았으며, 따라서

대사관으로서도 이들을 위한 별다른 지원 계획을

가지고 있지 않음. 아마도 한국내 교회나 인권

단체의 도움을 받아 독자적인 활동 계획을 추진하고

있는 것으로 보임.   끝.

예 고 : 1986.12.31. 일반

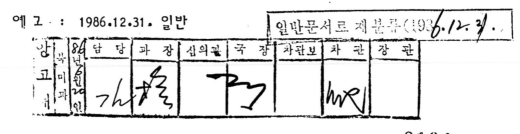

일반문서로 재분류(198 6.12.31.

	담 당	과 장	심의관	국 장	차관보	차 관	장 관
북미과 86년6월20일							

0134

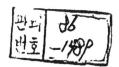

통 화 요 록
----

1. 일   시 : 86.6.23, 09:30

2. 송 화 자 : 김원수 북미과 사무관

3. 수 화 자 : Katheleen Stephens 주한미대사관 정무과 서기관

4. 제   목 : 남가주 교회협의회 인권조사단 방한 관계

김 원 수 : 표제 조사단에 대한 대사관 브리핑이 금 6.23
          오전중에 있을 예정이라고 들었음.

Stephens : 그러함. 본인도 동 브리핑에 동석 예정임.

김 원 수 : 금일 브리핑시 동 조사단이 정부측의 견해를 청취할
          의향이 있는지 여부를 문의하고 결과를 알려주기
          바람. 정부측으로서는 동 조사단이 아국 인권
          문제에 관하여 균형된 의견을 갖기를 희망하고 있음.

Stephens : 잘 알겠으며, 문의하겠음.

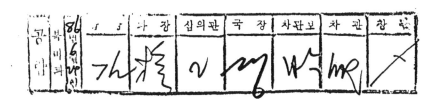

0135

(6.24. 10:30 Stephens 서기관 재차 통화)

Stephens : 작일 브리핑시 문의하였던 바, 동 조사단은
이 문제에 관해 정부측에 직접 연락하겠다고
하여 귀 사무관의 연락처를 주었음.

김 원 수 : 알겠음. 동 조사단중 누가 연락을 할 것인지?

Stephens : 동 조사단의 leader격인 Lester Kim
(한국계)임.   끝.

예 고 : 1986.12.31. 일반.

0136

미국 유학생 (양동화 , 김성만, 황대권) 간첩사건 , 1986. 6-11

0137

외 무 부   착신전문

번 호 : USW-2949   일 시 : 60616 1908   종 별 :

수 신 : 장 관 (미북)

발 신 : 주 미 대사

제 목 : 유학생 간첩사건

　　BERNARD KALB 국무성 대변인은 금 6.16(월) 정오 브리핑시 유학생 간첩사건 관련
자의 사형선고와 관련 질의에 대해 아래와 같이 답변함.

Q : AND SECONDLY, ON ANOTHER QUESTION UNRELATED TO THIS, ON MAY 31ST, TWO FORME
R STUDENTS OF WESTERN ILLINOIS UNIVERSITY, WHO ARE KOREANS, WERE GIVEN DEATH SEN
TENCES IN SOUTH KOREA ON CHARGES OF SPYING FOR NORTH KOREA, SOME OF IT WHILE THE
Y WERE IN THE UNITED STATES. A THIRD STUDENT HAD A LIFE SENTENCE. WHAT IS THE US
POSITION ON THE DEATH SENTENCE AND LIFE SENTENCE FOR THESE STUDENTS ?

MR. KALB : I DON'T HAVE ANYTHING NOW. LET ME TAKE THAT QUESTION.

Q : WELL, WHEN YOU TAKE IT, THE SECOND SECRETARY OF THE UNITED STATES EMBASSY, D
. KATHLEEN STEVENS, SAID AT THE END OF MAY THAT THE UNITED STATES --

MR. KALB : IN CONNECTION WITH THAT STORY ?

Q : IN CONNECTION WITH THIS CASE, THAT THE UNITED STATES HAS SO LITTLE INFORMATI
ON AVAILABLE TO US FROM THE SOUTH KOREA GOVERNMENT THAT WE'RE NOT IN A POSITION
TO COMMENT ON THE MERIT OF THE CASE. IS THE UNITED STATES REDOUBLING ITS EFFORTS
, OR DOING SOMETHING, TO FIND OUT MORE FROM THE SOUTH KOREAN GOVERNMENT ABOUT TH
E CASE OF THESE STUDENTS WHO ARE ALLEGED TO HAVE SPIED IN THE UNITED STATES ? OR
WILL THEY SIMPLY TAKE THE SOUTH KOREAN GOVERNMENT'S UNWILLINGNESS TO SUPPLY INF
ORMATION AS THE FINAL WORD WHILE THESE PEOPLE GET EXECUTED ?

MR. KALB : LET ME ADD THAT, TOO, DON, TO YOUR QUESTIONS.

(대사 김경원-국장)

미주국   1 차보   청와대   안 기   정문국

PAGE   1

86.06.17 10:15
외신 1과 통제관

0138

외 무 부 착신전문

번 호 : USW-2964   일 시 : 60617 1853   종 별 :

수 신 : 장 관 (미북)

발 신 : 주 미 대사

제 목 : 유학생 간첩사건

연: USW-2949

연호 6.16.(월) 국무성 브리핑시 유학생 간첩사건 관련 질문과 관련, 국무성 한국과
는 금 6.17.(화) 답변자료를 작성, 국무성 공보실에 게재하였다 하는바 아래 보고함.

TAKEN QUESTION

QUESTION TAKEN AT THE JUNE 16, 1986 DAILY PRESS BRIEFING KOREA -- STUDENTS SENT
ENCED FOR ESPIONAGE

Q : ON MAY 31 TWO FORMER STUDENTS OF WESTERN ILLINOIS UNIVERSITY, WHO WERE KOREA
NS, WERE GIVEN DEATH SENTENCES IN SOUTH KOREA ON CHARGES OF SPYING FOR NORTH KOR
EA, SOME OF IT WHILE THEY WERE IN THE U S. A THIRD STUDENT HAD A LIFE SENTENCE.
WHAT IS THE U S POSITION ON THE DEATH SENTENCE AND LIFE SENTENCE FOR THESE STUDE
NTS ?

A : ON MAY 31, A REPUBLIC OF KOREA APPELLATE COURT UPHELD DEATH SENTENCES FOR TW
O KOREAN MEN WHO, WHILE STUDENTS AT WESTERN ILLINOIS UNIVERSITY, ALLEGEDLY WERE
RECRUITED BY NORTH KOREAN AGENTS TO RETURN TO THE REPUBLIC OF KOREA TO ENGAGE IN
SUBVERSIVE ACTIVITIES ON BEHALF OF NORTH KOREA. A THIRD KOREAN MAN WHO ALSO STUD
IED AT WESTERN ILLINOIS UNIVERSITY HAS BEEN GIVEN A LIFE SENTENCE IN THE SAME CA
SE.

THE MEN HAD DISCONTINUED THEIR STUDIES IN THE UNITED STATES AND RETURNED TO RESI
DE IN THE REPUBLIC OF KOREA ABOUT A YEAR BEFORE THEIR ARRESTS. KOREAN PRESS REPO
RTS ALLEGE THAT ONE OF THE MEN TRAVELED TO NORTH KOREA FOR AGENT TRAINING, WHILE

미주국   1 차보   청와대   안 기   정문국

PAGE   1   86.06.18 09:39
                                                  외신 1과 통제관

                                                  0139

A SECOND RECEIVED SUCH TRAINING AT A NORTH KOREAN EMBASSY IN EASTERN EUROPE. BECAUSE OF THE U.S. CONNECTION, WE ARE FOLLOWING THIS CASE WITH PARTICULAR INTE REST. WE HAVE MADE A NUMBER OF INQUIRIES TO KOREAN AUTHORITIES AND OTHER CONCERN ED PARTIES IN AN ATTEMPT TO OBTAIN MOREINFORMATION ABOUT THE CHARGES AND THE EVI DENCE.

Q : THE SECOND SECRETARY OF THE US EMBASSY, D. KATHLEEN STEPHENS, SAID AT THE EN D OF MAY IN CONNECTION WITH THIS CASE THAT THE US HAS SO LITTLE INFORMATION AVAI LABLE TO US FROM THE SOUTH KOREAN GOVERNMENT THAT WE'RE NOT IN A POSITION TO COM MENT ON THE MERITS OF THE CASE. IS THE U S REDOUBLING ITS EFFORTS OR DOING SOMET HING TO FIND OUT MORE FROM THE SOUTH KOREAN GOVERNMENT ABOUT THE CASE OF THESE S TUDENTS, ALLEGED TO HAVE SPIED IN THE U S ? OR WILL IT SIMPLY TAKE THE SOUTH KOR EAN GOVERNMENT 'S UNWILLINGNESS TO SUPPLY INFORMATION AS THE FINAL WORD, AS THES E PEOPLE GET EXECUTED ?

A : WE ARE CONTINUING OUR EFFORTS TO OBTAIN MORE INFORMATIONA BOUT THE CHARGES A ND EVIDENCE IN THIS CASE. WE EXPECT THAT THIS CASE WILL BE APPLEALED TO THE KORE AN SUPREME COURT : DEATH SENTENCES UPHELD THERE ARE NORMALLY REVIEWED BY THE KOR EAN PRESIDENT.

(공사 한탁채)

0140

PAGE   2

기 안 용 지

분류기호 문서번호	미북 700-243 (전화 :)	시 행 상 특별취급	
보존기간	영구·준영구. 10. 5. 3. 1.	장 관	
수 신 처 보존기간			
시행일자	1986. 7. 12.		

보 조 기 관	국 장	전결
	심의관	V
	과 장	権
기안책임자	조백상	

협 조 기 관	

문서통제

발송인

경 유 수 신 참 조	법무부장관 검찰국장	발신명의	
제 목	자료요청		

대고문에 의거 일반공개 재분류 1987. 6. 30 서명

연 : 미북 700-566

주한미대사관은 별첨 양동화, 김성만, 황대권 사건에 관한

문서를 통해, 동인들이 미국 체류 유학생이었고 동인들의 기소 범죄

행위가 미국 체류중 활동과 관련되어 있을수 있음에 비추어 미측이

높은 관심을 갖고 있음을 상기시키며, 하기사항에 관하여 문의하여

왔는바, 이에대한 귀부의 의견또는 회신자료를 송부하여 주시기

바랍니다.

/계속/

1505-25 (2-1) 일(1)갑
85. 9. 9. 승인

190mm×268mm 인쇄용지 2급 60g /㎡
가 40-41 · 1985. 10. 29.

0141

- 아 래 -

1. 피고인들의 체포, 기소 및 공판일자

2. 피고인의 구체적 기소 범죄사실

3. 법정에 제출된 유죄입증 증거

4. 법정에서의 피고인 항변

5. 재판기록 입수 가능성 여부

6. 수사중 피고인이 신체적으로 부당대우를 받았다고

   피고 또는 변호인이 주장했는지 여부, 또는 피고인의

   구금중 기타 부당행위에 관한 주장이 있었는지 여부 및

   이에대한 법원의 판단

7. 동건이 항소 제기 되었는지 여부, 특히 김성만, 양동화의

   사형선고가 추후 재검토될지 여부

8. 피고인이 현재 구금되어 있는 장소 및 피고인에게

   방문객이나 변호인 면담이 허용되는지 여부

9. 피고인들의 현재 건강상태

   첨부 : 미대사관이 당부에 수교한 문서사본 1부. 끝.

Q142

<u>U.S. Government Request for Information</u>

The case of YANG Dong-Hwa, KIM Song-Man, HWANG Tae-Kwon, and their
co-defendants continues to draw considerable attention in the
United States. The Ministry of Foreign Affairs will recall that
the Embassy, on behalf of Senator Paul Simon, provided on February
24, 1986, a letter addressed to president CHUN regarding the case.
The Embassy and the Department of State have received numerous
other inquiries from congressmen and private American citizens,
most recently, on June 17, an inquiry from the Washington Post
regarding the case. Interest in the case is particularly strong
because Messrs. YANG, KIM and HWANG all were formerly students
in the United States and, according to Korean press reporting,
the charges against them, which have resulted in two death
sentences, are related in part to their activities while in the
U.S.

The Embassy appreciates the Ministry of Foreign Affairs' transmittal
on April 11 of information from the Ministry of Justice on the case.
In light of the continuing interest in this case and the fact that
according to newspaper accounts the defendants may have been
involved in activities in the U.S. requiring investigation by the
appropriate U.S. agencies, and because the carrying out of the
death sentences against Messrs. YANG and KIM would likely arouse
critical reaction in the United States if adequate explanatory
information is not available, we request the cooperation of the
Ministry in obtaining information on the following points:

--The precise dates the defendants were arrested, indicted and
  tried;

--The specific charges levied against the defendants;

--The nature of the incriminating evidence submitted at the
  trials;

--The pleas of the defendants at their trial;

--Whether trial transcripts are available;

--Whether the defendants or their lawyers alleged that they
  were mistreated physically during interrogation, or whether
  there were allegations of other irregularities during their
  detention, and the court's findings;

--Whether the case is being appealed, and in particular whether
  the death sentences of Messrs. KIM and YANG will be further
  reviewed;

--Where the defendants are now being held, and whether they are
  permitted to see visitors and their attorneys;

--The current state of health of the defendants.

0143

3. On the nature of the incriminating evidence
   submitted at the trials; Some 270 pieces of
   evidence were submitted at the trials.   They
   are composed of confessions of defendents,
   statements of other defendents, passports ~~made~~ prepared
   by North Korea for espionage activities in
   South Korea, seditious books, radio sets for
   listening to North Korean broadcast, and
   operational funds given by North Korea.

4. On the pleas of the defendents at the trials;
   They generally acknowledged the charges against
   them and requested clemency to the court, though
   there were some negations of the facts constituting
   offenses on the part of the defendents.

5. On whether transcripts are available;
   While
   ~~Because~~ the case is ~~being brought to~~ In the process of trial, it
   is in the domain of absolute authority of the
   court to approve the inspection and copy of the
   trial transcripts.   Current law permits lawyers
   to inspect and copy the documents related to
   on-going cases, otherwise, it does not permit
   transcripts of the trial to be sent to others.

0142

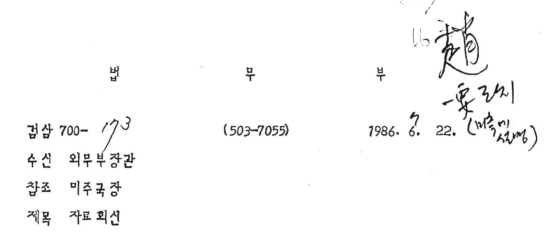

법 　 　 　 무 　 　 　 부

검삽 700-*173*　　　　(503-7055)　　　　1986. 6. 22.

수신　외무부장관

참조　미주국장

제목　자료회신

　　　귀부 미북 700-2439 (86. 7. 14) 와 관련, 공안사범 양동화외

2명에 대한 관계자료를 별첨과 같이 송부합니다.

　　첨부 : 자료 1부. 끝

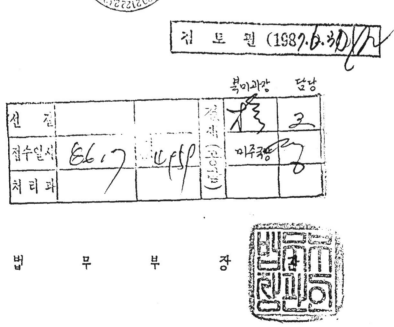

법　　무　　부　　장

0145

"별   첨"

ㅇ 피고인들의 체포, 기소 및 공판일자

    - 구속일자 : 85. 7. 30

    - 기소일자 : 85. 9. 4

    - 공판일자 : 1심 ┌─ 양동화, 김성만 : 86.1.20 : 사   형 ─┐

                        └─ 황대권   : "   : 무기징역 ─┘

                    2심 - 양동화, 김성만, 황대권 : 86.5.31 : 항소기각

                    3심 -   "   : 상고심계속중.

ㅇ 피고인의 구체적 기소 범죄사실

    - 양동화, 김성만 : 83. 9 - 85. 6간 유학차 체미중 재미 북괴

       공작책 서정균에게 포섭되어 동구마파를 경유 입북, 밀봉교육을

       받고 국내침투, 광주 및 서울지역 운동권 학생을 포섭, 폭력시위

       선동 및 공산주의 지하유인물 제작 배포하고 공공건물 폭파 및

       무장봉기로 제2의 광주사태 반발을 기도하는 한편, 우리나라의

       군사상황, 학생동향등 국가기밀을 탐지수집 하는등 간첩활동.

0146

- 황대권 : 유학차 도미, 83. 2 - 85. 5간 위 서정균 에게
  포섭되어 북괴선전영화 관람등 사상무장후 지명사항 수행코자
  국내잠입, 양동화에게 입북을 종용하고 불온서적 및 불온유인물을
  탐지수집 하는등 간첩활동.

o 법정에 제출된 유죄입증 증거

  - 피고인의 자백, 다른 피고인외 진술 및 압수된 북괴 대남공작용
    여권, 불온책자, 북괴방송 청취용 라디오, 공작금등 270여종의
    증거물.

o 법정에서의 피고인 항변
  - 범죄사실을 대체로 시인하고 선처를 바란다는 진술을 함.
    (일부 사실은 부인)

o 재판기록 입수 가능성 여부
  - 동사건은 현재 공판 계속중이므로, 동사건 기록의 열람,복사허가는
    재판부의 전권에 속하는 사항이며, 현행법상 변호인은 소송계속
    중의 관게서류를 열람 또는 등사할 수 있으나, 그 이외의 경우 에는
    재판기록의 사본을 송부할수없도록 규정되어 있음.

0147

° 수사중 부당한 대우를 받았다는 피고인 또는 변호인의 주장 유무등

  - 부당한 대우를 받았다는 주장 없었음.

° 항소제기 여부, 사형선고 재검토 여부

  - 85. 5. 31. 항소기각되고, 현재 상고심 계속중이므로 대법원

    에서 형량의 적정여부를 면밀히 재검토 할 것임.

° 피고인의 구금장소, 변호인등 면담 허용여부

  - 양동화, 김성만 : 서울구치소

  - 황대권   : 대전교도소

  - 면담가능   : 친족 및 변호인의 접견은 언제든지

                    허용됨.

° 피고인 현재 건강상태

  - 양호함.

                                                    0148

면 담 요 록

1. 일   시 : 1986년 7 월 25 일(금 요일) 11:00 시〜11:30 시

2. 장   소 : 북미과

3. 면 담 자 : 조백상 사무관

   Alexander Arvizu   주한미대사관 정무과 서기관

4. 내   용 :

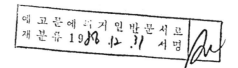

조백상 : 일전에 Dunlop 참사관이 미주국장에게 수고 했던 양동화,
        김성만, 황대권 사건에 대한 문의에 대해 설명코자 귀하를
        불렀음. 법무부로부터 상세한 답변이온 바, 귀하에게 설명
        하고자 함.   (별첨 법무부의 회신자료 설명)

Arvizu : 상세한 설명에 감사함. 동건관련 몇가지 질문을 하겠음.
         많은 미국인들은 자유 세계인 미국에서 한국의 유학생들
         (양동화등 3인)이 반정부 활동을 했던것에 대해 그렇게
         심한 사형선고를 내릴수 있는가에 대해 의아해 하고 있음.

공람	북미과	86년7월25일	담당	과장	심의관	국장
			조			

0149

조 백상 : (사견임을 전제하며) 단지 미국 내에서 반정부 활동을 했다고
해서 그러한 형을 내리는 것이 아님. 미국에 거주하는 많은
수의 반정부 고민, 학생들에 대해 한국정부는 그것을 이유로
어떠한 형사적 제재를 가하지 않음. 양동학, 감성만의
경우 문제는 미국 내에서의 활동이 아니라 미국을 떠나 동구
경유, 북한에 입국, 간첩교육을 받고 한국에 와서 명백한
간첩행위를 했다는 점임. 미국거주 교민들이 북한에간
경우가 있지만, 이산가족 재회를 위한 이들의 방북에
대해서도 한국정부는 어떠한 법적제재를 가하지 않음.
문제는 양동학, 감성만은 도미전 한국에서 고등교육 이상을
이수하여 북한에 가거나 북한을 위한 간첩행위가 얼마나
큰 이적행위인지를 잘 알고 있음에도 북한에가서 간첩교육을
받았고 입국하여 간첩행위를 했다는 점임. 미국에서도
소련을 위한 첩보행위에 대해 엄벌에 처하고 있는 점을
재미중 자주 목격했었음.

Arvizu : 귀하의 설명에 수긍이감. 이와관련 양인에 대한 사형선고가
감형될 가능성에 대해서는 어떻게 생각하는지 그리고 언제쯤
최종선고가 내려지는지 ?

조 백상 : 지금 대법원에서 최종 상고심이 진행중이란 사실외는 알고
있지 않음. 이미 설명했듯이 대법원에서 기존형량의
적절성에 대해 신중한 검토가 있을것임.   끝.

The following is *the* reply on the part of the Ministry
of Foreign Affairs to the inquiry made by U.S.
Embassy on the case of Yang Dong-Hwa, Kim Song-Man
and Hwang Tae-Kwon.

On (*The precise dates the defendants were arrested, indicted and tried;*)

1. Yong Dong-Hwa, Kim Song-Man and Hwang Tae-Kwon
   were arrested on July 30th, 1985, and indicted
   on September 4th, 1985. They were tried on
   January 20th, 1986 at the district court.
   Their appeal to the appellate court was rejected
   on May 31st, 1986 and the trial of the Supreme
   Court is in progress now.

2. The specific charges levied against the defendants
   are as follows;

   A) Yang Dong-Hwa and Kim Song-Man :

   While they stayed in the United States from
   September 1983 to June 1985, they were brought
   around to Suh Chung Kyun's side who ~~is~~ *was* a
   pro- North Korea's *collaborator* secret agent ~~operating~~ *residing* in
   the United States. They went to North Korea
   via Eastern European Communist Countries and
   returned to South Korea after being trained as
   espionages. They enticed some radical
   (In North Korea) *[sic]*

양고재	북미과	86년 7월 24일	담당	과장	심의관	국장
			2			

0151

activist students in KwangJu and Seoul into
stirring up violent demonstrations and into
producing and circulating underground printed
works praising Communist idealogy. They
attempted to initiate the second Kwangju
riots by blowing up official buildings and
through the armed insurrection. Furthermore,
they were engaged in espionage activities by
dectecting and gathering secrects for
National Security such as military situation
and student activities.

B) Hwang Tae-Kwon:

He stayed in the United States for study
from Feburary 1983 to May 1985. He was
brought around to Suh Chung Kyun's side and
indoctrinated by him by watching North Korea's
propaganda films while in the United States.
He returned to Korea to perform the missions
given by North Korea. He persuaded Yang
Dong-Hwa to enter North Korea while he also
was engaged in espionage activities by
detecting and gathering seditious books and
printing materials.

0152

6. On the allegations of the defendents or lawyers
   that they were mistreated during interrogation
   or on whether there were allegations of other
   ir regularities during their detention, and the
   court's findings; There were no allegations that
   they were mistreated.

7. On whether the case is being appealed, and in
   particular whether the death sentences of
   Messrs. Kim and Yang will be further reviewed;
   The appeal was rejected on May 31st, 1986.
   Now that the trial of the Supreme Court is
   continuing, the final court will carefully
   review the propriety of the sentence terms of
   them.

8. On where the defendents are now being held, and on
   whether they are permitted to see visitors and
   their attorneys;

   A) Yang Dong-Hwa and Kim Song-Man are being
      held in Seoul Detention Institution.
   B) Hwang Tae-Kwon is being held in Taejon Prison.
   C) Close relatives and attorneys are permitted
      to see the defendents.

0153

9. On the current state of health of the defendents;

They are in good helath.

기 안 용 지

분류기호 문서번호	미북 700-3103				시 행 상 특별취급	
보존기간	영구·준영구. 10. 5. 3. 1.	장			관	
수 신 처 보존기간						
시행일자	1986. 9. 9.					

(전화:)

보 조 기 관	국 장	전결	협 조 기 관		문 서 통 제	
	심의관				검열 1986. 9. 10	
	과 장					
기안책임자		조맹상				

경 유 수 신 참 조	법무부장관	발신명의	

제 목	인권관계 문의

대 : 검삼 700-173

현재 방한중인 미국무성 Blakemore   한국 과장은

양동화、김성만、황대권 사건에 대한 미국무성측의 문의사항을

아래와같이 전달한바、이에 대응하는 설명자료를 당부로 송부하여

주시기 바랍니다.

- 아 래 -

1. 동인들에 대한 죄목의 상세내용、특히 범죄구성 요건에

해당되는 일리노이주에서의 행위가 있는지 여부 및 행위가 있을경우

1505-25(2-1) 일(1)갑
85. 9. 9. 승인

0155

190mm×268mm 인쇄용지 2급 60g/㎡
가 40-41 1986. 2. 13.

한국 인권문제와 관련한 제 사안, 1985-86 **161**

상세한 범죄행위 (일리노이주에서의 행위는 미국의 관할권과도 관련이

있는 사항임.)

    2. 양동학, 김성만 양인에 언도된 사형에 대한 형량의 적절성

여부 (미국민이 일반적으로 관심을 가지고 있는 사항임)　　끝.

법 무 부

검삼 700- 205   (503-7055)   1986. 9. 12.

수신 외무부장관

참조 미주국장

제목 자료회신

　　　귀부 미북 700-3163 (86. 9. 10)와 관련, 공안사범 양동 확등에
대한 관련자료를 별첨과 같이 송부합니다.

첨부 : 관련자료 1부.   끝.

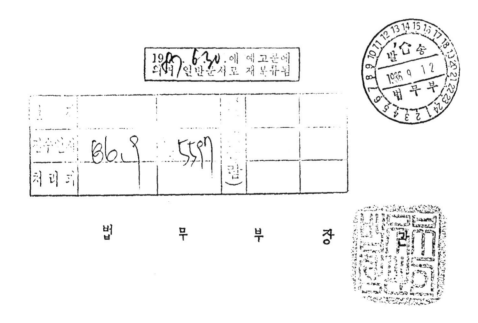

법 무 부 장

0157

관 련 자 료

○ 양동화, 김성만, 황대권등에 대한 구체적 범죄내용 및
  형량의 적정성 여부에 대하여는 당부 검삼 700-173
  (86. 7. 14.)을 참조 하시기 바람.

○ 동인들의 미국내에서의 범법행위에 관하여 :
  동인들은 82. 8.경 일리노이 주립대학에 입학, 수학
  하게됨을 기화로 그 경부터 북괴공작원 서정균에게
  포섭되어 동인으로부터 남한혁명을 위한 전략 전술 및
  투쟁방법인 요인암살방법등을 교육받고, 방학을 이용하여
  국내지하 혁명 조직을 점검지도 및 지하혁명 조직 결성
  가능성 탐지 등 간첩활동을 지령 받는등 범법행위를
  한 것임.

0158

관리번호 86-206

법　　무　　부

검사 700-206　　　　　503-7059　　　　　1986. 9. 13.
　　　　　　　　　　　　　　　　　　　　Blakemore 관계?

수신　외무부장관
제목　인권관련 문의에 대한 회신

　　미북 700-3162('86. 9. 9)에 의거 강종건에 대한 보안처분 현황을 별첨
과 같이 송부합니다.

　　첨부:　강종건 관련자료 1부. 끝.

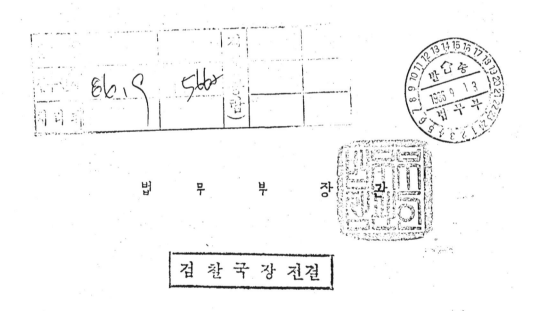

법　무　부　장

검 찰 국 장 전 결

0159

강 종 건 관 련 자 료
= = = = = = = = = = = = = = =

1. 범죄사실

   ° 1973. 4. 5. 서울대 제외국민연구소 수학중 학생들에게 북괴 찬양

   ° 1973. 8. 부터 1975. 10. 까지 4회 일본을 왕래하면서 대한민국의
      정치정세, 학생동향등을 조총련에 보고하는 등 간첩활동

2. 재판. 수형사항

   ° 1976. 12. 14. 대법원에서 국가보안법위반등으로 징역 5년, 자격
                    정지 5년 선고   '

   ° 1981. 2. 14. 출소

3. 보안처분 현황

   ° 1981. 2.14. 보안감호
   ° 1985. 2.14. 2차 기간갱신

4. 계속 보안감호에 처하는 근거

   ° 동인은 간첩활동을 하는 등 죄질이 중한 자 임에도 불구하고 현재
      까지도 개전의 정이 없이 사상전향을 극구 거부하고 있으며 감호중
      북괴를 찬양하고 관규를 어기는 등 동향이 불량하여 계속 보안감호

0160

중 임.

5. 외국 입법례

o 반국가사법에 대한 보안처분제도는 국가의 정치적 불행을 사전에
방지하기 위해 고안된 제도로서 선진제국의 경우에도 대부분 동
제도를 채택 실시중 임(엑, 일본의 파괴활동방지법, 자유중국의 징
치반란조례, 말레이지아의 국내안전법).

o 특히 우리나라가 처한 특수한 안보상황을 고려한다면 동 제도는
필수적임.

0161

기 안 용 지

분류기호 문서번호	미북 700- 3346	(전화 :)	시 행 상 특별취급	
보존기간	영구·준영구. 10. 5. 3. 1.		장 관	
수 신 처 보존기간				
시행일자	1986.9.22.			

보 조 기 관	국 장	전 결	협 조 기 관		문 서 통 제 검열 1986.9.24 외무부 보안담당자
	심의관				
	과 장				
기안책임자	조 백상				발 송 인

경 유 수 신 참 조	주 미 대사	발신명의		발송 1986.9.24 외무부

제 목	양동화 관련 자료 송부

Blakemore 미국무성 한국 과장은 방한시 양동화등

사건과 관련, 이들의 미국 내에서의 범죄행위 및 이들에 대한 형량의

적절성 여부를 문의하였는 바, 별첨 법무부의 의견을 송부하니

귀관에서 동인에게 적의 설명 바랍니다.

첨 부 : 양동화 관련 자료 1부. 끝.

1505-25(2-1) 일(1)갑
85. 9. 9. 승인

0162

190mm×268mm 인쇄용지 2급 60g/㎡
가 40-41 1986. 2. 13.

168 한국 인권문제 제 사안 1

1. 피고인들의 체포, 기소 및 공판일자

  ○ 구속일자 : 85.7.30

  ○ 기소일자 : 85.9.4

  ○ 공판일자 :

    - 1심 : 양동화, 김성만 : 86.1.20, 사형,

            황대권 : 86.1.20, 무기징역

    - 2심 : 양동화, 김성만, 황대권 : 86.5.31, 항소 기각

    - 3심 : 양동화, 김성만, 황대권 : 86.5.31, 상고심 계속중

2. 피고인의 구체적 기소 범죄사실

  ○ 양동화, 김성만 : 83.9-85.6간 유학차 체미중 재미 북괴
    공작책 서정균에게 포섭되어 동구라파를 경우 입북, 밀봉
    교육을 받고 국내침투, 광주 및 서울지역 운동권 학생을 포섭,
    폭력시위 선동 및 공산주의 지하유인물 제작 배포하고 공공
    건물 폭파 및 무장봉기로 제2의 광주사태 발발을 기도하는
    한편, 우리나라의 군사상황, 학생동향등 국가기밀을 탐지수집
    하는등 간첩활동

  ○ 황대권 : 유학차 도미, 83.2-85.5간 위 서정균에게 포섭
    되어 북괴 선전영화 관람등 사상 무장후 지령사항 수행코자
    국내잠입, 양동화에게 입북을 종용하고 불온서적 및 불온
    유인물을 탐지수집 하는등 간첩활동

0163

3. 피고인의 미국 내에서의 범법행위
   ○ 동인들은 일리노이 주립대학에 입학, 수학하게됨을 기화로
     북괴공작원 서정균에게 포섭되어 동인으로부터 남한혁명을
     위한 전략전술 및 투쟁방법인 요인암살 방법등을 교육받고,
     방학을 이용하여 국내지하 혁명 조직을 점검지도 및 지하
     혁명 조직 결성 가능성 탐지등 간첩활동을 지령받는등의 범법
     행위

4. 법정에 제출된 유죄입증 증거
   ○ 피고인의 자백, 다른 피고인의 진술 및 압수된 북괴 대남
     공작용 여권, 불온책자, 북괴방송 청취용 라디오, 공작금등
     270여종의 증거물

5. 법정에서의 피고인 항변
   ○ 범죄사실을 대체로 시인하고 선처를 바란다는 진술을 함.
     (일부 사실은 부인)

6. 재판기록 입수 가능성 여부
   ○ 동사건은 현재 공판 계속중이므로 동사건 기록의 열람, 복사
     허가는 재판부의 전권에 속하는 사항이며, 현행법상 변호인은
     소송 계속중의 관계서류를 열람 또는 등사할 수 있으나, 그 이
     외의 경우에는 재판기록의 사본을 송부할 수 없도록 규정되어
     있음.

0164

7. 수사중 부당한 대우를 받았다는 피고인 또는 변호인의 주장
   유무등

   o 부당한 대우를 받았다는 주장 없었음.

8. 항소 제기 여부, 사형선고등 형량 재검토 여부

   o 85.5.31, 항소 기각되고, 현재 상고심 계속중이므로 대법원
     에서 형량의 적정여부를 면밀히 재검토할 것임.

9. 피고인의 구금장소, 변호인등 면담 허용 여부

   o 양동화, 김성만 : 서울 구치소
   o 황대권   : 대전교도소
   o 면담가능   : 친족 및 변호인의 접견은 언제든지 허용됨.

10. 피고인 현재 건강상태

   o 양호함.

0165

발 신 전 보

번 호 : WUS-3984 일 시 : 60924 1830   전보종별 : _____

수 신 : 주   미   대사·병영사   사본 : 미주중요

발 신 : 장   관 (미북)

제 목 : 양동화 관련 자료 전달

연 : 미북700-3346

본부는 9·23. 주한미대사관 인권담당자를 불러 Blakemore
한국 과장이 방한시 거론했던 양동화 관련 자료를 전달했으니
참고 바람.

(미주국장대리 조 갑동)

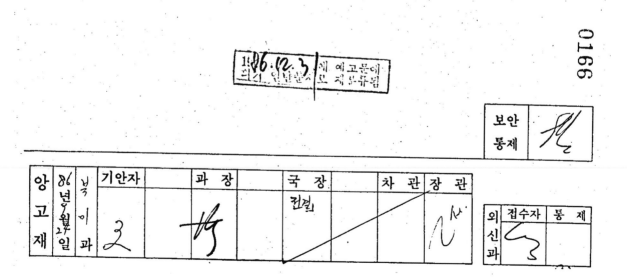

면 담 요 록

1. 일   시 : 1986년   9 월 23 일(화 요일)14:30 시 ~ 15:00시

2. 장   소 : 북미과

3. 면 담 자 : 김원수, 조백상 사무관
             주한미대사관 Arvizu 서기관

4. 내   용 :

　　　아측은 Blakemore   미국무성 한국과장 방한시 거론했던
양동화 관련 사건에 대한 법무부위 의견, 주한미대사관 Stephens 가
요청한 강종건 관련 자료 및 최근 논의되고 있는 헌법개정안의
민정당측 초안과 신민당측 초안을 미대사관측에 전달하였음.　　　끝。

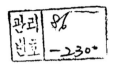

면 담 요 록

1. 일   시 : 1986년 10 월 6 일(월 요일)15:00 시 ～ 15:30시

2. 장   소 : 미주국장실

3. 면 담 자 : 미주국장

   Dunlop   주한미대사관 참사관

4. 내   용 :

   Dunlop : 시카고 유학생 간첩사건 관련、대법원이 양동화、김성만에
              대한 사형、황대권、강영주에 대한 종신형을 확정 판결
              했다는 사실을 동인의 가족으로 부터 들어서 알고 있음.

              미대사관은 동인들의 가족들로 부터 자주 진정을
              받고 있으나 본건은 사건의 성질상 미국이 개입할 문제가
              아니며 또한 동인들의 구명을 위해서 캠페인을 벌일수도
              없는 것이 미국의 입장임.

공람	복사미파	76년생원1일	담당	과장	심의관	국장	차관보	차관	장관
			3	테	2	7			

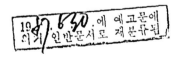

0168

미국의 인권단체등이 동건을 거론할지는 모르나
대사관으로서는 문제화할 의사가 전혀 없음. 다만 이와
관련 미국의 언론이나 여론이 문제로 제기할 경우 설명
자료로서 필요할지 모르니 동건 관련 대법원의 확정
판결문이나 동인들이 미국에서 간첩활동을 한것과관련된
추가 자료를 협조받을 수 있으면 고맙겠음.

미주국장 : 본건과 관련, 이미 관계부처로 부터 자료를 받아 미측에
　　　　　 협조 제공한 것은 귀하도 잘 알고 있으리라 생각함.
　　　　　 그러나 동건은 전적으로 사법부의 고유 관할권에 속하는
　　　　　 사항이며 외무부로서는 추가 자료가 입수되는 대로 귀측에
　　　　　 협조 하겠음.

* 참고 : 양동화, 김성만, 황대권등 미유 학생 간첩사건의 최종
　　　　 대법원 판결이 9.23 있었음. 　　　　 끝.

0169

기 안 용 지

분류기호 문서번호	미북 700-354 (전화:)	시 행 상 특별취급	
보존기간	영구·준영구. 10. 5. 3. 1.		
수 신 처 보존기간			
시행일자	1986.10.9.		

보조기관	국 장	전 결	협조기관		문 서 검동열 제 1986.10.10 외무부 보안담당관
	심의관				
	과 장				
기안책임자		조 백상			발 송 인 1986.10.10

경 유 수 신 참 조	수신처 참조	발신명의	

제 목	양동화 사건 관련 자료 협조

　　　1. 주한미대사관측은 9·23 확정된 양동화등 미유학생

간첩단 사건과 관련 미 인권단체나 언론 기관의 문의에 대비 동건의

대법원 최종 판결문과 미국 내에서의 간첩활동에 관해 법원에 제출 된

증거에 대한 협조가 가능한지를 문의하여 왔읍니다.

　　　2. 동건에 대한 상기 자료 제공은 동건으로 인해 야기될 수

있는 한·미 양국 간의 불필요한 문제를 사전에 방지하는 의미에서

필요할 것으로 판단되어 요청하오니 관련 자료를 당부로 송부하여

주시기 바랍니다. 1986.12.31에 예고문에 의거 일반 서로 재분류됨 / 계속 /

수신처 : 법무부장관 (참조 : 검찰국장)、

국가안전기획부장 (참조 : 제1국장)

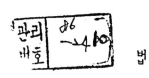

법   무   부

검삽 700- 227   (503-7055)   1986. 10. 21.

수신 외무부장관

참조 미주국장

제목 자료회신

1. 미북 700-3541 (86. 10. 10) 과 관련입니다.

2. 양동확등 사건의 판결문등은 현행법상 피고인등 소송관계인

이외에는 교부할 수 없으므로, 이를 송부할 수 없으니 양해하시기

바라며, 동 사건의 기타사항에 대하여는 당부 검삽 700-205 (86. 9. 12)을

참조 하시기 바랍니다. 끝.

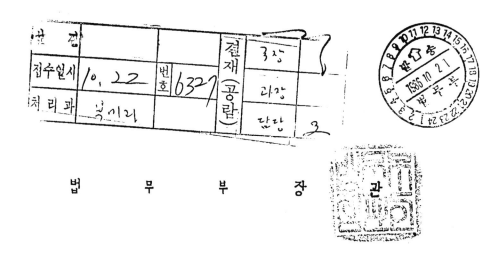

법   무   부   장

0172

통 화 요 록

일   시 : 1986.10.14. 15:00

송 화 자 : 안기부 수사 1과장

수 화 자 : 외무부 북미과장

제   목 : 양동화 사건 관련 자료 협조

수사 1과장 : 양동화사건에 대한 대법원 최종 판결문은 법원에서
            관할하는 것으로 알고 있음. 아직 미측에서 문제시
            하지 않고 있으니 반응을 기다렸다 다시 공식 거론할
            경우 관계부처 대책회의를 통해 의견 조정을 함이
            바람직할 것으로 봄.

북미과장 : 동감임. 미측의 반응을 유의하겠음.   끝.

0173

外　務　部　착신전문

관리번호 86-137

번 호 : USW-4843　　　일 시 : 610231653　　　종 별 :

수 신 : 장관(미북) 사본:김경원주미대사

발 신 : 주미대사대리

제 목 : 양동화등 감형요청

대: 미북 700-784, 334 6

　　STEPHEN SOLARZ　하원 아태소위원장은 김성만 및 양동화에 대한 감형을 탄원하는 아래 멧세지를 대통령 각하께 상달해 줄것을 금 10.23. 자 주미대사앞 서한으로 요청하여 왔음을 보고함.

DEAR MR. PRESIDENT:

I AM WRITING CONCERNING KIM SONG MAN AND YANG DONG HWA, TWO CITIZENS OF THE REP
UBLIC OF KOREA WHO HAVE BEEN CONVICTED ON ESPIONAGE CHARGES AND SENTENCED TO DE
ATH.

I UNDERSTAND AND RESPECT THE KOREAN GOVERNMENT S LAWS ON THESE QUESTIONS. MY CO
NCERN IS WITH THE HARSHNESS OF THE PUNISHMENT. IF ALL THAT WERE INVOLVED IN THESE
CASES WERE MEETINGS WITH NORTH KOREAN AGENTS, AND NOT ANY OVERT ACTS OF ESPIONA
GE OR TREASON, I HOPE THAT YOU WILL CONSIDER ON HUMANITARIAN GROUNDS COMMUTING T
HE DEATH PENALTY TO A PRISON TERM.

THANK YOU VERY MUCH.

SEPTHEN J. SOLARZ

(공사 한탁채-차관)

예고 : 1987.6.30. 일반

미주국　차관실　1 차보　청와대　안 기

PAGE　1

86.10.24　09:43
외신 2과　통제관

발 신 전 보

번 호 : WUS-4447   일 시 : 6103 01230   전보종별 : _____

수 신 : 주   미   대사 (총영사)

발 신 : 장   관   (미북)

제 목 : 양동학 관련 각하 앞 서한

대 : USW-4843

연 : 미북 700-3346 (86.9.24)

1. 연호 Solarz 의원의 양동학등 관련 각하 앞 서한에
대해서는 연호 참조, 귀관 명의로 적의 회신하고 보고바람.

2. 9.23. 최종심에서는 원심대로 양동학, 김성만은 사형,
황대권은 무기형이 확정되었음.

(차관 오재희)

예 고 : 1987.6.30. 일반.

앙고재	86년 10월 27일	북미과	기안자	과 장		국 장	제1차관보	차 관	장 관	발신시간 :		
								전결		외신과	접수자	과 장

0175

관리
번호 86 -□□777

趙, 鐘

주 미 대 사 관

미국(정) 700- 3/2   1986. 11. 12.

수신 : 미주국장

제목 : 양동화등 관련 서한

대 :   WUS-4147 (86.10.30)

　　　Stepen J. Solarz   하원 외무위 아태쏘위원장 (민주-뉴욕)의

양동화 및 김성만 관련 서한에 대하여 별첨과 같이 회신하였음을 보고합니다.

첨부 : 상기 회신 사본 1부. 끝.

예고 : 87.6.30. 일반

　　　　주　　　　　　미　　　　　대

선 결			결 재 (공 람)		
접수일시	1986.11.13	번호 148			
처 리 과					

0176

THE AMBASSADOR

November 7, 1986

The Honorable Stephen J. Solarz
Chairman
Subcommittee on Asian and
   Pacific Affairs
House of Representatives
Washington, DC 20515

Dear Chairman Solarz:

In response to your letter of October 23, 1986, I should like
to inform you of the following facts concerning the case of Mr.
Yang, Dong Hwa and Mr. Kim, Song Man.

Messrs. Yang and Kim were sentenced by the courts for having
actively engaged in espionage activities against our national security. Infiltrating the South after undergoing intensive training
in North Korea, they recruited student activists to produce and
disseminate communist propaganda materials and stage violent demonstrations. In so doing, they attempted to bomb public buildings, create
public disorder and incite violent riots. They were also involved
in collecting state secrets on, among other things, the military
situation.

Their sentences were carefully examined by the Supreme Court,
which finally confirmed the judgement of the lower courts on September
23, 1986.

While we are appreciative of your humanitarian concern over
this case, we sincerely hope that you also understand the need for
vigilance on our part for our national security.

With my warmest regards, I remain,

Sincerely yours,

Kyung-Won Kim

0177

November 7, 1986

The Honorable Stephen J. Solarz
Chairman
Subcommittee on Asian and
    Pacific Affairs
House of Representatives
Washington, DC 20515

Dear Chairman Solarz:

     In response to your letter of October 23, 1986, I should like
to inform you of the following facts concerning the case of Mr.
Yang, Dong Hwa and Mr. Kim, Song Man.

     Messrs. Yang and Kim were sentenced by the courts for having
actively engaged in espionage activities against our national security. Infiltrating the South after undergoing intensive training
in North Korea, they recruited student activists to produce and
disseminate communist propaganda materials and stage violent demonstrations. In so doing, they attempted to bomb public buildings, create
public disorder and incite violent riots. They were also involved
in collecting state secrets on, among other things, the military
situation.

     Their sentences were carefully examined by the Supreme Court,
which finally confirmed the judgement of the lower courts on September
23, 1986.

     While we are appreciative of your humanitarian concern over
this case, we sincerely hope that you also understand the need for
vigilance on our part for our national security.

     With my warmest regards, I remain,

                                   Sincerely yours,

                                   Kyung-Won Kim

                                                    0178

6. Amnesty Int'l 인사 면담, 1986.8.11

0179

미 주 국

1 9 8 6 . 8 . 20 .

북미 담당 관실	담 당	과 장	심의관	국 장	차관보	차 관	장 관
	己	书	~7				

제 목   국제사면위원회 (AI) 인사 면담

요 약

1. AI 미국지부 대표 8.11 주미대사관 방문, 광복절 41주년 사면을 청원하는 1,800명이 연서한 각하앞 청원서를 제출

2. AI 측은 구속중이던 피의자(이을호)의 치료목적을 위한 석방조치등 인권 차원에서의 긍정적인 조치를 환영하며, 임동규등 양심수 및 정치범의 광복절 사면을 청원

3. 아측은 한국의 안보현실을 설명하며 아국에 대한 폭넓은 이해를 요청

조치사항

0180

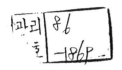

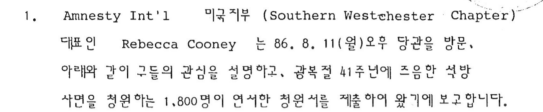

주 미 대 사 관

미국(정)700- 24/   1986. 8. 12.

수 신 : 장 관
참 조 : 미주국장, 구주국장
제 목 : 국제사면협회 (AI) 인사면담

1.   Amnesty Int'l   미국지부 (Southern Westchester Chapter)
      대표인   Rebecca Cooney 는 86. 8. 11(월)오후 당관을 방문,
      아래와 같이 그들의 관심을 설명하고, 광복절 41주년에 즈음한 석방
      사면을 청원하는 1,800명이 연서한 청원서를 제출하여 왔기에 보고합니다.

      º AI 는 세계 모든국가의 인권문제에 관심을 가지고 있을뿐, 타국의
        국내정치에 관여하려는 의도가 전혀 없음.   북한에 대한 보고서도
        낸바 있음. (별첨 2)

      º 최근 한국정부가 고문사례를 근절하겠다고 한바 있고, 구속중이던
        피의자(이을호)를 치료목적으로 석방하는등 일련의 인권차원에서의 긍정
        적인 노력과 조치를 환영함.

      º 8. 15. 41주년을 즈음하여 모든 양심수(임동규를 명시적으로 거론)와
        정치범에 대한 석방, 사면을 청원함.

      º 헌법에 명시된 표현의 자유존중, 고문의 중지, 피의자가 신속히 변호인의
        보호를 받을 권리존중등 인권차원의 발전을 기대함.

                                          0181

신 결			결		
접수일시	86 . 8 . 51성				
치 리 과			인		

0182

2. 이에 당관 김참사관은 아래 요지로 정부입장을 설명하였읍니다.

o 한국에는 정치범이 없으며, 많은 인권단체들이 주장하는 인권위반
사례는 어떤 저의를 가진 집단들의 일방적 주장을 그대로 되풀이
하고 있는 경우가 많다고 보며, 이런 경우 명망있는 국제단체의 권위
와 권능을 의심케 함.

o 한국은 옳바른 방향으로 나가기 위해 노력하고 있으며, 지금은 매우
중요한 과도기에 있음.   한국의 현실은 미국이나 영국과는 다르며,
남북분단과 실존하는 공산위협으로 인해, 자유라는 어휘가 갖는 개념상
에 차이가 있음이 사실이며, 직접적으로 폭력을 행사하지 않더라도
폭력이나 사회혼란을 선동하는 것 자체가 실정법상 위법임.

o 세계 어느 국가도 완전한 국가는 없으며, 과오는 범할 수 있을 것임.
한국에 대한 관심에 감사하나, 한국은 주권국가로서 법, 질서, 정의가
지배하는 사회임을 분명히 하고자함.   우리의 우방이나 친구들이 한국의
현실에 대한 이해의 폭을 넓히는 것이 중요한 과도기에 처해 있는 한국의
민주발전과 인권 향상에 더욱 도움이 될 것임.

첨 부 : 1. 청원 서명록 2부.
        2. AI 측 북한인권 보고서 1부.   끝.

주   미   대   사

0183

EXTERNAL

AI Index: ASA 24/01/85
Distr: SC/PO/CO/PG

AMNESTY INTERNATIONAL CONCERNS IN THE
DEMOCRATIC PEOPLE'S REPUBLIC OF KOREA

May 1985

Amnesty International
International Secretariat
1 Easton Street
London WC1X 8DJ
UNITED KINGDOM

0184

· EXTERNAL

AI In━ : ASA/24/01/85
Distr: SC/PO/CO/PG

Amnesty International
International Secretariat
1 Easton Street
London WC1X 8DJ
United Kingdom

May 1985

AMNESTY INTERNATIONAL CONCERNS IN THE

DEMOCRATIC PEOPLE'S REPUBLIC OF KOREA

BACKGROUND

Any consideration of human rights in the Democratic People's Republic of Korea must first take account of the difficulties involved in gathering information about the country. The media operating in the country appears to be under total state control; Amnesty International has monitored it for years, but only rarely does it include any information relating to arrests, trials, death sentences or any other event relevant to Amnesty International's concerns*. Inquiries made by Amnesty International to the DPRK authorities regarding, for example, the imprisonment of former government officials, use of the death penalty and legislation relating to detention for "re-education" purposes, have met with no response.

The absence of information from official sources is compounded by the lack of other available sources of information on the human rights situation. There is no significant overseas community of North Koreans who have left the country in recent years and might report on the situation. Official emigration, it appears, is not permitted, and the few people known to have left the country illegally since 1953 have gone to the Republic of (South) Korea, the Soviet Union or the People's Republic of China. No reliable information, however, is available on the numbers of people who have illegally left the country. The poverty of information emanating from the country has meant that few scholars have specialized on North Korea.

Probably the fullest account of political imprisonment in the DPRK is Ali Lameda: a Personal Account of the Experience of a Prisoner of Conscience in the Democratic People's Republic of Korea published by Amnesty International in 1979. This report is still frequently quoted in other organizations' reports on the human rights situation in DPRK.

Ali Lameda, a Venezuelan poet and member of the Communist Party of Venezuela, went to the DPRK in 1966 to take charge of the Spanish language section of the Department of Foreign Publications run by the North Korean Ministry of Foreign Affairs. He was arrested in September 1967 and held for a year without charge or trial. Following his release he was placed under house arrest, but two months later he was re-arrested and put on trial charge with attempted sabotage and espionage. He was sentenced to 20 years' imprisonment. Amnesty International adopted him and a French colleague Jacques Sedillot, also sentenced to 20 years',

*Amnesty International is an independent worldwide movement working impartially for the release of prisoners of conscience, those imprisoned by reason of their political, religious or other conscientiously held beliefs provided they have not used or advocated the use of violence. It works for fair and prompt trials for all political prisoners and an end to torture and the death penalty.

as prisoners of conscience and campaigned for their release. Ali Lameda was released in 1974. Jacques Sedillot died in Pyongyang in January 1976, a few months after his release.

On 14 September 1981 the DPRK acceded to the International Covenant on Civil and Political Rights and the International Covenant on Economic, Social and Cultural Rights. Reports submitted by the DPRK in October 1983 and April 1984 under article 40 of the International Covenant on Civil and Political Rights do not significantly alter or add to the information already available on the human rights situation in the country.

In late 1982 three North Koreans who had fled the DPRK between 1977 and January 1982 wrote to Amnesty International in general terms about human rights violations in North Korea. An attempt to open a correspondence with these men met with no response. Subsequently the South Korean authorities published a short document which included allegations that seven prominent North Korean officials who had disappeared from public life had been detained. In December 1982 Amnesty International wrote to President Kim Il Sung inquiring about the reported detention of four of these men. No reply was received.

A North Korean soldier who defected to the Republic of Korea in July 1984 reported public executions for robbery, rape, murder and sabotage, and, specifically, the trial and public execution by shooting of alleged leaders of violent disturbances which occurred in 1982.

CONSTITUTIONAL AND LEGAL SYSTEM

Amnesty International has been able to collect some materials relating to the Constitution and Legal System of the DPRK. The Constitution provides for freedom of speech, the press, assembly, association and demonstration (article 53). Freedom of religious belief is guaranteed by article 54 while another article guarantees "genuine democratic rights and liberties" (article 50). Several other articles in the Constitution, however, specifically articles 11, 49, 67 and 68 (see Appendix), would appear to limit individual rights by emphasizing the rights of the community or the "collective principle".

Chapter X of the Constitution deals with "the Court and Procurator's Office". The right of defence and the independence of the judiciary are provided for by articles 138 and 140 respectively:

"Cases are heard in public and the accused is guaranteed the right to defence. Hearings may be closed to the public as stipulated by law". (Article 138)

"In administering justice, the Court is independent, and judicial proceedings are carried out in strict accordance with the law". (Article 140)

The Constitution however does not appear to include any right of the individual to be presumed innocent until proved guilty nor would there appear to be any right to an effective remedy by competent tribunals for acts violating the fundamental rights granted by the Constitution. There is no prohibition of torture or cruel, inhuman or degrading treatment in the Constitution, although it is possible that these are prohibited under other legislation.

The Constitution does not include any guarantee of the right to leave the country. Foreign visitors have reportedly been told that no citizen of the DPRK has ever legally asked to leave the country, although many citizens of the DPRK have relatives abroad in Japan, the Republic of (South) Korea, the USA, the People's Republic of China and the Soviet Union. The number of people known to have left the country illegally since the conclusion of the Korean War in 1953 is very small. It is not clear what sanctions the authorities would bring against an individual who attempted to leave the country illegally. Legal provisions for the punishment of adult relatives of a soldier who flees the country are described below.

Information on specific criminal justice procedures and practices in the DPRK is scarce. The Penal Code of the DPRK was promulgated on 3 March 1950 and reportedly revised in the 1970s. There is also a Code of Criminal Procedure, which establishes a system of preliminary investigation, indictment, trial, judgment and appeal. Article 7 of the Penal Code defines a crime as "a punishable act committed through intent or negligence which has a social danger infringing upon the DPRK and the legal order established therein". Punishments, defined in article 28, are the death penalty, penal servitude, correctional labour, money fine, deprivation of certain rights (for example voting or standing for office), prohibition against engaging in a certain trade occupation or trade, total or partial confiscation of property. Penal servitude may be imposed for a term of one to 20 years, and the sentence served in "a certain place of confinement or in a special labour camp" (article 30).

The Code of Criminal Procedure requires the agency making an arrest to notify the Procurator within 24 hours and state the reason for the detention. The Procurator must within 48 hours after receiving such a report either approve the arrest or disapprove it and order the suspect's release. This statutory limit does not apply, however, to those suspected of having committed crimes against the State. The pre-trial investigation of these crimes falls under the exclusive jurisdiction of the state security agency, that is, the police belonging to the Ministry of Public Security also known as the Ministry of Social Safety. The Code of Criminal Procedure states that the procedure for approval of the detention of those persons suspected of anti-state crimes shall be regulated by a "special statute". These "special statutes" have not, apparently, been published and no other law requires the state security agency to report such arrests to the Procurator.

TRIALS

The only substantial information on trials in the DPRK which has come to the attention of Amnesty International is the testimony of Ali Lameda, who was arrested in September 1967 and held for a year without charge or trial. Two months after his release he was again arrested, and tried before a tribunal. He described his experiences:

> "The tribunal was under the direction of the Ministry of Internal Security and, apart from members of the tribunal, there was a representative from what they call the High Court who acted as the judge and a prosecutor; I was provided with a so-called defence counsel. The only people present apart from members of the tribunal were two uniformed policemen and a young man who acted as interpreter. The trial lasted for one day, from nine o'clock in the morning till five o'clock in the afternoon. I was suffering from fever and did

committed a political offence, which was considered far worse than
offences by common criminals.

"The pattern of my trial followed the interrogations I had undergone.
It was demanded that I confess my guilt. The tribunal did not make
any specific accusations - there were no formal charges - but the
accused has to accuse himself before the tribunal. Thus there was
no necessity for the tribunal to produce any evidence. I had no
right to defend myself, I could only admit guilt. The basis for
the tribunal's condemnations is the confession of the prisoner and
the prosecutor told me that I should speak out and confess everything, to rid myself of my crimes. I insisted that I had committed
no crimes, that I had only come to Korea as a servant of the
government. During the trial, I asked for a lawyer of my choice
and that the tribunal should be made open, but such demands were
dismissed as bourgeois. When I tried to ask questions, I was
abruptly interrupted and told that I had no rights in defending
myself. The prosecutor eventually informed me that I had been in
Korea to sabotage, spy and introduce infiltrators. To this I could
only reply that I had been invited to Korea by the government and
that allegations that I was under the control of the CIA were
absurd. The prosecutor read a small extract from the Penal Code,
which emphasized the gravity of my crime. As a political offender,
I had committed a crime against the basis of the Korean state.
In summing up, the prosecutor demanded the maximum penalty for the
crimes I had committed. The so-called defence counsel, whom I had
seen for just half an hour, made a lengthy eulogy of Kim Il Sung,
and in lodging my plea, asked for 20 years' imprisonment. The
tribunal retired for just five minutes and then returned to sentence
me, to 20 years' imprisonment with forced labour."

Since the end of the Korean War in 1953 a number of officials have been
removed from office, and some reportedly put on trial. They include:

Between 3 and 6 August 1953 twelve officials were tried by a Military   -
Tribunal on charges of espionage. The trial was said to be public and was reported
in the North Korean newspaper Nodong Sinmun. Ten of the twelve were reported
to have been sentenced to death and executed: Yi Sung-yop, formerly Minister
of Justice and secretary of the Central Committee of the Korean Workers'
Party (KWP); Cho Il-myong, Vice-minister of Culture and Propaganda; Yim Hwa,
a poet and KWP official; Cho Yong-bok, a senior member of the People's
Inspection Committee; Maeng Chong-ho, an army officer; Pae Chol and Pak Sung-won,
officials with the Liaison Department of the Central Committee of the KWP;
Paek Hyong-bok, an official with the Security Department; Sol Chong-shik, an
official of the Supreme Command of the Korean People's Army; Yi Kang-guk,
director of the Bureau of Foreign Affairs. The remaining defendants were
Yun Sun-dal, an official with the Liaison Committee of the Central Committee
of the KWP, sentenced to 60 years' imprisonment, and Yi Won-ju, an official
in the Department of Propaganda and Agitation, sentenced to 33 years'
imprisonment.

On 15 December 1955 Pak Hon-yong, Deputy Premier and Minister of Foreign
Affairs, was tried by a special session of the Supreme Court on charges of
espionage and attempting to overthrow the government. He was reportedly
sentenced to death and executed.

0188

.../...

Between 1956 and 1959 some 35 officials were accused "of factional, anti-revolutionary activities", removed from office and expelled from the KWP. Some fled to the People's Republic of China or to the Soviet Union. There are reports that Kim Tu-bong, chairperson of the Central Committee of the KWP, and Pak Chang-ok, a Deputy Premier, were sent to work as ordinary labourers. Amnesty International has no information on their trial, if any.

In April 1967 Pak Kum-chol, a high ranking member of the Central Committee of the KWP, was removed from office, and reportedly sent to work as the manager of a provincial factory. Amnesty International has no details of his trial, if any.

In December 1968 Kim Chang-bong, a Deputy Premier and Minister of Defence was removed from office, and reportedly detained. Amnesty International has no details of his trial or sentence.

In October 1975 Ryu Chang-shik, an alternate member of the Political Committee and secretary to the Central Committee of the KWP, was removed from office and reportedly detained. Amnesty International has no details of his trial or sentence.

In October 1977 Yi Yong-mu, a member of the Political Committee of the KWP, was removed from office and reportedly detained. Amnesty International has no details of his trial or sentence.

IMPRISONMENT

Several detention centres for political detainees have been reported, as well as prison facilities in Pyongyang. Ali Lameda was detained in a camp near the town of Sariwon, in North Hwanghae Province. Defectors to South Korea in 1982 described the location of eight camps, three of them in North Hamkyong Province, two in South Hamkyong Province, two in North Pyongan Province and one in Chagang Province. Another report stated that the Chagang camp housed prisoners considered guilty of various political crimes, and located a further camp in Yanggang Province where political prisoners were reportedly accompanied by their families.

Little information about conditions in prisons or detention camps is available. Ali Lameda reported meagre food rations (no more than 300 grams of food per day), inadequate sanitary facilities and heating, and restricted medical attention. Describing his first term of imprisonment he said: "There are no rights for the prisoner, no visits, parcels of cigarettes or food or opportunity to read a book or newspaper, or write. The process of 'rehabilitation', as they call it, must start straightaway, the 'self-examination' of the crimes the prisoner has reportedly committed, to purify the self". According to his account of the Sariwon detention camp, prisoners are required to work for 12 hours a day.

Exile to remote areas of the country is reported from time to time for both criminal and political offences; it is not clear whether this is a different punishment from penal servitude in a detention centre in a remote part of the country, as described in article 28 of the penal code. The only reference to exile in the Penal Code is in article 70, where exile to a

0189

remote region, and suspension of voting rights, for five years is specified
as a punishment for adult relatives of a soldier who flees or crosses the
border, if they are resident with him at the time. Adult relatives who help
him, or who have knowledge of his flight, and do not report it to the
authorities are punishable by a minimum term of three years' penal servitude
plus total confiscation of their property.

THE DEATH PENALTY

The 1950 Penal Code contains provisions for the death penalty to be applied
as the maximum penalty for a considerable number of "crimes against state
sovereignty". These are:

> "... the organization of an armed uprising or invasion of the
> territory of the Republic by armed detachments or bands for anti-
> state purposes in an attempt to seize power at the capital or
> local level. ..." (Article 65)

> "... inducing a foreign state or any social organization in it to
> militarily intervene in the affairs of the Republic, or to engage
> in any other hostile act, especially blockade, seizure of state
> property of the Republic, severance of diplomatic relations,
> abrogation of any treaty concluded with the Republic, ..."
> (Article 66)

> "... communicate with a foreign power, or its individual repre-
> sentatives, which has unfriendly relations with the Republic or who
> in some way assist the foreign power or individual groups of people
> for this purpose. ..." (Article 67)

> "Treason against the fatherland, that is, an act committed by a
> citizen of the Republic to the detriment of the independence of the
> fatherland as a state, its military might, or its territorial
> inviolability, espionage, transmission of a state or military
> secret (to a foreign state), going over to the side of the enemy
> or flight abroad. ..." (Article 68)   This offence carries a
> mandatory death sentence if committed by a soldier (Article 69).

> "Espionage, that is, an act of transfer, or the acquisition or
> collection by stealing, or any other means for the purpose of
> transfer to a foreign state or anti-state organization, of infor-
> mation constituting an important state secret.... under especially
> aggravating circumstances, that might have caused serious conse-
> quences to the state's interest." (Article 71)

> "... committing terroristic acts against representatives of the
> state authority or of democratic parties and public service
> organization for the purpose of resisting the people's sovereignty
> or disrupting the democratic reform that took place after the
> liberation, ..." (Article 72)

0190

"Wrecking, that is, an act directed toward the subversion of state industry, transportation, trade, monetary circulation, or the credit system for the purpose of undermining the state by means of using state institutions and enterprises or impeding their normal activities, or an act of using state institutions and enterprises or impeding their normal operations in the interests of the former ownership system, ..." (Article 73)

"Destruction, that is, the destroying or damaging, by explosion, arson or other methods, of railways, and other routes, means of transportation, water supply system, warehouses and other instal- lations, and buildings of the state and social organization, ..." (Article 74)

The death penalty is additionally specified as the maximum penalty under "crimes against state administration", which articles include:

"The organization of banded groups, or participation therein or in organized attacks on state and private institutions or individual citizens, or participation in destruction and robbery of railroads or other means of transportation and communication, ..." (Article 82)

"Mass disorders accompanied by clear disobedience to the lawful demands of the state authorities ... attended by murder, arson, destruction of means of communication, or by other acts ..." (Article 83)

"A person who carries on propaganda or agitation designed to arouse national or religious emnity or hatred, or who disseminates, prepares or possesses literature of such character ... if committed on the occasion of mass disturbances or in time of war. ..." (Article 101)

Criminal offences, including intentional homicide (articles 112 and 114), may also be punished by death.

The account of a North Korean who defected to the south in July 1984 referred to public executions by shooting. He stated that two persons, Kim Ji-su, age 37, and one other, were tried, sentenced and executed for instigating violent disturbances that occurred at Um Dok mine in South Hamkyung province in November 1982. Other public executions were reportedly carried out after riots in Haeneung-gun, South Hamkyung Province, also believed to have taken place during 1982. Death sentences are not publicly announced, and no figures are available as to the number of executions carried out.

0191

EXTRACT FROM THE

SOCIALIST CONSTITUTION

OF

THE DEMOCRATIC PEOPLE'S
REPUBLIC OF KOREA

Adopted at the First Session
of the Fifth Supreme People's
Assembly of the Democratic
People's Republic of Korea

27 December 1972

CHAPTER 1

POLITICS

Article 11

The State defends the socialist system against the subversive activities of the hostile elements at home and abroad and revolutionizes and working-classizes the whole of society by intensifying the ideological revolution.

CHAPTER IV

BASIC RIGHTS AND DUTIES OF CITIZENS

Article 49

In the Democratic People's Republic of Korea the rights and duties of citizens are based on the collectivist principle of "One for all and all for one."

Article 50

The State substantially guarantees genuine democratic rights and liberties as well as material and cultural welfare to all citizens.

In the Democratic People's Republic of Korea the rights and freedoms of citizens increase with the consolidation and development of the socialist system.

Article 51

Citizens all enjoy equal rights in the political, economic and cultural and all other spheres of State and public activity.

Article 53

Citizens have the freedoms of speech, the press, assembly, association and demonstration.

The State guarantees conditions for free activities of democratic political parties and social organizations.

Article 54

Citizens have freedom of religious belief and freedom of anti-religious propaganda.

0193

Article 55

Citizens are entitled to make complaints and submit petitions.

Article 67

Citizens must strictly observe the laws of the State and the socialist norm of life and the socialist rules of conduct.

Article 68

Citizens must display a high degree of collectivist spirit.

Citizens must cherish their collective and organization and establish the revolutionary trait of working devotedly for the sake of society and the people and for the interests of the homeland and the revolution.

CHAPTER VI

THE PRESIDENT
OF THE DEMOCRATIC PEOPLE'S
REPUBLIC OF KOREA

Article 94

The President of the Democratic People's Republic of Korea promulgates the laws and ordinances of the Supreme People's Assembly, the decrees of the Central People's Committee and the decisions of the Standing Committee of the Supreme People's Assembly.

The President of the Democratic People's Republic of Korea issues orders.

CHAPTER X

THE COURT AND THE PROCURATOR'S
OFFICE

Article 133

Justice is administered by the Central Court, the Court of the province (or municipality directly under central authority), the People's Court and the Special Court.

Verdict is delivered in the name of the Democratic People's Republic of Korea.

0194

Article 140

In administering justice, the Court is independent, and judicial proceedings are carried out in strict accordance with law.

Article 141

The Central Court is the highest judicial organ of the Democratic People's Republic of Korea.

The Central Court supervises the judicial work of all the Courts.

Article 142

The Central Court is responsible for its work to the Supreme People's Assembly, the President of the Democratic People's Republic of Korea and the Central People's Committee.

The Court of the province (or municipality directly under central authority) and the People's Court are responsible for their work to their respective People's Assembly.

Article 143

Procuration affairs are conducted by the Central Procurator's Office, Procurator's Offices of the province (or municipality directly under central authority), city (or district) and county and Special Procurator's Office.

Article 144

The Procurator's Office exercises the following functions:

1. to supervise if the State laws are properly observed by the State insitutions, enterprises, social cooperative organizations and by citizens;

2. to supervise if the decisions and directives of the State organs conform with the Constitution; the laws and ordinances of the Supreme People's Assembly, the orders of the President of the Democratic People's Republic of Korea, the decrees, decisions and directives of the Central People's Committee, the decisions of the Standing Committee of the Supreme People's Assembly and with the decisions and directives of the Administration Council;

3. to expose and institute legal proceedings against the criminals and offenders so as to safeguard the power of the workers and peasants and the socialist system from all sorts of encroachment, and to protect the property of the State and social cooperative organizations and the rights of people as guaranteed by the Constitution and their lives and property.

0195

Article 134

The judges and people's assessors of the Central Court are elected by the Standing Committee of the Supreme People's Assembly.

The judges and people's assessors of the Court of the province (or municipality directly under central authority) and the People's Court are elected by the People's Assembly at the corresponding level.

The term of office of judges and people's assessors is the same as that of the People's Assembly at the corresponding level.

Article 135

The President and judges of the Special Court are appointed or removed by the Central Court.

The people's assessors of the Special Court are elected by the servicemen and employees at their respective meetings.

Article 136

The Court exercises the following functions:

1. to protect through judicial activities the power of the workers and peasants and the socialist system established in the Democratic People's Republic of Korea, the property of the State and social cooperative organizations, the rights of people as guaranteed by the Constitution and their lives and property against all infringements;

2. to guarantee that all the State institutions, enterprises, social cooperative organizations and citizens strictly observe the State laws and actively struggle against class enemies and all the law-breakers;

3. to execute judgements and findings with regard to property and conduct notarial work.

Article 137

Justice is administered by the Court composed of one judge and two people's assessors. In special cases the number of judges may be three.

Article 138

Cases are heard in public and the accused is guaranteed the right to defence.

Hearings may be closed to the public as stipulated by law.

Article 139

Judicial proceedings are conducted in the Korean language.

Foreigners may use their own languages in court proceedings.

0196

Article 145

Procuration affairs are conducted under the coordinated leadership of the Central Procurator's Office, and all the Procurator's Offices are subordinated to their higher offices and the Central Procurator's Office.

The procurators are appointed or removed by the Central Procurator's Office.

Article 146

The Central Procurator's Office is responsible for its work to the Supreme People's Assembly, the President of the Democratic People's Republic of Korea and the Central People's Committee.

His Excellency
President Chun Doo-hwan
The Blue House
Seoul, Republic of Korea

Your Excellency:

We, the undersigned, appeal to your Excellency to use the occasion of
the 41st anniversary of National Liberation Day, 15 August 1986, to take
immediate steps to ensure that anyone taken into custody is treated in
accordance with internationally accepted standards, and that guarantees of
basic rights enshrined in the 1980 Constitution in the Republic of Korea and
safeguards provided by the Code of Criminal Procedure and other laws are
fully respected.

We further appeal to Your Excellency to use your authority as President
by releasing unconditionally all those imprisoned for the non-violent
exercise of their rights to freedom of expression and association; ensuring
that all political prisoners are tried by judicial procedures that conform
to international norms; ensuring that no one is tortured or ill-treated; and
commuting all death sentences.

Respectfully,

Name	Signature	Address
Joanne E. Belanger	Joanne E Belanger	41 Seymour St. Roslindale Ma 02131
Arlene H. Kelly	Arlene H. Kelly	4 Litchfield St Brighton, Ma 02135
Heidi Wilkinson	Heidi Wilkinson	32 Victory Rd. Dorchester, MA 02122
Roberta Cabral	Roberta Cabral	41 Lincoln Way, Camb. 02140
Kelly Gilrnine	Kelly Gilrnine	16 Prince St. Brookline, ma 02146
Kathy Killilea	156 Kathy Killilea	1569 Washington St W Newton ma 02165
Denise Constantne	Denise Constantni	
Robin Jeghelian	Robin Jeghelian	881 Main St. Apt 7 Walpole ma 02081
Josie Blake	Josephine Blake	247 Wales St Abington, Ma 0351
Lisa M Fisher	Lisa M. Fisher	182 Margaret Rd, Abington. MA
Amanda Solomon	Amanda Solomon	19 Michmod Dr Framingham
Lisa M. Flynn	Lisa M. Flynn	6 Keystone St., W. Roxbury, MA 02132

Please return to Korea Petition, Northeast Regional Office, AIUAS, 1675
Massachusetts Avenue, Cambridge, MA 02138 by June 25, 1986.

0198

한국 NCC 인사   출국 규제문제, 1986.11-12.

면 담 요 록

1. 면담일시 : 1986년 12월 2일 (화) 11:00-11:40
2. 면담장소 : 북미과
3. 면담인사 : 김원수 북미과 사무관
   Alexander Arvizu 주한미대사관 2등서기관
4. 면담내용 :

    사무관 : 금일 귀하를 초치한 것은, 그동안 귀측에서 관심을 표명했던
                  문의사항에 대해 관계부처 (법무부) 에서 회신한 아래자료를
                  전달키 위한것임.

          o 86. 9. 30-10. 3 호놀루루 개최 한. 북미 NCC
            회의 참가 예정이던 한국 NCC인사 24명중 6명의
            출국규제 사유 (별첨1)

          o 화란개최 WCC 회의에 참가예정이던 오재식의 출국정지
            사유 (별첨2)

          o 강종건 관련자료 (별첨3)

          o 임동규, 조일지, 이철, 이돈명, 박종진, 박종석 관련자료
            (별첨4)

          o 미문화원사건 관련자중 광복절 특사자 명단 (별첨5)

Arvizu : o 귀측의 협조에 감사함.

o 개인적인 견해이지만 상기자료에 포함된 인사중 이돈명의
경우에는 유성환의원의 경우와 같이 단순한 범법자라기
보다는 정치범으로 봐야되지 않나 생각됨.

사무관 : o 이돈명의 경우, 법을 위반한 혐의로 수배중인 인물을
은닉해준 사실은 명백한 실정법 위반이므로 정치범이라고
할수 없음.

o 유성환의원의 경우, 통일문제에 대한 논의는 이념및
체제에 대한 논의와 연계되어있는 문제로서 50년대이후
전통적으로 매우 민감하게 다루어져 왔음.
─ 따라서 북한의 통일정책에 동조하는 주장은 아국의
안보현실상 매우 위험한 것으로서 아국 관계법규 (국가
보안법) 의 적용이 불가피함.

Arvizu : o 귀하가 지적한대로, 이돈명의 경우 법위반 사실이 있고,
유성환의원의 경우 현시점에서 민감한 문제에 대해 그러한
주장을 한것이 현명했느냐 하는데 대해서 의문이 존재함이
사실임.

o 그러나, 자신의 생각하는 바를 밝힌것을 이유로해서
구속되는 경우, 일반 범법자와는 다르지 않나 하는
것이 본인의 개인적 견해임.

0201

사무관 : o 이미 설명한 바와같이, 상기인들은 아국의 실정법을
위반한 사실이 있고, 또한 그러한 사실을 근거로
구속이 집행되었기 때문에 어떠한 기준에 의하더라도
정치범이라고 볼수 없음을 다시한번 밝히는 바임.

o 현재 아국내 일부 수감자에 대해 인권단체 등에서
정치범 또는 양심범이라고 주장하는 경우가 있으나,
아국의 실정법을 위반한 사람에 대해 여사한 주장은
타당치 않음.

예 고 : 1987. 12. 31. 일반.

한국 NCC인사 출국 규제 관련 문제

1. 문제제기

   ○ 86.9.30-10.3 호놀루루 개최 한·북미 NCC회의 참가 예정
   이던 한국 NCC인사 24명중 6명 출국 규제

   - 한·북미 NCC회의시 협의된 결의안중 한국정부의 출국
   규제 조치에 항의 내용 포함

2. 주한 미국 및 카나다 대사관 문의 사항

   가. 미대사관

   ○ 10.22 Dunlop 정무 참사관, 미주국장에 협조 요청

   - 미교계로 부터 문의가 있는 바, 출국정지 사유 파악
   등에 관한 외무부 협조 부탁

   나. 카나다 대사관

   ○ 10.22 Gwozdecky 3등 서기관, 북미과에 출국정지
   사유 파악 요청

3. 출국 규제자별 대응논리 (안)

   가. 여권 미소지자

   ○ 대상자 : 박형규, 강신석, 김향자

   ○ 대응논리

   - 여권발급 절차 미필

나. 병역 미필자
  ○ 대 상 자 : 장윤재
  ○ 대응논리
    - 병역 미필자로 병역법상 해외여행 규제 대상

다. 단수 여권소지자
  ○ 대 상 자 : 김상근
  ○ 대응논리
    - 단수여권 소지하고 있으나 과거 다른 목적으로 발급

라. 복수여권 소지자
  ○ 대 상 자 : 홍성현
  ○ 대응논리
    - 복수여권 소지하고 있으나 출입국관리법 4조 1항
      (출국의 금지) 해당
      · 그 출국이 대한민국의 이익을 현저하게 해할 염려가
        있다고 인정되는 자

4. 향후 조치 예정사항
  ○ 미대사관 및 카나다 대사관에 대해 출국 규제자별 상기 대응
    논리 설명 및 일부 한국 NCC인사 활동의 문제점을 일반적
    으로 언급
    - 아국의 통일정책에 상치되고 북한의 통일정책에 동조하는
      일부 NCC 인사의 주장은 한국 국내관계 법규에 위반

0204

o 특히 복수여권 소지자 홍성현에 대해 상기 대응논리 이상의
  설명 요구시에는, 출국금지 사유 판단은 아국정부 관계부처의
  재량사항이므로 외무부가 답변할 위치에 있지 않음을 설명

0205

(지난번
　다른 문건으로 바침)

- 25180 (　　　)
- (신원조회받고)
- 신원조회

26240

0206

(지난번
다른 목차로 발송)

25180 (   )

2b240

0206

- 출입국관리법 4조
  1항
- 출입국관리법 시행령
  3조 1항

＊66년생:

5연생
F-100828
- 86. 9. 13접수.
- 여권번호없.

99313

0207

- 출입국관리법 4조
  1항
- 출입국관리법 시행령
  3조 1항

* 66 연령:

F-100828
-86. 9. 13접수
- 여권 ...

99313

정리보존문서목록					
기록물종류	일반공문서철	등록번호	21620	등록일자	1995-06-02
분류번호	701	국가코드	US	보존기간	영구
명 칭	한국 인권문제와 관련한 제 사안, 1987				
생산과	북미과	생산년도	1987~1987	담당그룹	북미국
내용목차	1. 미국 변호사 입국 사증 발급 규제문제 - 김근태 외 재판참관차 2. Schifter 미국 국무부 인권차관보 발언 3. Amnesty Int'l 관계 - 수감자 관련 문의 등 4. 김대중에 대한 죠지.미니 인권상 수여				

0001

1. 미국변호사 입국 사증발급 규제문제

　　─ 김근태 외 재판참관차

0002

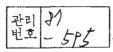

외 무 부 착신전문

번 호 : USW-0860   일 시 : 702241834   종 별 :

수 신 : 장관(미북,영사,아일)사본:주일대사(중계필)

발 신 : 주미대사

제 목 : 미국인 입국사증 발급문제

경위 check
VISA review?

1. 국무성 한국과는 WORTLEY 하원의원(공,뉴욕)으로부터의 요청이 있어 당관에 아기
참고로 알리는 사항이라고하면서 일본거주 미국인의 아국입국 문제에 관해 2.24(화)
다음과같이 알려왔음.

가. 재일 미국인 ▇▇▇▇▇▇(남,변호사)는 과거 수차에 걸쳐 변호사업무로 방
한한 경험이 있는바, 86년 가을(9월 또는 10월)이후 주일 한국대사관에 입국 사증을
신청하였으나 거부되고 있다함.

나.동인은 자신에 대한 입국 불허가 86.2. 소위 김근태사건 재판참관 활동과 관련된
것으로 생각, 동 활동에 대해 해명하기 위해 주일 미국대사관을 통해 한국대사관에 면
담을 신청하였으나 상금 면담이 이루어지지않고 있음.

다. ▇▇▇ 는 ▇▇▇▇▇▇ 의 부탁으로 상기 86.2월 재판에 참관 활동에
관여된바 있으나,정치적 동기나 특별한 목적이 없었던것이었으므로 이에 대한 자신의
입장과 활동경위를 한국 대사관측에 설명할 기회를 갖고 싶어함.

2.국무성측은 동건에대해 WORTLEY 의원에게 설명해줄 필요가 있음을 감안, 아측의
입장을 알려주기를 요망하고 있음.

(대사 김경원)

예고:87.12.31까지

예고문에 의거 재분
직위   성명

검토필 (87. 6. 30)

미주국   차관실   2차보   영교국   아주국   청와대   안기

PAGE 1   87.02.25 10:35
                                                     외신 2과 통제관

0003

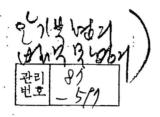

외 무 부

착 신 전 문

번 호 : JAW-1318   일 시 : 702261758   종 별 :

수 신 : 장관(미북,영사,아일)   사본: 주미대사-중계필

발 신 : 주일 대사(일영)

제 목 : 미국인 입국사증

대 : WJA-1003(USW-0860)

대호관련 아래 보고함.

1. 대호 미국인 ████████████████ 생)는 86.11.4. 당관에 관광목적 입국사증을 신청하였으나, 동인이 사증발급 규제자인 관계로 입국사증 발급을 거부한바 있음.

2. 이와관련, 주일 미대사관측은 최근 전화로 상기인이 입국사증 재신청시 발급받을 수 있는지 여부와 입국사증이 거부된 이유를 알려줄것을 요청하여왔는바, 당관으로서는 재신청시에도 본부의 허가없이는 발급이 불가할 것이라고만 하였음.

3. 본인이 주일 미대사관을 통해 한국대사관에 면담을 신청해온 사실이 없음을 참고 바람. 끝.

(총영사 강신무-국장)

예고: 87.12.31. 까지

예고문에 의기 재분 (19   )
직위   성년

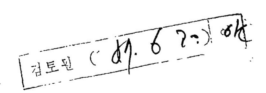

검토필 (87. 6 ?) 애

미주국   2차보   잉고국   청와대   안 기

PAGE   1   87.02.27   08:59
                                                     외신 2과   통제관

0004

외 무 부   착 신 전 보

번 호 : USW-1009   일 시 : 703031853   종 별 :

수 신 : 장관(미붕,영사,아일,대사) 사본:주일대사-중계필

발 신 : 주 미 대사대리

제 목 : 미국인 입국사증   ? why ?

대 : WUS-863(JAUS-06)

연 : USW-860

국무성 한국과는 대호 재일 미국인 ████████ 의 아국 입국사증 문제 관련

아래사항을 확인해줄 것을 재차 요청하여온바 회보 바람.

-동인이 사증발급 규제자로 되어있는 사유

-동인의 주일 아국대사관 면담 가능 여부   - 「김남익」대 쓴편.

-동인에 대한 사증 발급거부 재검토 가능여부   - 렌라느라로 회비 딱 목록. 3/8. 14:00
                                              3/10. 문서리보 통보
(공사 한탁채)

예고:87.12.31까지

예고문에 의거 서문 (187.12.31.
격위   성명

대조필 (87. 6.30.) 완료

미주국   차관실   2차보   아주국   대 사   안 기 법무부 출입비로 (출입30여3)

기 안 용 지

분류기호 문서번호	미북 0160-739 (전화:)	시 행 상 특별취급	
보존기간	영구·준영구. 10.5.3.1.	장 관	
수신처 보존기간			
시행일자	1987. 3. 3.		

보 조 기 관	국 장		협 조 기 관		문 서 통 제	검 열 1987.3. 3 통제관
	심의관					
	과 장				발 송 인	
기안책임자	조 백 상					

경 유 수 신 참 조	법무부장관 출입국관리국장	발신명의		

제 목	미국인 입국사증 발급규제관련 의견문의

1. 미국무성 및 Wortley 하원의원(공화당·뉴욕)은 일본

거주 미국인 변호사 ▮▮▮▮▮ 가 86년 10월 이후 주일

한국대사관에 입국사증을 신청하였으나 거부되고 있다는 점을

알려오며 동인에 대한 입국 거부이유 및 입국 가능성을 타진해

왔읍니다.

2. 미국무성 및 동인의 문의에 대한 회답시 참고코자 하니

동인의 입국사증발급 규제 대상인 이유 및 방한 가능성등 관련

검토필 (1987. 6. 20) 여백계속 / 0006

1505-25(2-1) 일(1)갑
85. 9. 9. 승인　　190mm×268mm 인쇄용지 2급 60g /m'
가 40-41 1986. 10. 20.

222　한국 인권문제 제 사안 1

사항을 지급 회보하여 주시기 바랍니다.

3. 이와관련 86.2. 김근태사건 재판방청시도 이후

동인의 방한시 동향을 고려, 입국 사증 발급 규제 대상에서

제외하는 문제에 대한 귀부의 의견도 아울러 회보하여

주시기 바랍니다.

첨 부 : 관련 전문 사본 2매. 끝.

0007

법　　무　　부

입국 23621-58　　　(503-7096)　　　1987· 3· 11·

수신　외무부장관

참조　미주국장

제목　사증발급규제 관련 의견회신

1. 미북 0160-739('87·3·4)로 문의하신 재일 미국인 변호사 ███
███의 사증발급규제 건에 대하여 아래와 같이 회신합니다.

　　　가· 사증발급규제조치

　　　　o 상기인은 '83·8·29- '85·6·30까지 국내 중앙국제특허법률
사무소 법률자문역으로 근무할 당시 취득한 고용자격의 사증(9-11)으로 입국('85·
12·28)하여 국제 인권법률가협회(사무총장 : 미국인 AMY YOUNG)소속변호사
들과 연계, 김근태 공판참관을 시도하고, 문익환목사를 방문하면서 인권관계를
운운하는등 체류자격외 활동을 하여 사증발급규제 조치한 바 있음.

　　　　o "사증발급규제"란 입국을 금지하는 조치가 아니고 재외공관에
사증신청이 있을시 당부의 사전승인을 받아 사증을 발급하도록 하는 제도임.

　　　나· 방한 가능성 여부

　　　　o 상기인이 재차 사증발급을 신청하는 경우 담당영사가 본인을
직접 면담 입국목적 및 동향등을 상세히 심사, 당부에 승인상신하면, 공관장의
의견을 참작하여 사증발급 여부나 규제조치 해제등을 종합 검토하겠음.

　　　2. 참고사항

　　　　o 동인에 대한 사증발급규제 조치('86·1·14) 이후 친구방문을 위해
입국코자하여 2회('86·2·27、'86·6·20)에 걸쳐 입국을 하려한 사실이 있음.

법　　무　　부　　장

출입국관리국장 전결

0008

선 결			결재 (공람)		
접수일시	1987. 1. 12	번호 1203			
처 리 과					

0009

	분류번호	보존기간

발 신 전 보

번 호 : 2US-1073 일 시 : 703131210   전보종별 : _____

수 신 : 주   미   대사·총영사!

발 신 : 장   관 (미북)

제 목 : 미국인 입국 사증

대 : USW-0860, 1009   예고문에 의거 재분류 (1987.12.31.)
                           직위   성!

1. 재일 미국인 변호사 ▮▮▮▮▮ 에 관한 법무부의 입장은

아래와 같은 바, 국무성 및 Wortley 상원의원측에 설명시 참고 바람.

  가. 사증 발급 규제 사유 : 동인은 83·8·29-85·6·30까지

          중앙국제특허법률 사무소 법률자문역으로 한국에서

          근무할 당시 취득한 고용자격의 사증(9-11)으로 85·12·28·

          입국, International Human Rights Law Group

          소속 변호사들과 연계, 김근태 공판참관을 시도하고,

          문익환목사를 방문하는등 체류자격외의 활동을 하여

          사증 발급 규제대상이 되었음.

  나. 방한 가능성 및 규제조치 해제 가능성 여부

       o 사증발급 규제란 입국을 금지하는 조치가 아니고 방한을

          희망하는 외국인이 재외공관에 사증을 신청할 경우

          법무부의 사전승인을 받아 사증을 발급 받을 수 있도록

          한 조치임.

검토필 (1987.6.20.)   /계속/

			기안자	과 장	국 장	차 관	장 관	0010
앙고재	87년 월 13일	북미과	2		전결			

보안 통제	9

외신과	접수자	통제

ㅇ 따라서 동인이 재차 사증발급을 신청하는 경우,
  주일대사관의 담당영사가 동인을 면담, 입국목적,
  동향등을 상세히 심사, 법무부에 승인 신청을
  하면 법무부가 종합적으로 검토, 사증발급 여부
  또는 규제조치 해제등을 결정할 수 있음.

ㅇ 동인 86.1.14. 사증발급 규제 조치가 된 이후에도
  친구 방문을 위해 입국을 ~~허락~~ 하여 법무부는 86.2.
  27 및 86.6.20. 2회에 걸쳐 입국을 허가한 바 있음.

  인도적인 고려로

(미주국장 장선섭)

0011

외 무 부

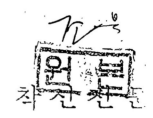

번 호 : JAW-1562   일 시 : 703111515   종 별 :

수 신 : 장관(미북,영사,아일,법무부) 사본: 주미대사-중계필

발 신 : 주 일 대사(일영)

제 목 : 미국인 입국사증

대: USW-1009

1. 주일 미대사관은 대호 ████████ 의 아국 입국사증 문제와관련, 동인이
당관을 방문, 본인의 입장을 설명하는 기회를 가질수있는지 여부를 문의하여 왔는바
당관은 동인의 입국사증 문제에 관해 구체적으로 설명할 입장은 아니라고 하고 그러
나 동인이 입국사증 담당영사의 면담을 희망해올 경우 면담은 가능할것이라 하였음

2. 이와관련, 동인의 당관 방문시 입국문제에 관한 본부설명 지침 하시바람. 끝

(총영사 강신무-국장)

예고: 87.12.31 까지

예고문에 의거 재분류(19 .12. .)
직위   성명

검토필 (1 . 6. 20.)

미주국   영교국   아주국   법무부

87.03.12   09:55
외신 2과   통제관

0012

	분류번호	보존기간

발 신 전 보

번 호 : WJA-1282   일 시 : 103 131210   전보종별 : ＿＿＿＿

수 신 : 주   일   대사·총영사

발 신 : 장   관   (미북)

제 목 : 미국인 입국 사증

        대 : JAW-1318, 1562

    1. 재일 미국인 변호사 ▇▇▇▇▇▇ 의 사증 규제에
대한 본부의 입장은 아래와 같은 바 주일미대사관 문의 및 동인의
면담 신청시 참고 바람.

        가. 사증발급 규제 사유

        ㅇ 동인은 83.8.29-85.6.30간 중앙국제 특허 법률
          사무소 법률자문역으로 한국에서 근무할 당시
          취득한 고용자격의 사증 (9-11)으로 85.12.28. 입국
          하여 미국소재 인권단체인 국제인권법률 가협회
          (International Human Rights Law Group)
          소속 변호사들과 연계, 김근태 공판참관을 시도하고
          문익환목사를 방문하는등 체류자격외의 활동을 하여
          ＿＿＿＿＿＿ 4. 이래 사증발급 규제 대상이 되었음.

＿＿고군에 의기 재본 (1987.12.31.) 이
직위

검토필 (1987.6.20.) 이원 PR

/계속/

보안 통제

이주장 :

양 고 재	87 년 3 월 13 일	63 미 과	기안자 3	과 장	국 장 전결	차 관	장 관

0013

외 신 과	접수자	통 제

나. 방한 가능성 및 규제조치 해제 가능성 여부

　　ㅇ 사증발급 규제란 입국을 금지하는 조치가 아니고
　　　외국인이 재외공관에 사증신청시 (　　) 법무부의
　　　사전승인을 받아 사증을 발급하는 제도임에 비추어,
　　　동인이 사증신청을 위해 귀관 담당영사 면담을
　　　희망할 경우, 동인을 직접 면담 입국목적 및
　　　동향등을 상세히 심사, 본부에 승인 상신하면 법무부가
　　　이를 종합적으로 검토하여 사증발급 여부 및 사증
　　　발급 규제 해제등을 검토할 것임.

다. 동인은 86.1.14. 사증발급 규제가된 이후 친구 방문을
　　위해 입국 사증 없이 86.2.27 및 86.6.30. 방한 하였
　　으나, 법무부는 인도적인 고려로 입국을 허가한 바
　　있음.

　　　　　　　　　　(미주국장 장선섭)

0014

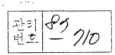

외 무 부   착 신 전

번 호 : JAW-1677   일 시 : 703161722   종 별 :

수 신 : 장관(영사,미북,아일,법무부)

발 신 : 주일대사(일영)

제 목 : 사증발급 승인요청

대 : USW-1009,WJA-1003

연 : JAW-1562

1.

2.

3. 남

4.

5. 미국

6. 변호사

7.

8. 미국

9. 미국 뉴욕

10. 일본 지바현

11. 관 광

12. 가급적 빠른시기

13. 무

14. 서울 뉴용산호텔

15. 60일

16. 상기인은 3.13 당영사관을 방문 아래입장을 표명함,

- 자신에대한 입국불허가 86.2. 김근태재판 참관과 관련 된것으로 생각되나, 본인은

정치적 동기나 특별한 목적은 전혀 없었으며 앞으로도 유사한 활동을 할 의도는 없음

- -

영교국   미주국   아주국   안 가   법무부

PAGE   1   87.03.17 09:28
                                        외신 2과 통제관

                                        0015

- 금번 방한은 개인적으로 결혼 상대자와의 재회를위한 방한인바, 86.2. 이후에도 특별 허가로 2차례 방한한점을 감안, 입국 히가하여 주기바람.

상기 방한 목적에 극한된 입국사증 발급 허가를 건의함. 끝

(총영사 강신무-국장)

예고: 87.12.31 까지 ~

발 신 전 보

번 호: WJA - 1355   일 시: 70318 2020   전보종별: 지급

수 신: 주   일   대사 ·1총영사 /

발 신: 장   관 (미북)

제 목: 미국인 사증 신청

　　　1· 주한미대사관은 미국 변호사 협회 소속 Mr. Harold McElhiny
변호사가 3·24로 예정된 유성환 의원 재판 방청을 위해 주 일대사관을
통해 방한 사증을 신청할 예정임을 알려오며 사증 발급에 대한 협조를
요청하여 왔음·

　　　2· 동건은 법무부에서 방침을 결정할 예정인 바、 사증 접수
되는 대로 보고 바람·

　　　　　　　　　　　　(미주국장 장선섭)

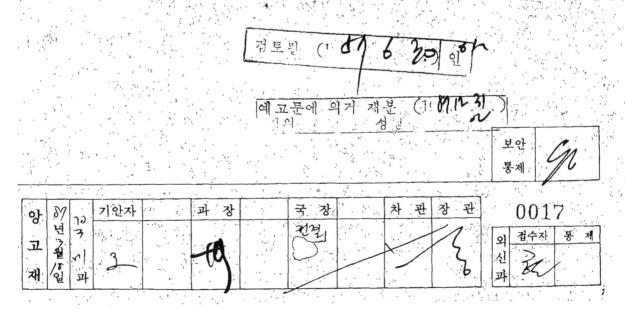

OFFICE OF THE PRESIDENT
EUGENE C. THOMAS
AMERICAN BAR CENTER
750 N. LAKE SHORE DRIVE
CHICAGO, ILLINOIS 60611
TELEPHONE: 312 / 988-5100
ABA / NET: ABAOIO

PLEASE REPLY TO:
1800 M STREET, N.W.
WASHINGTON, D.C. 20036

M E M O R A N D U M

TO: Harold McElhinny

FROM: Eugene C. Thomas
           President
           American Bar Association

RE: Authorization to be the official representative
           of the American Bar Association to observe the
           legal proceedings concerning Assemblyman Yoo
           Sung-hwan in South Korea

DATE: March 18, 1987

        I hereby designate you as the official representative of
the American Bar Association (ABA) and its over 320,000 member
lawyers as observer at the appellate proceedings in South Korea
concerning Assemblyman Yoo Sung-hwan. You may give copies of
this memorandum of credential to any appropriate South Korean
or American government officials or others in South Korea to
request their cooperation and assistance regarding your
responsibilities as a trial observer on behalf of the ABA.

        Your mission is part of the ABA International Human Rights
Trial Observers Project, administered by the ABA Section of
Individual Rights and Responsibilities, which has been
authorized by the Board of Governors of the ABA. The purpose
of this project is to fulfill Goal VIII of the American Bar
Association by encouraging adherence to the rule of law
throughout the world by sending prominent American lawyers
overseas to observe trials with significant human rights
implications. Your mission is also in furtherance of the
resolution adopted by the ABA House of Delegates on February
25, 1975, reaffirming our Association's support for the rule of
the law in the international community and its recognition of
the need for an independent judiciary and for the independence
of lawyers as essential elements in maintaining the rule of law.

0018

Memorandum to Harold McElhinny
Page Two
March 18, 1987

Among the objects of your mission are the following:

1) To make known to the court, to the authorities of South Korea, to the prosecutors, defense counsel and the defendant in this case, and to the general public the interest and concern of the American legal profession and the American Bar Association in the trial in question;

2) To obtain information about the conduct of the trial, the nature of the case against the accused and the laws under which he is being tried; and

3) To collect more general background information concerning the circumstances leading to the trial.

The primary concern of our Association is for the maintenance of the rule of law and the elements necessary to sustain it. On behalf of the American Bar Association, I thank you for volunteering for this important mission, and I look forward personally to receiving your report.

cc: The Honorable George Shultz
     U.S. Secretary of State
     U.S. Department of State
     Washington, D.C.   20520

4827P

0019

외 무 부

착신전보

번 호 : JAW-1774 일 시 : 703201517 종 별 : 지급

수 신 : 장관(미북,영사,법무부)

발 신 : 주일대사(일영)

제 목 : 사증발급 승인요청

대 : WJA-1355

1. ▮▮▮▮▮▮

2. ▮▮▮▮▮▮

3. 남

4. ▮▮▮▮▮▮

5. 미국

6. 변호사

7. ▮▮▮▮▮▮

8. 미국

9. 미국 켈리포니아

10. 미국 샌프란시스코

11. 유성환의원 재판방청

12. 87.3.23

13. 무

14. 롯데호텔

15. 5일

16. 대호지시에 의한 보고인바, 입국허가여부 지급 하시바람. 끝

(총영사 강신무-국장)

예고: 87.12.31 까지

정보심 (1. 87. 6. 20) 한

예고문에 의거 재분
직위 성 (1. 87. 12. 31.)

- -

미주국 영교국 안 기 법무부

PAGE 1

분류번호	보존기간

발 신 전 보

전보종별: 긴급

번 호: WJA-1449 일 시: 70923 1000

수 신: 주 일 대사·총영사

발 신: 장 관 (미북)

제 목: 미국인 사증발급

대 : JAW - 1774
연 : WJA - 1355

1. 대호 인사에게 아래와같이 아국 정부의 입장을 주지 시킨후
허가 번호 852.9-4, 10일로 사증 발급하기 바람.

　가. 아국의 출입국 관리법상 채류 자격에 재판절차 방청이
　　　없기 때문에 관광 또는 연고자 방문등으로 입국 목적을
　　　변경기재 하여야 사증을 발급받을 수 있음.

　나. 입국 목적에 위배되는 일체 정치 활동은 금지됨.

　다. 재판 방청 허용문제는 재판부에서 결정할 사항이므로
　　　입국후 방청을 신청하여야 함.

(미주국장 장선섭)

검토필 (1. 87. 6. 20.) 완

예고문에 의거 재분 (19   )
직위   성명

	보안 통제	유

앙고재	87년 3월 21일	북미과	기안자 3	과장	국장	차관	장관	0021

외신과	접수자	통재

공   란

통 화 요 록
----

1. 통화일시 : 1987.3.23(월) 08:50-08:55

2. 송 화 자 : 법무부 입국심사과 박기식 계장

3. 수 화 자 : 외무부 북미과 조백상 사무관

4. 제   목 : 미국인 변호사 사증 발급

○ 아래와 같이 사증 발급하기로 결정하였음.

○ 재판방청 목적을 관광 또는 연고자 방문등으로 변경한후 사증
  발급

   - 허가번호 : 852

   - 사증종류 : 9-4 (방문)

   - 체류기간 : 10일 .   끝 .

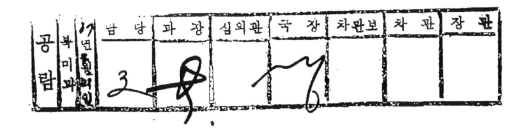

공 란

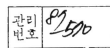

관리
번호 82510

외 　무　부

원본
착 신 전 보
긴급

번 호 : JAW-1815　　　　일 시 : 703231608　　　　종 별 : 긴급

수 신 : 장관(미북, 영사)

발 신 : 주일대사(일영)

제 목 : 미국인 사증발급

대: WJA-1419

1. 당관은 3.23. 대상자를 면담하면서 대호사항을 주지시킨바, 동인은 이를 충분히 인지하고 한국 변호사협회 간부 방문목적으로 수정, 사증을 신청하면서 금일 18:00 동경발 NW-009 편 입국예정이라 첨언함

2. 따라서 당관은 동인에게 87-852, 9-4, 10일 단수 입국사증을 발급하였음. 끝

(총영사 강신무-국장)

예고: 87.12.31 까지

예고문제 회기 사분 (19
적위　　　　성

(　여. 6 2.여

미주국　영교국　안 기

PAGE 1

'87.03.23　17:14
외신 2과　통제관

외 무 부

번 호 : JAW-1915   일 시 : 70326 1804   종 별 :

수 신 : 장 관(미북, 영사, 법무부)

발 신 : 주 일 대사(일영)

제 목 : 미국인 입국사증

대: WJA-1419

연: JAW-1815

1. 대호 미국인 H.J.MCELHINNY 는 대리인을 통하여 재차 한국 변호사협회 간부
면담 목적으로 87.4.?. 재입국을 위한 사 증을 신청 하였는바, 사증 발급 허가 여부
하시 바람.

2. 본인은 현재 한국에 체류중인바, 87.3.27.(금) 당지 도착 예정임. 끝

(총영사강신무-국 장)

예고:87.12.31.까지

미주국   영교국   법무부   안 기

PAGE 1

공   란

공   란

면 담 요 지

o   일 시 : 1987.3.24. (화) 11:10-11:50

o   장 소 : 외무부 북미과

o   면담자 : 아측 : 유명환 북미과장, 조백상 북미과 사무관 (배석)

　　　　　　　미측 : Harold J.McElhinny 미 변호사협회 소속 변호사

　　　　　　　　　　 Edward Dong 주한미대사관 2등 서기관 (배석)

McElhinny :　o   입국사증 발급 협조에 대해 외무부에 감사함.

　　　　　　　o   미국변호사 협회를 대표하여 유성환의원 재판
　　　　　　　　　 방청 및 관계자 면담등 자료수집차 방한 하였음.

　　　　　　　o   본인의 방한은 미변호사협회 인권 재판 참관단
　　　　　　　　　 계획의 일환임.

　　　　　　　o   현직 국회의원의 기소에 대해 미국 인권단체에서
　　　　　　　　　 많은 관심을 표명하고 있음.

북미과장　 :　o   정부로서는 ABA 소속변호사의 방한이 정치적
　　　　　　　　　 의도를 가진 것일 경우 환영할 수 없는 입장임.

　　　　　　　o   유성환의원은 반공국시 발언 및 인천사태에
　　　　　　　　　 대한 왜곡등 국가보안법 위반혐의로 기소 현재
　　　　　　　　　 재판 진행중임.

공람	북미과	서면월4일	담당	과장	심의관	국장	차관보	차관	장관
			3						

0029

o 유의원의 위법성에 대해서는 재판부가 결정할
   것임.

o 공산주의자와의 전쟁을 겪은 한국으로서는 반공은
   국가목표중 가장 중요한 것임.

o 체한중 법적 재약을 받고있는 사람을 제외하고는
   누구나 만나도 좋음.

o 법무부등 관계자 면담을 통해 동 사건에 대한
   정확한 인식을 하기 바람.

0030

면담참고자료

○ 면담인사 : ○ Harold J.Mce㎢hinny (1947. 40세)

　　　　　　 ○ 미국변호사 협회 (ABA) 소속변호사

　　　　　　 ○ 상황법률회사 근무

○ 방한목적 : 유성환의원 재판 방청 (1987.3.24. 14:00 예정)

○ 유성환의원 발언 사건에 대한 정부입장

1. 기소 이유 (상세 별첨 참조)

　　 -　 86.10.14. 국회질의시 동인은 '국시는 반공이 아니고 통일
　　　　 이어야 한다 ' '통일과 민족은 공산주의나 자본주의보다
　　　　 상위에 위치해야 한다 '는등 반공 국시에 어긋난 발언과
　　　　 함께 인천사태는 민중 수탈에 대한 민중의 생존권 쟁취
　　　　 투쟁, 이라고 왜곡하는등 국가 기본 질서에 반하는 발언을
　　　　 하여, 검찰은 국가보안법 위반 혐의로 동인에 대한 구속영장을
　　　　 법원에 신청, 10.15. 국회에 체포동의를 요청하였음.

2. 정부입장

　　 -　 사법부의 독립원칙 및 현재 재판이 진행중에 있으므로
　　　　 유의원 발언의 위법성에 대해서는 외무부의 실무자가
　　　　 언급할 입장이 못됨.

0031

-   사안의 중대성에 비추어 재판부(서울형사 지법 합의 14부,
    재판장 박영부 부장판사)도 23일 쟁점이 되고 있는 「국시」
    부분과 관련 서울대 사회학, 정치학, 법학 교수등 관계
    전문가에게 사실 조회를 의뢰하는등 최대한의 신중을
    기하고 있음.

3. 외국인의 재판 방청요청에 대한 정부입장

-   대한민국의 사법제도는 비록 미국의 기준으로 볼때 완벽
    하다고 할 수 없을지는 모르나 분단국 이라는 특수상황과
    여러제약속에도 국가의 기본을 유지하고 국민의 기본권을
    보장하기 위하여 그 기능을 발휘하고 있음.

-   헌법에 보장된 공개 재판의 원칙에 따라 특수한 경우를
    제외하고는 누구나 적절한 절차를 걸쳐 재판에 방청
    할 권리가 있음..

-   외신기자나 주한 외국공관 직원등 상주 외국인의 경우
    재판을 자유롭게 방청할 수 있음.

-   그러나 외국의 변호사나 인권단체가 특정재판의 방청을
    위하여 방한한다는 사실 그 자체가 자주 독립국의 자존심과
    특히 재판부의 권위를 손상시키는 점이 있어 이를 환영치
    못하는 것임.

-   미국의 재판에 한국이나 기타 국가의 변호사가 방청을
    목적으로 미국을 방문한다고 할때 미국 관리나 재판부는
    이를 어떻게 받아들일지 묻고 싶음.

0032

- 한국은 비록 미국의 기준에서 볼때 인권등의 분야에서
  몇가지 문제점이 있다는 것은 우리도 인정하고 있음.

- 그러나 주어진 상황에서 국민의 기본권 보호를 위해서
  나름의 최선을 다하고 있으며, 문제점이 있다고 해서 북한
  이나 동구 공산국가, 또는 제3세계 독재국가 처럼 우리의
  체제를 폐쇄 시키거나 하지 않음.

- 방한 기회에, 동 의원 재판에 방청, 분위기를 느껴보고
  아울러 피고측과 법무부측의 견해를 고루 청취하여 균형된
  시각을 갖게 되길 희망함.

0033

공   란

공   란

공 란

공   란

공   란

공   란

공　　　　란

공   란

1. 인권 보장에 관한 아국정부의 입장

　　가. 아국은 세계인권선언이 구채화된 경제적 사회적 및 문화적 권리에
　　　　관한 국제규약 (1976년 부터 발효)에 가입함으로써 인권을 존중
　　　　하는 아국정부의 입장 천명

　　나. 대한민국헌법 2장(국민의 권리와 의무)을 통해 국민의 기본권에
　　　　대해 광범위하게 보장

2. 국내 인권문재와 아국의 입장

　　가. 김근태 사건

　　　　1) 김근태는 85.1-85.6간 폭력혁명에 의한 국가전복 및 노동자,
　　　　　　농민등이 주채가된 사회주의 국가건설을 목적으로 하는 소위
　　　　　　" 민청련" 이란 반국가단채를 조직, 불법집회, 시위등
　　　　　　활동을하여 북괴의 대남혁명 노선에 동조한 명백한 반국가적
　　　　　　범죄자로서 86.9.23. 대법원에서 징역 5년, 자격
　　　　　　정지 5년의 형이 확정되어 복역중에 있음.

　　　　2) 고문은 헌법상 금지되어 있고, 관계법률에서 고문등으로
　　　　　　인한 자백은 유죄의 증거로 사용할 수 없고, 고문을 중한
　　　　　　범죄로 규정하는등 인권보장에 관한 완벽한 장치를 두고있고,
　　　　　　나아가 정부는 이와같은 법정신에 입각하여 국민의 인권옹호에
　　　　　　최대한 노력을 기울이고 있음.

0042

ㅇ 김근태가 경찰수사과정에서 고문을 당했다는 주장에 대해
　　서는, 고문을 당했다고 인정할만한 사실이나 혼적이
　　없으며 이를 정치적으로 이용하기위한 재야운동권 단체의
　　악의적으로 왜곡 전파에 기인한것임.

나. 권인숙 (부천서 성고문) 사건

1) 권인숙은 노사분규를 일으킬 목적으로 타인의 주민등록
　　증을 변조해 위장취업한 범죄자로 8 6 . 1 1 . 2 1 .
　　1심에서 3년형이 구형되어 현재 2심 대기중임.

2) 권양에 대한 조사과정에서 야기되었던 소위 ' 성고문 ' 은
　　조사담당자가 직무에 집착, 우발적으로 저지른 폭행으로
　　정부는 관련 형사의파면 및 부천서장의 면직등 엄중한
　　조치를 취하였음.

3) 동 사건에 대한 사법절차가 진행중에 있으므로 이에 영향
　　을 줄 외부적 개입은 적절하지못함.

다. 문익환 목사 사건
3) 문익환 목사는 민중봉기에의한 정부타도를 목표로하는
　　불법이적 단체인 민통련의 의장으로서 인천사태 소요주도
　　및 서울대학 내에서의 학생소요를 선동한 혐으로 1 1 . 4
　　선고 공판에서 징역3년이 확정되어 현재 복역중임.

0043

라. 미유학생 간첩단 사건

　　1) 양동화, 김성만등은 83.9-85.6 유학자 체미중
　　　　재미복귀 공작책 서정균에 포섭되어 동구라파경유 입북,
　　　　밀봉교육을 받고 국내침투, 간첩활동 및 정부전복을
　　　　기도한 범죄로 86.9.23. 최종심에서 양동화,
　　　　김성만은 사형, 황대권은 무기형이 확정되었음.

　　2) 형량의 적절성등에 대해서는 3심을 통해 충분히 고려되었
　　　　으나, 북한 공산집단과 대치하고있는 현 상황에서 간첩활동
　　　　등의 이적행위에 대해서는 중형이 불가피함.

마. 보안 감호 관련자

　　1) 서준식
　　　－ 제일교포 간첩사건 관련자
　　　－ 공산주의 사상 고집으로 보안 감호 조치가 연장되고있음.

　　2) 강종곤
　　　－ 1976.12. 대법원에서 국가보안법위반혐의로 징역
　　　　5년, 자격정지 5년 선고
　　　－ 간첩죄를 저질렀던자로 사상전향거부, 북괴 찬양지속으로
　　　　감호조치가 연장되고있음.

　　3) 정부 입장
　　　－ 반국가사범에 대한 보안처분 제도는 여타 선진국에서도
　　　　채택하고 있으며 우리나라의 특수한 안보상황을 고려할때
　　　　동 제도는 필수적임.

0044

	분류번호	보존기간

발 신 전 보

번 호 : WJA-1534   일 시 : 032781330   전보종별 : 지급

수 신 : 주 입   대사·총영사

발 신 : 장   관   (미북)

제 목 : 미국인 입국 사증

대 : JAW - 1915

대호, McElhinny 측에 입국 예정(일)   체류 예정 기간 확인, 지급

보고 바람.

(미주국장 장선섭)

검토 : (87. 6. 20.) 안

	보안 통제	

| 앙
고
재 | 87
년
3
월
28
일 | 63
제
과 | 기안자

3 | 과 장

 | 국 장
전결 | | 차 관 | 장 관 | 0045 | 외
신
과 | 접수자 | 통제 |

외 무 부

번 호 : JAW-1976   일 시 : 703301340   종 별 :

수 신 : 장관(미북,영사,법무부)

발 신 : 주 일 대사(일영)

제 목 : 미국인 입국사증

대: WJA-1534

연: JAW-1915

대호 MCEILIINNY 는 87.4.6(월) 입국예정이며, 체류 예정기간은 1주일 임. 끝

(총영사 강신구-국장)

예고: 87.12.31 까지

기도 (87. 6. 20. 안

문에 의거 재분 (1
직위   성

미주국   영교국   법무부   안 기

	분류번호	보존기간

발 신 전 보

번 호: 2JA-1601   일 시: 1104021200   전보종별: 지급

수 신: 주 일   대사·총영사//

발 신: 장   관   (미북)

제 목: 미국인 입국 사증

대 : JAW - 1976

1. 주한 미대사관측은 대호.McEhlinny 가 일정상 4.6 방한이 불가하여 대신 미변호사협회 소속의 Stephen Schrader 가 방한할 예정임을 알려오며, 사증발급에 대한 협조를 요청하여 왔는 바, 사증 신청 접수 되는 대로 보고 바람.

(미주국장 장선섭)

보고필 (87. 6. 20) 안

예고문에 의거 재분 (1)
직위   성명

	보안	
	통제	81

앙고재	87년4월2일	북미과	기안자	파장	국장 건결	차관	장관	0047	외신과	접수자	통제
		3									

통 화 요 록

o 4. 2. 10:20 - 30

   송화자 : 주한미대사관 K. Stephens 1등 서기관

   수화자 : 북미과 조백상 사무관

   (ABA 소속 변호사 방한)

0 Stephens : • 4.6 입국 예정이던 Mr. McEhlinny는 중공

              방문 일정 때문에 예정대로 방한하지 못하고 그 대신

              미변호사협회는 동인과 일본에서 같이 일하고 있는

              Stephen Schrader를 파한키로 했다함.

              동인의 방한목적은 4.6 유성환 의원 재판방청이라함.

              • 미변호사협회 워싱턴 지부장 Stephen Raiken

              은 아침 국제전화로 이와같은 사실을 알려오며 사증

              발급에 대한 협조를 요청해 왔음.

0   조 백 상 : • 사증 신청이 4.6 입국 예정일에 비추어 지나치게

              촉박한 감이 있음.

              • 동인으로 하여금 가능한 빨리 주일 한국 대사관에

              사증 신청하도록 하기 바람.

              • 관계부처 협의후 결과 알려주겠음.

              • 금후 방한사증 신청은 적어도 7-10 이전에

              이루어지도록 협조하여 주기 바람.

                                                      0048

관리
번호 87
- 917

외 무 부

번 호 : JAW-2116   일 시 : 704031344

수 신 : 장관(미북,영사,법무부)

발 신 : 주일대사(일영)

제 목 : 사증발급 승인요청

대 : WJA-1601

1. SCHRADER

2. STEPHEN J

3. 남

4. 1956.7.26

5. 미국

6. 변호사

7. 일반 C1488329

8. 미국

9. 미국 아이오와주

10. 일본 동경

11. 유성환의원 재판방청 및 한국변호사협회 간부방문

12. 1987.4.4

13. -

14. 프로자호텔

15. 7일간

16. 대호에의한 입국사증 신청인바, 허가여부 지급 하시바람. 끝

(총영사 강신무-국장)

예고 : 87.12.31 까지

예고문에 의거 재분류
직위   실명

미주국   영교국   안 기   법무부

PAGE   1

87.04.03 16:49
외신 2과 통제관

0049

외 무 부

착 신 전 보

번 호 : JAW-2153   일 시 : 704051205   종 별 :

수 신 : 장관 (미북,영사)

발 신 : 주 일 대사 (일영)

제 목 : 미국인 사증발급

대 : WJA-1646

1. 당관은 금 4.5 (일) MR.SCHRADER 와 면담 대호 (WJA-1419) 아국정부 입장을 설명하였는바, 동인이 입국목적을 한국변호사협회 간부 방문목적으로 수정신청함에 따라 동인에게 대호지시에 의거, 사증발급하였음.

2. 동인은 금 4.5.18:00 동경발 NW-009 편으로 입국키 위해 WAITING LIST 에 올려놓았으나, 여의치 못 할경우 다른 비행기편으로 라도 금일중 입국예정이라함. 끝.

(총영사 강신무-국장)

예고: 87.12.31. 까지

예고문에 의기 재분류
직위   성명

미주국   차관실   1 차보   영교국   청와대   안 기

공 란

공   란

공 란

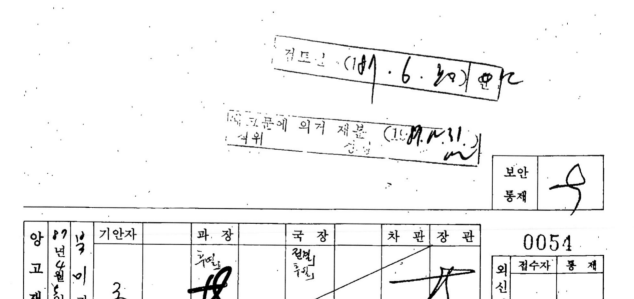

분류번호	보존기간

발 신 전 보

번 호 : WJA-1646   일 시 : 7040550930   전보종별 : 긴 급

수 신 : 주 일   대사·총영사

발 신 : 장 관 (미북)

제 목 : 미국인 사증신청 승인

대 : JAW-2116

연 : WJA-1419

○ 대호 인사에게 연호 아국정부 입장을 설명, 유성환의원 재판방청 목적은

지우고   허가번호 87-1025 , 9-4 , 10일로 사증발급 바람.

(미주국장   장세섭)

검토 (87.6.20) 한

.....문에 의거 재본
....위

보안
통제

앙 고 제	87년 4월 6일	북 미 과	기안자		과 장		국 장		차 관	장 관	0054			
			3								외신과	접수자	통재	

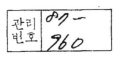

관리
번호
960

외 무 부

착 신 전 보
종 별 : 지 급

번 호 : JAW-2212　　　　일 시 : 704081655

수 신 : 장 관 (영사, 미북, 법무부)

발 신 : 주 일 대사 (일영)

제 목 : 사증 발급

1. MC ELHINNY

2. HAROLD J,

3. 남

4. 1947.1.5

5. 미국

6. 변호사

7. 일반 050960498

8. 미국

9. 미국

10. 일본 동경

11. 한국 변호사협회 간부 방문

12. 1987.4.12

13. 무

14. 조선호텔

15. 2 일간

16. 한국 변호사협회 간부 방문 목적인바, 입국허가 가하다고 판단됨. 아울러 동일

목적의 복수사증 발급 여부 하시 바람. 끝

(총영사 강신무-국장)

예고:87.12.31 까지

검토 (87. 6. 20.) 안

- -

영교국　미주국　아주국　안 기　법무부

PAGE 1

87.04.08 20:19
외신 2과 통제관

0055

통 화 요 록

1. 통화일시 : 87.4.6(월) 11:05-11:10

2. 송 화 자 : 주미대사관 Dong 2등서기관

3. 수 화 자 : 북미과 조백상 사무관

4. 통화내용 :

(방한 ABA 소속 변호사 관련)

Dong : ○ Schrader 변호사는 사증발급에 대한 외무부의 협조에
　　　　　감사하며 채한중 외무부 방문을 희망하고 있음.

　　　　○ 또한 동인은 김두희 검찰국장 ○김진세 법무과장○등과의
　　　　　면담을 희망하여 왔는 바 동 일정 주선에 외무부가 협조해
　　　　　주길 바람.

초백상 : ○ 면담 방침은 관계당사국에서 결정할 예정이나, 가능한
　　　　　협조를 요청해 놓겠음.

　　　　○ 외무부는 출국전 적절한 기회에 방문하는 것이 좋겠음.

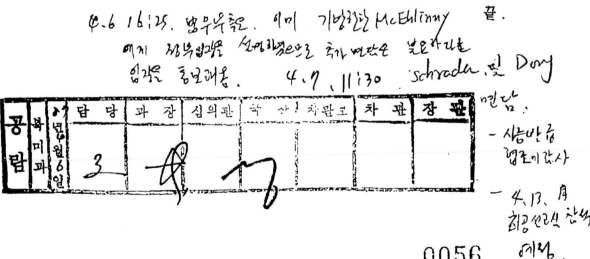

0056

통 화 요 록
----

1. 통 화 일 시 : 1987.4.6(월) 09:55-10:05

2. 송 화 자 : K. Stephens 주한미대사관 1등서기관

3. 수 화 자 : 외무부 북미과 조백상 사무관

4. 통화내용 :

(ABA 소속 변호사 방한 관련)

Stephens : ○ Stephen Schrader 가 어제 저녁 입국, 곧 대사관에

              올 예정임.

           ○ 주말인데도 동인의 입국을 위하여 노력해준데

              감사함.

조 백 상 : ○ 미대사관측이 유성환 의원 사건에 대한 전반적

              설명을 해주길 희망함.

           ○ 동인이 법무부등 관계기관 방문 희망시 협조해

              주겠음.

공람	북미과 87년 4월 6일	담 당	과 장	심의관	국 장	차관보	차 관	장 관
		3						

0057

('말' 사건 관련 구속자 관련)

Stephens :　○ Deconcini 상원의원은 의회 청문회시 '말'특집호
　　　　　　　관련 3인이 구속, 재판을 받고 있는것 외에 3월
　　　　　　　정석모, 박우정등 2명의 언론인이 추가로 구속
　　　　　　　되었다고 하며 국무성측에 확인을 요청하였음.

　　　　　　○ 상기 2인이 언제, 어떠한 이유로 구속되었는지
　　　　　　　알려주기 바람.

조 백 상 :　○ 관계부처에 문의, 알려주겠음.　　　　끝.

0058

분류번호	보존기간

발 신 전 보

번 호 : WJA-1736   일 시 : 10410 1900   전보종별 : 지급

수 신 : 주   일   대사·총영사·

발 신 : 장   관   (미북)

제 목 : 사증발급

대 : JAW - 2212

대호 인사에게 허가번호 87-1096, 9-4, 10일로 단수 사증

발급하기 바람.

(미국3과장 장선섭)

검토필 (89. 6. 20.) 미안

보안
통제

0059

앙 고 재	87 년 6 월 8 일 북미 과	기안자 조	과 장	국 장 련팽	차 관	장 관		외 신 과	접수자	통재

통 화 요 록

일 시 :

    o 87. 4. 10. 18:10

    o 송화자 : 법무부 입국심사과 송계장

    o 수화자 : 외무부 북미과 조백상 사무관

    o 내 용

    McEhlinny 에게 허가번호 87-1096, 9-4, 10일간

    단수 사증 발급 바람.

0060

2. Schifter 미 국무부 인권차관보 발언

외   무   부   착 신 전 문

번 호 : USW-2260   일 시 : 8705062313   종 별 : 긴급

수 신 : 장관(미북)

발 신 : 주 미 대사

제 목 : 하원 아태소위 청문회

연 : USW-2258

금 5.6(수) 저녁 이기백 국방장관 주최 리셉숀(대사관저) 석상에서 LILLEY 대사는 박수길 차관보에게 연호 청문회 결과에 대해 다음과 같이 언급하였음

1. 금일 청문회 증언에서 SIGUR 차관보는 미리 준비한바와 같이 균형된 입장에서 발언하였으며, SOLARZ 위원장도 아국에 대해 그렇게 크게 비판적으로 발언하지는 않은 것으로 평가됨

2. 한편 SCHIFTER 인권차관보의 경우 의외로 인권관계 질문에 대해 예상외의 답변을 하였는바, LILLEY 대사 자신은 물론 국무성 관계자들도 그의 발언에 대하여 크게 당황하였으며 유감으로 생각하고 있다함

3. 동 인권관계 발언부분에 대해 SIGUR 차관보는, SCHIFTER 차관보가 너무 많은 질문을 받아 당황한 나머지 실제 의도와는 다른 발언과 필요이상의 비유를 하게 된것으로 보인다고 하면서 예상치 못했던일이라는 반응을 보였음.

(대사 김경원)

예고:87.12.31일반

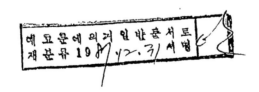

미주국   차관실   1 차보   2 차보   정문국   청와대   총리실   안 기

주 미 대 가 관

번호 : USW(F)-623 0506 1P20

수신 : 장관 머봉   ) 발신 : 주미대사

제목 : 하원 청문회 질거응답요지 (2후-5매)

1

Hearing, Wed. Afternoon

Statement of Gaston Sigur, Asst. Sec. for Pacific and Eastern Affairs

Richard Schifter, Asst. Sec. of State for Human Rights and Human Affairs
gives a short presentation.

Solarz: Is our idea of democracy compatible with the Korean people's
         concept?

Sigur: They're equally capable of developing democracy as they are
         of developing a strong economy.
Schift: I share Sigur's views...

Solarz: The US has an interest in stability in Korea with 40,000
         US troops there and 70,000 North Korean troops over the border.
         What are the prospects for stability with the maintenance of
         more or less of an authoritarian regime in South Korea?
Sigur: Development on all levels (economic and political) are important
         for stability. But political development, particularly
         political participation is the key.

Solarz: Do you feel that concensus (political) would serve all conerned
         (US and Korea)? Do you favor dialogue to achieve an agreement
         on political developments in the country?
Sigur: Yes...Yes Dialogue essential...must be resumed.

Solarz: We would like to see dialogue resume soon.
Sigur: No queston of that.

Solarz: You would like to see this dialogue to begin immediately, as
         opposed to a two year delay?
Sigur.   Dialogue is most important to develop fundemental rights (press,
         fair election laws and local autonomy)

0063

Solarz: Would we object to the conflicting parties conducting a dialogue on the Constitution?
Sigur: We don't want to impose a decision on them. but yes.

Solarz: I'm confused, it's good to press the issue when it comes to the press, election laws or political prisoners, but not the Constitution?
Sigur: No this is fine to talk about on the same level as other concerns.
Solarz: We should take this show on the road.

Solarz: Do you advocate restoring political rights and removing Kim Dae Jung from house arrest?
Sigur: Yes.

Solzarz: Then would you object to having a report made by the State Department on Dae Jung's trial.
Sigur: I haven't looked at it, and I would have to.

Solarz: Under the existing electoral system, the opposition says that it doesn't have a fair chance in the upcoming elections. Do You agree? Is there a need for a change in the Constitution and election laws to make fair elections?

Sigur: They have to determine this for themselves, but there is currently a strong imbalance between rural and urban areas.

Solarz: Mr. Schifter, you have the responsibility of monitoring Human rights abuses around the world. A comparative analysis please, between Chile and South Korea?
Schift: There are a lot of similarities in the two situations. In both cases, institutions independent of the government exist (as opposed to totalitarian regimes), leadership is in the hands of the military. In both cases too, there is the problem of torture, and the return of the military to its barracks would be essential to a return to democracy.

Solarz: Compare the two countries with regards to torture and Political prisoners.
Schift: The two are the same. The press is more open in Chile, and there are fewer political prisoners. Torture occurs at roughly the same level

Yatron: Have you visited Korea Mr. Schifter?
Schift: No.
Yatron: It would be helpful if you went there.
Schift: I have met with both sides here in the US.

Yatron: After the case of a student being tortured to death by the police, three officers were fired but now have been reinstated. Two others were not tried yet. Do you have additional info. on This?

Schift: I spoke with the Koreans yesterday about this.
Yatron: Do you have any more information on the police situation.
Schift: No.

0064

Yatron: Could you describe the judicial system in Korea, the degree of autonomy it has, for example?
Schift: No.

Yatron: Has our administration taken any action on the emprisoned labor leaders in South Korea?
Schift: We've addressed this to Korean representatives and we addressed this in our country report on South Korea.
Yatron: Do you make representations on this matters in other forums?
Schift: Yes to different South Korean Officials and during our noon statements.

Yatron: Any guess as to how many political prisoners there are in South Korea now? Are there likely to be retributions following the revoked promise on the Constitution?
Schift: Approx. 1,000 prisoners (political). A political prisoner in our classification is someone who has done nothing other than express himself, as one might under our First Ammendment. People who have received a punishment which is not at all commensurate with their crimes are also considered to be political prisoners.

Yatron: How many students detained?
Schift: Many.

Yatron: Mr. Sigur, how is our friendly advice received/considered in Seoul. Has Mr. Chun accepted our criticism of the revocation of promised Sonstitutional changes.
Sigur: He sees it as coming from a fiend.

Yatron: And what is the labor situation like now?
Sigur: We have seen some improvement here. The National Assembly has revised some of the labor laws (Welfare & Nat. Indust. Relations).

Yatron: Have we received formal replies to our advice/criticism?
Sigur: No, and we never expect this type of reply.

Yatron: The Olympics are tainted by the troubles (political ones) that Korea is having. What can the US do to encourage Korea to become a shwocase for political change/the poltical process?
Sigur: As Mr. Schifter said, there is an overwhelming desire for opening up the poltical process in Korea. All leaders understand this. The question is, how to get there. The question is, can people start compromising.

Leech: The Reagan Administration's policy on Human Rights has come a long way. According to Mr. Schifter's [prepared] testimony, much has changed and little has changed.. What do you think all concerned parties will have to do in Korea to show good faith.

Sigur: The government must move toward implementing a number of measures. Press laws must be changed.(espec. TV and radio) The government must move to revise the election laws, and the prisons must be opened. We's hope that the opposition would see all of this assan act of good faith.

0065

Leech: What is the role for a Third party (the US) as an inter-
          mediary here, or for that matter, the role of an internat-
          ional organization acting in this capacity?
Sigur: There is no role for the US here. The US must be very careful.
Leech: We all hope that Korea will appreciate your views and role
          [that of the State Department's].

Atkins: One would hope that Korea would take the same path as the
          Phillipines. One thing I noticed while I was in the
          Phillipines right before Marcos fell was that repression
          could be very subtle. There is no need for it to be overt.
          There, the press was excersizing self-censorship, following
          government guidelines. Now, in South Korea, we have censor-
          ship in the Stars and Stripes and AFKN, to avoid offending
          the Korean government. What are your thoughts on this? What
          are your thoughts on our ability to broadcast with AFKN and
          use it as a means to create dialogue?

Schift: That's the role of the VOA.
Atkins: Wait -- we send our soldiers to Korea to defend Freedom, but
          a Nightline telecast of Mr. Kim Dae Jung is censored. Do you
          see an irony in this?
Schift: To accurately broadcast the news is necessary. But if you are
          asking if we should overtly use telecasting abilities to
          influence -- NO.

Atkins: Are you concerned about censorhsip problems at AFKN?
Schift: Yes.
Atkins: What are your feelings on this subject Mr. Sigur?
Sigur: Well, we broadcast there with the permission of the government.
Athin: But we have leverage over that.
Sigur: Yes.

Atkins: It seems to me with the government's rigid controls over the
          electronic media, AFKN would be the one place where it is
          possible to do an accurate reporting of the news.
Sigur: I have no qualms about that. But there is a fine line so far
          as interfering with their process.

Solarz: Could you submit for the record, Mr. Sigur, a supplemental
          statement on how many times the AFKA has consciously refrained
          from broadcasting?
Sigur: YEs.

Atkins: On the subject of our IMET program with Korea. It's a $2 million
          year program. Can you assure us that the trainees in the program
          are not the ROK officers who tortured prisoners?
Schift: The problems stem from the police, not the military.
Atkins: IMET funding covers Police too, no?
Schift: No.
Atkins: So it would be easy to assure us that our taxpayers $$ are not
          being used to train officers who torutre prisoners?
Schift: I'll check into it.

0066

282 한국 인권문제 제 사안 1

Soloman: My concern is violent demonstrations. Kim Dae Jung has never come out against violence. Democratic Progress impossible with violence.

Sigur: They (the opposition) do not approve of violence to my knowledge. They have clearly stated this. Violence comes from the extreme left. They believe that violecne is the only way to bring about change.

Soloman: Isn't North Korea instigating this violence in the student movement?

Sigur: That is speculation.

Solarz: The sincerity of the government's stated desire for democracy in Korea is at question here. The Opposition says that he is not serious. Why doesn't he take steps towards Democracy now? What is your assessment of this?

Sigur: Hopefully, there is an understanding in the government of a need for reform.

Solarz: So they agree on the need for reform?

Sigur: Yes.

Solarz: The government tried to make a big deal out of the fact that it was allowing the press to cover provincial capitols again. This can't be interpretted as a relaxation of press restrictions. Mr. Schifter, how do you account for the discrepancy between the difference between your numbers and the opposition's numbers on the number of political prisoners being held in Korea?

Sigur: Discusses methodology again (p. 3). They know the Secreatary of State's views on this matter.

Solarz: I have heard that our views on human rights abuses have been seen to be the views of mid-level bureaucrats. Perhaps the Sec. of State or the President should say something, in the proper forum on this..

Leech: The role of Congress and the Executive are both important here. Did Congress weaken or strengthen its credibility by passing the Gepardt ammendment? Sigur: Bad move.

Solarz: What about suspending GSP exports from Korea. Is there wisdom in this approach? Sigur: could fuel anti-American sentiment.

Solarz: What about instructing representatives to Wordl Bank to vote against loans to South Korea (CHile analogy). Sigur: Bad idea.

Solarz: What about terminating CPEC loan guarantees, in order to lend credibility to our words?

Sigur: There is a problem with that approach too. We have to realize that Chun has promised to step down.

Solarz: What if Congress adopted a resolution which expresses interest toward further progress toward democracy and calls for dialogue?

Schrift: That would be helpful. You (Congress & Solarz) are well-respected over there.

Solarz: I'm pleased to here that. I think that this move could show strong congressional/executive concensus. We would like to get together with you to put out a text which merits your endorsement.

0067

발 신 전 보

번 호 : CUS-1776 일 시 : 7058 1890   전보종별 : _____

수 신 : 주   미   대사 /총영사/

발 신 : 장   관   (미북)

제 목 : 시프터 인권차관보 발언 ( )

대 : USW - 2260

1. 대호 하원 청문회시 시프터 차관보는 솔라즈 의원의 질문 (아국과 칠레의 비교분석)에 대해 아래와 같이 답변한 바 있음.

"There are a lot of similarities in the two situations.
In both cases, institutions independent of the
government exist (as opposed to totalitation regimes),
leadership is in the hands of the military.
In both cases too, there is the problem of torture
and the return of the military to its barracks would
be essential to a return to democracy.
The press is more open in Chile, and there are fewer
political prisoners. Torture occurs at roughly
the same level"

/계속 /

앙고재	87년 월 일	북미과	기안자 황태	과 장	국 장 전결	차 관	장 관	발신시간 :

외신과	접수자	과 장

0068

2. 시프터 차관보가 상기와 같이 한국 실정에 관하여 특히
군부의 지도충 지배、고문·정치범 등 부정확하고 왜곡된 증언을
한데 대하여 유감의 뜻을 표명하지 않을 수 없는 바、이와 관련
동 차관보의 주의를 환기 시키고 금후 여사한 기회가 있을 경우
아국 실정을 보다 정확하게 증언할 수 있도록, 요청하고 결과 보고바람.

(미주국장   장선섭)

예 고 : 87. 12. 31. 일반.

외 무 부

착신전문

원 본

번 호 : USW-2295   일 시 : 8705081451   종 별 :

수 신 : 장관(미북)

발 신 : 주미대사

제 목 : 시프터 인권차관보 발언

대 : WUS-1996

1. 대호 하원청문회 관련, 본직이 5.6(수) 저녁 안보협의회 참석자들을 위한 대사 관저 리셉션에 참석한 SIGUR 차관보에게 SCHIFTER 차관보의 발언내용이 전적 으로 잘못되었음을 지적하고 강력항의 하였던바, SIGUR 차관보는 SCHIFTER 차관보가 크게 실언하였으며, 의원들의 질문공세에 말려든것같다고 언급 한바 있음. 또한 CLARK 부차관보에게도 유감을 표명한바, 동부차관보도 SHIFTER 차관보 가 실언하였음을 인정하였음

2. 본직은 이와관련 SHIFTER 차관보에게도 유감의 뜻을 표할계획이며 결과 보고 하겠음.

3. 한편 SCHIFTER 차관보는 SIGUR 차관보와는 달리 의원들의 질문공세에 말 려드는 경향이 있으므로 가능한한 청문회에 증인으로 출두하지 않는것이 가장 바람직 하나, 앞으로 증언을 피할수 없는경우 사전 접촉, 올바로 발언하도록 요청하겠음

(대사 김경원)

예고: 87.12.31일반

검 토 필 (1987.6.3.

미주국   차관실   1차보   2차보   정문국   청와대   총리실   안 기

발 신 전 보

번 호: WUS-2063   일 시: 7051 22000   전보종별: _____

수 신: 주   미   대사 · 총영사 ////

발 신: 장   관 (미북)

제 목: 국무성 인권담당 직원 접촉 강화

       연 : USW - 2260

       대 : USW - 1609

     연호관련, Schifter 차관보, ⟨⟩ Montgomery 부차관보 및 Farrand 인사국 부국장(몽고메리 후임예정), Rackmales 과장, Murphy 부과장등 국무성 인권담당 직원들이 아국 인권상황에 대해 좀더 정확한 인식을 가질수 있도록 동인들과의 평소 접촉활동을 적극 강화 하기 바람.

                        (차관   오재희)

    예고 : 87. 12. 31. 일반.

앙 고 재	87년 2월 2일	북미과	기안자	과 장		국 장	차 관	장 관	발신시간:
									외신과 접수자 / 파 장

0071

NYT. 87. 5.12.

State Department

'Quiet Diplomacy' In a Loud Voice

By NEIL A. LEWIS
Special to The New York Times

WASHINGTON, May 8 — Richard P. Schifter, the Assistant Secretary of State for human rights, converses barely above a whisper.

It is perhaps a fitting manner for the official charged with conducting "quiet diplomacy," the Reagan Administration's preferred approach for persuading governments to let political opponents out of jail and desist from torture and repression.

Yet in testimony before a House subcommittee last week, Mr. Schifter offered something other than quiet diplomacy as he denounced the Government of South Korea, an important ally, for torturing its political opponents, suppressing legitimate dissent and imprisoning more than 1,000 people improperly on political charges.

The man who delivered this blistering verdict is someone who says he has a deeply personal understanding of how governments abuse their citizens. A native of Austria, he was sent to the United States in 1938 by his parents, who hoped to join him soon afterward. When World War II ended, he learned that his entire family had been shot by the Nazis in 1942.

'Something We Try First'

His remarks on South Korea were a vivid demonstration of just how far the Administration has moved on the issue of human rights.

"Quiet diplomacy is something we try first," Mr. Schifter, 64 years old, said after his testimony last week. "We resort to public condemnation when quiet diplomacy fails."

In a sense, the Administration has found itself with a human rights policy when it originally never intended to have one.

Michael Posner, director of the Lawyers Committee for Human Rights and a frequent antagonist of the Administration's policy, credits Mr. Schifter with some of the change in approach. "The Reagan Administration is never going to be a human rights champion," he said, "but Schifter is at least trying to improve the record."

The people who assumed office with Ronald Reagan in 1981 were determined to undo the human rights policy of Jimmy Carter. They said the Carter policy of criticizing the internal policies of non-Communist allies was foolish and naïve.

Alexander M. Haig Jr., the Administration's first Secretary of State, said resources would be better used combatting terrorism. And Mr. Reagan's first choice for the human rights job, Ernest W. Lefever, said he thought the United States "had no responsibility to promote human rights in sovereign states."

The events that produced a change in the human rights policy began when Mr. Lefever's nomination was rejected by the Senate Foreign Relations Committee and he was eventually forced to withdraw.

The post was then given to Elliot Abrams, who brought an ideological

The New York Times/George Tames
Richard P. Schifter testifying before House subcommittee.

cast to his stewardship of human rights policy and eagerly sought confrontation with liberal human rights activists like Mr. Posner.

Mr. Abrams was an exponent of the view that friendly "authoritarian" regimes are preferable to "totalitarian" regimes, such as those in Communist countries. According to this theory, authoritarian regimes, like many in Latin America, have the potential to become democracies but Communist regimes do not.

It was considered wrong to "hector" friendly anti-Communist regimes about rights abuses, for that might result in such regimes being replaced by Communist regimes and all hope of reform being lost.

Mr. Abrams, for example, disputed the idea that death squads in El Salvador were connected to the government.

"Elliot Abrams always contended the government had nothing to do with it," said Aryeh Neier of Americas Watch, a group that monitors human rights violations. Mr. Neier added that these particular abuses largely abated after Vice President Bush visited El Salvador in December 1983 and admonished the military to end the death squad activities.

By contrast, Mr. Neier was delighted at the testimony Mr. Schifter delivered on South Korea last week.

"The Administration today solidly accepts the principle that it is the responsibility of the United States to

---

'We resort to condemnation when quiet diplomacy fails.'

Richard P. Schifter

---

promote human rights worldwide," Mr. Neier said. "That was not the view in 1981."

Despite the Administration's preference for quiet diplomacy, Congress has forced it to be conspicuous in its criticism of human rights practices abroad. The State Department's annual survey of torture and repression around the world, mandated by Congress since 1977, is often startling in the frankness of accusations leveled against some of Washington's closest allies. It criticizes Israel for abuse of Arabs in the occupied territories, for example, and Britain for denial of due process in Northern Ireland.

Mr. Posner of the Lawyers Committee and other activists say, however, that the Administration is unable to separate human rights concerns from other elements of its foreign policy in several key areas.

The Lawyers Committee, Americas Watch and other allied groups publish a review of the State Department report. In its 1985 critique, the coalition commended the department for professional and fair reporting but said that a notable exception was the assessment of Central America, where it said abuses were played down in friendly countries and exaggerated in Nicaragua.

Activists like Mr. Neier say they find Mr. Schifter, who assumed the job in November 1985, far less difficult to work with than his predecessor. "Elliot Abrams attracted fire and that is not at all Dick Schifter's style," Mr. Neier said. "He is relatively low key."

In private, friends say, Mr. Schifter is an unremitting hardliner on foreign affairs, especially the Soviet Union.

A Washington lawyer, he was a protégé of both Senator Hubert H. Humphrey of Minnesota and Senator Henry M. Jackson of Washington.

He is also one of several Democrats from the defense-minded wing of the Democratic Party who complained that the party was becoming too liberal. "I didn't leave the Democratic Party," he once said. "The Democrats left me."

시프터 美国務省 人権次官補 発言関聯 措置

- 5.6 下院 聽聞會時 我國과 칠레 比較-

87.5

外 務 部

0074

시프터 美國務省 人權次官補는 5.6 下院 聽聞會 質疑應答時 我國을 칠레와 비교하는 歪曲 發言을 한바 이에 대한 當部 措置事項을 아래 報告드립니다.

聽聞会 発言内容

o 시프터 次官補는 5.6 美下院 亞太小委 및 人權
   小委 合同 聽聞會時 韓國과 칠레의 政治 및 人權
   狀況이 유사하다고 言及
   (솔라즈 委員長의 質疑에 대한 答辯)

当部 措置事項

o 5.8 駐美大使에게 시프터 次官補의 不正確하고
   歪曲된 證言에 대해 유감의 뜻을 表明하고 注意를
   喚起시키도록 訓令함

   - 駐美大使는 우선 5.6 시거次官補 및 클라크
      副次官補에게 各各 시프터 次官補의 發言內容이
      全的으로 잘못되었음을 指摘하고 強力 抗議

   - 駐美大使는 시프터 次官補와도 面談, 直接
      유감의 뜻을 表明할 豫定

0075

美側反応 및 対策

○ 시거 次官補 및 클라크 副次官補는 共히 시프터
次官補가 크게 失言하였으며, 議員들의 質問攻勢에
말려든것 같다고 解明함

○ 今後 유사한 聽聞會時 시프터 次官補의 證言이
不可避할 경우, 我國實情을 보다 正確히 答辯할
수 있도록 事前 對備 豫定임

- 끝 -

0076

시프터 미국무성 인권 차관보 발언관련 조치보고

- 5.6 청문회시 아국과 칠레 비교 -

87. 5.

외 무 부

시프터 미국무성 인권차관보는 5.6. 하원 청문회 질의응답시 아국을 칠레와 비교하는 왜곡 발언을 한바 이에 대한 당부 조치사항을 아래 보고드립니다.

청문회 발언내용

o 시프터 차관보는 5.6. 미하원 아태소위 및 인권소위 합동 청문회시 한국과 칠레의 정치 및 인권상황이 유사하다고 언급 (솔라즈 위원장의 질의에 대한 답변)

당부 조치사항

o 5.8 주미대사에게 시프터 차관보의 부정확하고 왜곡된 증언에 대해 유감의 뜻을 표명하고 주의를 환기시키도록 훈령함.

ø 주미대사는 5.6 <ins>우선</ins> 시거차관보 및 쿨라크 부차관보에게 각각 시프터 차관보의 발언내용이 전적으로 잘못되었음을 지적하고 강력 항의 제기

- 주미대사는 시프터 차관보와도 면담, 직접 유감의 뜻을 표명할 예정

0078

o 상기 양인은 공히 시프터 차관보가 크게 실언 하였으며, 의원들의
   질문공세에 말려든것 같다고 해명함.

o 금후 유사한 청문회시 시프터 차관보가 가급적 증인으로 출두하지
   않도록 대처 예정임.
   - 증언이 불가피할 경우에는 아국실정을 보다 정확히 증언할 수
     있도록 사전 대비   끝.

0079

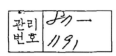
외 무 부 착 신 전 문

원 본

번 호 : USW-2397   일 시 : 705121952   종 별 :

수 신 : 장 관 (미북,정홍,해신)

발 신 : 주 미 대사

제 목 : 국무성 인권과장 면담

연 : USW-2258

1. 연호 하원 아태소위 청문회에서 SCHIFTER 인권차관보의 아국 인권관계 발언
과 관련, 금 5.12 (화) 당관 정태익 참사관은   ROBERT RACKMALES   인권과장을 면담,
 SCHIFTER 차관보가 의회에서 아국과 칠례를 비교할수 있느냐는 솔라즈 의원의
질문을 받고 아국의 자존심을 자극할 우려가 있는 발언을 한데 대해 유감을 표시하고,
아래와같은 점들을 지적하면서 인권관계 실무자로서 여사한 발언이 되풀이 되지 않
도록 협조해줄것을 당부하였음. (송민순 서기관, MURPHY 인권부과장 동석)
가. 아국은 정치사상 처음으로 있을 평화적 정권교체를 준비해가는 과정에서 보다
민주적인 정치사회적 여건 조성을 위해 언론법, 지방자치제등 제도적 개선과 국민화
합을 위한 과감한 사면조치를 위해 많은 노력을 기울이고있음.
 또한 경찰의 범죄수사과정에서 발생할수 있는 물리적 힘의 사용을 방지하기 위해
제반 개선책을 마련, 실시 또는 준비중에 있음을 잘알려진 사실임.
나. 이러한 싯점에서 인권차관보가 공개적으로 아국 인권상황을 부정적 시각에서만
관찰, 평가하는것은 아국의 개선노력에 도움이 되지 않을뿐아니라 국민의 자존심을
자극할 우려가 있음.
다. 특히 아국과 칠례는 사회문화적 배경과 안보상황등 제반 비교 판단요소가 상이
함에 비추어 비교대상이 될수 없음에도 불구하고 양국을 비교 평가한것은 합당치 못
한일로 생각함.
2. 이에대해 RACKMALES 과장은 아측의 유감을 SCHIFTER 차관보에게 전달하겠
다고 하면서 아래와같이 언급하였음.

미주국   차관실   1 차보   2 차보   정문국   청와대   총리실   안 가   문공부

PAGE   I

87.05.13 13:38
외신 2과 통제관
0030

가. 개인적으로는 한국과 칠레를 비교하지 않는것이 좋았을것 (PERSONALLY SHARE YOUR PREFERENCE NOT TO COMPARE) 으로 생각하나, 아주 교묘한 (TRICKY) 질문에 빠진것으로 생각함. 한편 행정부가 나라별로 다른 기준에 따라 평가할경우 의회의 비판을 면하기 어려운점에 비추어 의원들의 질문을 기술적으로 회피하는것이 그렇게 쉬운일은 아님 (SIMPLY NOT POSSIBLE TO AVOID WHEN ASKED) 을 이해해 주기바람.

나. 국무성으로서도 한국의 인권상황 (특히 언론분야) 개선노력을 인정하지 않는것은 아니며, 실제 금번 하원청문회에서 SIGUR 차관보는 주로 밝은면을, SCHIFTER 차관보는 어두운면을 언급한바, 의회증언에서는 이러한 역할 분담 (DIVISION OF WORKS) 이 필요한바, 양 차관보의 증언을 종합적으로 평가하는것이 바람직할것으로 생각함.

다. (금일자 N.Y.T. 지의 SCHIFTER 차관보 발언 인용 관련, 레이건 행정부가 QUIET DIPLOMACY 에서 OPEN DIPLOMACY 로 정책을 변경하는것이냐고 질문한데 대해) 동 NYT 보도는 현행 정부 정책을 잘못설명 (MISINTERPRETATION) 한것이라고 하면서, 의회 청문회는 행정부측이 하나의 의무로서 임하는것이지 각국 인권상황에 대해 능동적으로 공개 거론하는것은 아니며, 현행정부는 조용한 인권외교를 계속할것이라고 설명함.

라. 88올림픽이 다가옴에 따라 아직 알려지지 않은 한국의 여러가지 상황이 대외적으로 알려지게 될것인바, 미국의 일반대중이 국무성 브리핑등 행정부 쏘스기사 보다는 현장감이 있는 현지 특파원의 보도를 더 선호하는 경향이 있음을 감안 한국정부 고위관리와 미 언론 특파원과의 보다 빈번한 접촉을 통해 대한국 인식개선 (CONVEY SENSE OF OPENESS) 을 도모하는것이 효과적일것으로 생각함. 이러한 관점에서 근래 한국정부가 실시하고 있는 외신기자들에 대한 수시 브리핑은 가치있는것으로 보임.

3. 한편 정참사관은 작 4.11(월) BLACKEMORE 한국과장과 면담, 상기 인권차관보의 의회 증언에 관해 유감을 표시한바, 동 과장은 SCHIFTER 차관보가 한국의 인권상황 자체만 언급하고 비교 평가하는것은 회피했으면 좋았을것이라고 하면서, 유감스럽게 생각한다고 말하였음.

(대사 김경원)

PAGE 2

0031

3. Amnesty Int'l 관계

－ 수감자 관련 문의 등

0082

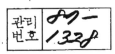

외 무 부

착 신 전 보

원 본

번 호 : USW-2786   일 시 : 705281826   종 별 :

수 신 : 장관(미북)

발 신 : 주미대사

제 목 : 수감자 관계 문의

SOLARZ 아.태 소위원장 사무실 은 금 5.28 동위원장이 AMNESTY INTERNATIONAL

측(USA GROUP 205)으로 부터 문의 요청을 받고 있다고 하면서 수감자 김상복의 수

감장소,협의등 사실관계를 확인해줄수 있는지 당관에 문의해온바, 동 설명자료를 회

보하여 주시기바람.

(대사 김경원)

예고:87.12.31까지

검토필 (87. 6. 30 가안)

예고문에 의거 ....본 (1....
직위   성

─────────────────────────────────────

미주국   차관실   1차보   청와대   안기

PAGE   1   87.05.29 10:19
                                              외신 2과   통제관

0083

22135

기 안 용 지

분류기호 문서번호	미북 20002-	(전화 :　　　　)	시 행 상 특별취급	

보존기간	영구·준영구. 10. 5. 3. 1.		장　　　　관

수 신 처 보존기간	

시행일자	1987. 5. 29.

보 조 기 관	국 장	전 결	협 조 기 관		문 서 통 제
	심의관				검 열 1987. 6. 2 통제관
	과 장				발 행 인
기안책임자		조백상			

경 유		발 신 명 의		발　송 1987. 6. 2 외무부
수 신	법무부장관			
참 조	검찰국장			

제 목	인권관계 문의

Amnesty International 워싱톤 지부는 주미대사관을

통하여 수감자 김상복에 관해 문의해 왔는 바, A.I측에 설명시

참고코자 하니 수감장소, 혐의등 관련자료를 당부로 송부하여

주시기 바랍니다.

0084

1505-25(2-1) 일(1)잡
85. 9. 9. 승인

190mm×268mm 인쇄용지 2급 60g /㎡
가 40-41 1986. 10. 20.

공 란

공 란

외　무　부　착신전문

번　호 : SFW-0337　　　일　시 : 706201130　　　종　별 :

수　신 : 장　관(국연,기정)

발　신 : 주 상항 총영사

제　목 : AI 대표 접촉보고

연 : SFW-316

대 : WSF-312

1. 본직은 6.19. AI 미국 서부지부 J.RENDLER 및 한국문제　COORDINATOR E.BAKER 의 방문을 받고 김현장문제에 관하여 대호에 따라 아국입장을 설명한바 결과 아래 보고함.

2. 상기 양인은 김현장이 82년 고문에 의해 얻어진 자백으로 사형선고를 받았으며 그후 무기징역형으로 감형되어 현재 복역중에 있으며 AI 로서는 동인이 부당한 대우를 받고있는 양심범이므로 한국이 그를 석방하기를 희망한다는 종래 입장을 주장하였음

3. 이에 대해 본직은 김현장이 광주사태 불법집회 주동(80.5월), 문부식, 김은숙에 대한 의식화교육(81.12월)과 미문화원 방화교사 및 이들의 은익(82.3월)으로 아국 실정법을 위반을 위반한 범죄자로서 아국의 적법절차에 따라 유죄판결을 받은자임을 설명함

4. 또한 본직은 김현장이 AI측 주장과 같이 고문에 의한 자백을 받은것이 아니고, 문,김등의 증인 진술 및 본인 자신의 방화교사 인정및 범인은익사실등에 따라 재판이 이루어진것 임을 설명 하고, 헌법 제11조 6항 및 형법309조, 310조 내용(고문에 의한 자백을 증거로한 처벌불가)등 대인권 보호에 관한 아측입장을 상세히 설명함

5. 상기 본직 설명에도 불구 AI 대표는 김현장에 대한 아국 사직당국의 편견관련, AI 측이 보유한 자료에 따르면 고문에 의한 자백임이 들어나 있음을 계속 주장하면서, 김의 석방을 요청하는 한편, AI 상항회의 개최후 당관 또는 주미대사관을 통하

국기국　차관실　1차보　정문국　청와대　안기　미주국

여 문서로 동인석방을 탄원할것임을 시사하였음.

(총영사 현희강-국장)

예고 : 87.12.31일반

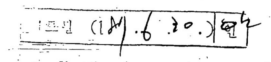

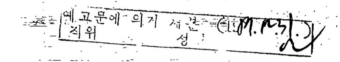

주 뉴 욕 총 영 사 관

주뉴욕(정) 700-**2023**   1987. 7. 2.

수 신 : 장 관

참 조 : 미주국장

제 목 : 인권관계 서한 송부

　　　　당지 Amnesty International USA(Group 253) 및 뉴육주
웨스체스터 카운티의 입법의원은 별첨 본직앞 서한을 통해 현재 복역중인
임동규, 박석걸, 김종삼등의 건강상태 악화소식에 관해 우려를 표명하고
여사한 소식이 사실인지의 여부를 문의함과 동시에 이들의 석방을 탄원하여
왔는바 회답 작성에 참고코저 하니 동건 관련사항을 회시하여 주시기
바랍니다.

첨 부 : 상기 서한 2매.

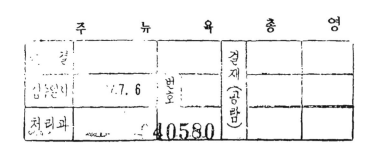

주	뉴	육	총	영
결		번호	결재 (공람)	
십수일시	7. 7. 6			
처리과	40580			

0089

49 Van Wyck
Croton, New York 10520
June 15, 1987

Consul General Gong Ro-myung
The Consulate of the Republic of Korea
460 Park Avenue
New York, NY 10022

Dear Consul General Gong,

I write to you on behalf of my chapter's 35 members and 100 or so supporters
about a disturbing report we received three days about from the Tokyo-
based Rescue Committee for the Prisoners Involved in the Case of the "South
Korean National Liberation Front". The report alleges that Im Tong-gyu,
Park Sul-gul and Kim Jong-sam are seriously ill and are in need of urgent
medical attention. I have enclosed the contents of what we received for
your review.

We are deeply concerned, as I am sure you must be, about this report's contents.
Unfortunately, we do not as of yet have any confirmation -- one way or the
other -- of the report's veracity. Nonetheless, its assertions are so
serious that we would like to meet with you to discuss its contents further
and to find out if your government can confirm it. Would the week of
June 29th be possible? I will call your office next week to confirm.

We are particularly concerned about this report because it mentions
Im Tong-gyu for whose release our chapter has worked since 1983. As you
may know, both Im Tong-gyu and Kim Jong-sam have both been adopted by
Amnesty International as "prisoners of conscience". In its in-depth
study into this case, Amnesty International has found no convincing evidence
that either used or advocated violence. Rather Amnesty believes they have
been imprisoned for the peaceful expression of their political views.
Amnesty International also remains concerned about the fairness of the
procedures used at Park Suk-gul's trial. I have enclosed a summary of
Im Tong-gyu's case. Unfortunately I have no information other than what
I mentioned here about the cases of the other two.

I thank you in advance for the attention you give this most pressing matter
and look forward to speaking with your office next week.

Sincerely and Respectfully,

George Klein

George Klein
Chapter President

0090

April 15, 1987

Dear Sirs,

We would like to pay great respect on your activities to save
the lives of the prisoners of conscience all over the world and give
many thanks especially for your concern on the detained persons
connected with so-called "South Korean National Liberation Front"
case.

We must tell you about the most severe circumstances of Mr.
Park Suk-gul. He was arrested in October 1979, and sentenced to
life imprisonment. He has been suffering from duodenitis more than
four years. In spite of his eager request for medical treatment
together with his family, the prison authorities did nothing but
leave him in the prison.

Recently what is worse, he also suffers from pancreatitis.
He has loose bowels 3-10 times a day, and cannot digest even a cup
of milk. He fell into a serious condition, but the attitude of
the prison authorities remains unchanged. He says to his family,
"Does a prisoner of life imprisonment not have a right even to
survive?"

Moreover we must tell you about Mr. Kim John-sam and Mr. Ihm
Tong-gu. Mr. Kim was sentenced to 15 years. He has been suffering
from serious otitis media by torture. Besides since 1985 he has
been attacked by sharp pain in his heart so-called angina pectoris.
He says, "I can't stand such a pain any more. Please cut down my
heart with a knife". Mr. Ihm was sentenced to life imprisonment.
In August 1986, He was tortured so cruelly that bleeding through
the anus has not stopped since then. They demanded that the prison
conditions must be improved and struggled with hungerstrike in the
prison, so they were tortured in retaliation of it.

Considering that three persons connected with this case have
already died in the prison, we cannot stand any more the death of
these three persons who are suffering from heavy desease now. We
have not enough time. We would like to beseech you to take whatever action so that they can be released and have adequate medical
treatment as soon as possible.

Sincerely yours,

Ikeda Keiko

0091

AMNESTY INTERNATIONAL USA

Southern Westchester Chapter, Adoption Group 253

IM TONG-GYU: A SUMMARY OF HIS CASE

Im Tong-gyu, a labor relations specialist at Korea University, is serving two life imprisonment sentences for belonging to two banned political parties. He has not, however, used nor advocated any violence, according to Amnesty International.

Mr. Im was first arrested in 1979 and charged with belonging to the banned "Unification Revolutionary Party". Other charges against him were that he was attempting to instill "anti-government" ideas through articles he had written in an agricultural magazine and at lecture meetings and for possessing "non-approved" books such as a history of German farmers' struggle against feudalism and the medieval church.

In 1980, he was charged with being a member of the "South Korean National Liberation Front" and accused of having taught martial arts to other alledged members of the "Front". At his trial Mr. Im stressed that he had adamantly opposed any plans to raise funds through robberies or stealing arms and that he had never taken part in such ventures. The evidence against him consisted only of his confession and those of his co-defendants, made during interrogation.

At various stages of the trials of the hundred or so prisoners accused of belonging to the South Korean National Liberation Front, the defendants reportedly testified that they had been tortured by police interrogators to make them confess and that their statements to the prosecutor were made under threat of further toture and were also false. Several defendants appeared in court with broken limbs and one with a broken spine. Amnesty International received reports that Mr. Im was held in isolation for about a month after his arrest in 1979 and that he was ill-treated and deprived of sleep during his interrogation.

Originally from a farming family near Kwangju, Im Tong-gyu was working on agricultural issues at the Labor Research Institute of Korea University in Seoul. He was known to have been critical of his government's agricultural policy. Amnesty International believes this case to follow a pattern common in the Republic of Korea where people who have peacefully criticized the government are convicted on "anti-state" charges.

Amnesty International is an independent worldwide movement working impartially for the release of all prisoners of conscience, fair and prompt trials for political prisoners and an end to torture and executions. It is funded by donations from its members and supporters throughout the world.

CHAIR BOARD OF DIRECTORS
James David Barber

EXECUTIVE DIRECTOR
John G. Healey

0092

WESTCHESTER COUNTY BOARD OF LEGISLATORS

800 MICHAELIAN OFFICE BUILDING
148 MARTINE AVENUE
WHITE PLAINS, NEW YORK 10601
(914) 285-2813
(TTY: THIS PHONE NUMBER CAN ALSO
BE USED BY DEAF/HEARING IMPAIRED)

PAUL J. FEINER
Legislator, 12th District
565 Broadway, Apt. 4-h
Hastings-on-Hudson, N. Y. 10706
(914) 478-1219

Member
Committee on Health
and The Medical Center
Committee on
County Officers and
Departments

June 19,1987

Consul General Gong Ro-myung
Consulate of the Republic of Korea
460 Park Ave
New York, New York 10022

Dear Consul General Gong Ro-myung:

I would be most grateful to have the opportunity to meet with
you and a group of my constituents.

We're very concerned about Im Tong-gyu, who has been in a
Republic of Korea prison since 1979. There are many allegations of
torture and others have reported back that his health is very poor.

We, in Westchester, are very concerned ---we are worried that Mr.
Im Tong-gu may die in prison and we demand his release.

An appointment with you would be greatly appreciated so that the
representatives of the thousands of Westchester residents who are concerned
about Mr. Im Tong -gyu's conditions could discuss our feelings with you
and so that we could get an update on what the government's position is
on this prisoner of conscience.

Thank you for your attention. I would be willing to meet with you anytime,
any place ---at your convenience.

Sincerely,

Paul Feiner
Legislator
Westchester County

0093

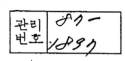

외 무 부

착 신 전

번 호 : ANW-0172   일 시 : 707311630   종 별 :

수 신 : 장 관(미북,영재)   사본:주미대사—직송필

발 신 : 주 아틀란타 총영사

제 목 : AMNESTY INT.

1. AMNESTY INT. 의   SOUTHERN REGIONAL DIRECTOR 인 HERRICK 는 요지 다음과

같은 7.30자 공한을 당관에 보내옴

-귀정부가 인권문제에 관하여 취한 최근의 조치는 매우 고무적임

-8.10-14 기간중 편리한 날에 수명의 대표가 귀관을 방문하여 아직도수감중인 양심

수의 상황, 귀정부의 조치계획 등에 관하여 협의하고자함

2. 상기와 관련, 당관직원의 동 대표단면담에 응할지 여부를 회시바라며, 면담시 참

고자로등 송부바람

(총영사 박련—국장)

예고:87.12.31.까지

- 87. 8/ .

- Atlanta 총영사가 AI. 인사면담도록

진도 바람 . (8.3)

《가중권의 》.

안기부다 협의 요

차요 요망

미주국   차관실   1 차보   영교국   청와대   안 기

PAGE   1   87.08.01 10:20
                                  외신 2과 통재관

                                  0094

관리
번호 87-1984

발 신 전 보

번 호 : WAN- 0221 일 시 : 70803 1520   전보종별 : _____

수 신 : 주   아틀란타   대사·총영사

발 신 : 장   관 (미북)

제 목 : 인권단체 면담

대 : ANW - 0172

1. 대호, Amnesty International 측 요청 대로 동단체 인사를 면담, 정부위 7.9 사면·복권등 민주화 조치를 상세히 설명하고 결과 보고바람.

2. 관련자료 파편 송부 예정임.

(미주국장   신두병)

예고문에 의거 재본
직위   성)

보안
통제

0095

		기안자	과 장	국 장	차 관	장 관
앙고재	87년 월 일 북이과	3		전결		

외신과 접수자 통제

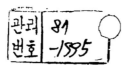

기 안 용 지

분류기호 문서번호	미북 0160- 245	(전화 :)		시 행 상 특별취급	
보존기간	영구·준영구. 10. 5. 3. 1.		장 관		
수 신 처 보존기간					
시행일자	1987. 8. 3.				

보 조 기 관	국장	전 결	협 조 기 관		문 서 통 제
	과장				비밀문서 1987. 8. 04 통제관
기안책임자		조 백상			발 인

경 유 수 신 참 조	주 아틀란타 총영사	발 신 명 의		발송 1987. 8.04 발송 1987. 8.04 외무부

제 목	인권단체 면담 참고자료 송부

대 : ANW - 0172

대호, Amnesty International 인사 면담시 활용할 인권관계

자료를 별첨 송부하니 참고하시기 바랍니다.

첨 부 : 1. 7.9 특별사면 조치 관련 정부 대변인 발표문 (국·영문)

　　　　2. 동 해설자료

　　　　3. 7.9 사면 대상자 명단. 끝.

0096

사면·복권 조치 (87.7.10)

1. 배경 및 목적

가. 국민적 대화합과 전향적 민주발전을 위한 대통령 각하의 결단에
   따라 시국 관련 사범에 대한 대폭적인 특별사면 및 복권

나. 이미 석방된 시국관련 사범들에게 국가발전에 동참할 수 있는
   기회를 부여함으로써 국민적 화해의 촉진과 민주발전의 실천 입증

2. 범위 및 기준

가. 원칙적으로 유신이후의 시국관련 사범 전원에 대하여 실시
   다만, 사직당국의 조사와 사법부의 재판을 통해서 명백하게 간첩
   사건에 연루되어 있거나 좌경 이적단체의 핵심인들이거나 또는
   극렬한 폭력 파괴 행동 주동자는 제외됨.
   ○ 자유민주주의 체재를 부정하고 폭력혁명을 기도한 인혁당,
      남민전 사건등의 핵심인물
   ○ 전민련 핵심인물
   ○ 부산 미문화원 방화사건 등 인명살상 형사범 경합자
   ○ 현재 재범으로 복역중에 있는 자
   ○ 집행유예 선고를 받고 출소한 자에 대하여는 다시 죄를 범하여
      현재 복역중인 자

0097

3. 사면.복권내역

가. 총 대상자 2,541 명
  ○ 실시예정자 2,335명
  ○ 제외자 206명

    * 제5공화국 출범이후 이미 총 17회, 10,029명 사면.복권 실시

나. 세부내역
  ○ 복권대상자 401명
  ○ 사면대상자 1,819명
  ○ 사면.복권대상자 115명

다. 주요대상자
  ○ 김대중 내란음모사건 관련자 18명 전원
    · 김대중, 김상현, 문익환, 예춘호, 김종완, 이석표, 조성우,
      이시범, 이해찬, 김옥두, 함운식, 한희갑, 손주항, 김흥일,
      김대현, 오대영, 권혁중, 서원석
    · 정동년등 광주사태 관련자 17명 전원
    · 권호경등 긴급조치 위반자 13명
    · 백기완 등 YWCA 위장결혼 사건 관련자 5명
    · 이협등 계엄법 위반자 9명
    · 범인 은닉 이돈명

0098

4. 7.10. 사면.복권의 특징

 o 민주발전과 국민화합의 염원을 수렴한 제5공화국 출범이후 최대

    규모의 사면

 o 70년대 이후의 시국관련 사범 거의 구제

 o 특히 광주사태 관련자 전원 사면.복권으로 대화해 실현

0099

1987. 8.

1. 김근태 사건

가. 김근태 고문 보도사건

ㅇ 발 단

- 85.10.2-7.   국제사면협회, AP 통신, 동아일보,
  N.Y. Times 지등 김근태 고문에 관한 보도

- 85.10.4.   동아일보, 변호인단의 김근태에 대한 고문
  혼적 보전 신청 보도

ㅇ 미측반응

- 85.10.4.   Dunlop 주한 미참사관 동건에 유감 표명

- 85.10.11.   Isom 미 국무성 한국과장 동건 제기

- 85.10.16.   Sherman 미국무성 부차관보, 동건에 유감 표명

- 85.10.18.   미국무성, 논평을 통해 동건에 대한 우려 전달

ㅇ 아측 대응조치

- 85.10.16.   주미대사관, Sherman 부차관보 면담시 고문
  보도 사실무근 설명 및 국내문제 간섭중지 요청

- 85.10.18.   주미대사관, 미국무성 논평, 관련, 동건 공개
  거론의 위험성 지적

ㅇ 경 과

- 86.3.6.   김근태 1심에서 징역7년 자격정지 6년 선고

0100

나. 김근태 항소심 재판 방청허용 문제

　ㅇ 발　　단
　　　- 86.6.12.　　　미국변호사 협회 (ABA) 대표단 일행 주미
　　　　　　　　　　 한국대사관에 김근태 사건 방청을 위해 입국
　　　　　　　　　　 사증 신청

　ㅇ 미측반응
　　　- 86.6.25.　　　ABA 측, 주한 미대사관 제보에 의거 한국의
　　　　　　　　　　 재판부가 재판방청권 부여권한이 없다고
　　　　　　　　　　 한 사실에 대해 주미대사관에 해명 요청
　　　- 86.6.27.　　　ABA 측, 7.3. 종결되는 김근태 항소심 방청을
　　　　　　　　　　 위한 방한이 어려움을 주미대사관에 통보
　　　- 86.7.1.　　　 ABA 측, 주미대사관 방문, 김근태건등에 대한
　　　　　　　　　　 질문
　　　- 86.7.2.　　　 International Human Rights Law group,
　　　　　　　　　　 ASIA WATCH, 주미대사관에 김근태건 제기

　ㅇ 아측 대응조치
　　　- 86.6.7.　　　 ABA 대표단, 김근태 항소심 방청시도에 대한
　　　　　　　　　　 관계기관 실무대표회의 개최, 입국은 허용하되
　　　　　　　　　　 재판방청 허용문제는 재판부의 고유 결정권한
　　　　　　　　　　 임을 ABA 측에 명백히 통보키로 결정
　　　- 86.6.9.　　　 주미대사관, ABA 측에 입국사증 발급,
　　　　　　　　　　 재판방청 허용문제에 대한 아측의 입장 전달

0101

- 86.6.28.   ABA 대표단 방청허용 문제 관련, 관계부처
             회의, ABA 국무성 및 주한 미대사관에 진상
             해명키로 결정
- 86.6.30.   본부, 주한 미대사관 담당직원 초치, 잘못된
             보도로 아국정부와 ABA 측간의 오해가 야기
             되었음을 지적하고 ABA 측에 해명 조치토록
             촉구
- 86.7.1.   주미대사관, ABA 측에 아측입장 설명

ㅇ 전망 및 대책
- 김근태 공판 종결로 ABA 대표단의 재판방청 관련 입국
  가능성은 희박
- 김근태, 최종심에서 원심보다 감형이 확정되었고, 현재
  경주교도소에 수감중임.
- 그러나 7.10. 사면.복권대상에서 재의된 바, 미 주요인사
  또는 인권단체에 의한 동건 진정 가능성은 많으며, 이경우
  법무부의 의견을 관계인사에 회보할 예정
  · 87.2 Feighan 미 민주당 하원의원, 외부의사 진료가능
    문의 (자비로서 가능)

0102

2. 부천서 성고문 (권인숙) 사건

  가. 경   위

    ○ 7.16, 검찰의 부천서 사건 수사결과 발표이후, 재야세력은
       1차 7.18 명동성당 집회, 2차 7.27 성공회집회 및 3차 8.14
       신민당 중앙당사집회를 통해 권인숙 사건의 폭로 및 대정부
       비난시도

  나. 미국무성 반응

    ○ 7.25자 논평 : 아국의 명동성당 집회 저지에 유감표명

    ○ 7.29자 논평 : 권양의 학대에 대한 개탄(deplorable) 과
                      전율(appalling) 을 금치 못한다고 언급,
                      관련 책임자 처벌 및 재발방지 조치를 한국에
                      촉구

  다. 아측 대응조치

    ○ 7.30, 주미대사관 Blakemore 한국과장 접촉, 7.29자 논평에 대한
       아측 유감 표시

    ○ 8.1, 미주국장 Dunlop 주한 미 참사관 초치, 아측 유감전달
       및 동건의 신중 대처 미측에 요청

    ○ 8.14, 미주국장 Pierce 주한미 1등서기관 (참사관 대리) 초치,
       신민당사 집회에 대한 아측입장 전달, 여사한 미측의 논평
       재발 방지 요청

0103

라. 경   과

  o 8.19. 인천지검, 부천서 사건관련 문귀동 경장에 대해
    기소유예, 불기소 처분

  o 8.5. 인천지검 및 서울고법, 부처서 사건관련 변호인단이
    제출한 재정신청을 기각

  o 현재 대법원에서 재정신청 계류중

마. 아측의 입장

  o 검찰은 동사건에 대해서 엄격한 수사를 통해 관련사실을
    밝혀내고, 조사과정에서 폭행사실이 드러난 담당관들에 대해서는
    파면등 엄중한 조치를 취하였음.

  o 정부는 어떠한 조사과정에서든지 고문.폭행 행위는 용납치
    않음.

  o 동건관련 국무성의 논평은 일부 야권 및 반체제 과격인사들에게
    정치적으로 악용되어 대화와 타협을 통한 현재 정국의 안정에
    역행하는 사례가 될 우려가 있음.

  o 동 사건에 대한 사법절차가 종료되지 않고 현재 진행중에
    있으므로 이에 영향을 줄 여사한 외부적 개입은 적절치 못함.

0104

3. 기타 주요 인권문제 (7.10. 조치 제외자)

인 명	관심표명인사	비 고
양동화 김성만 황대권	- Mike Lowry 하원의원 주미대사 앞 서한 - Paul Simon 의원 각하 앞 서한 - 미국무성, 주한 미대사관	- 미 Illinois 대 유학생, 간첩 죄로 사형.무기 선고 - 미측의 지속적인 관심대표 - 최종 상고심 계속중 - 270여종의 유죄입증 증거물이 제출되었음. - 82.8. 유학시 북괴공작원 서정균에게 포섭되어 남한 협멸전술 및 요인 암살법등을 교육받고 입국, 간첩활동을 하였음.
김종삼	- Solarz, Mineta 의원 각하앞 서한 - Porter 의원 주미대사 앞 서한 - Fascell 의원 주미대사 앞 서한 (단식등 건강 악화를 이유로 석방 진정)	- 79년 납민전관련 무기형 - 600여점의 유죄 입증자료가 제출되었음. - 86.5.25-27간 단식한 적이 있었으나 현재는 건강 양호함.
서 승 서준식	- A.I. - American Friends Service Committee, 일본의 서형제 구명 운동회	- 재일교포 간첩사건 관련 서승 (무기) 서준식(보안감호) - 공산주의 사상 고집으로 보안 감호 조치가 연장되고 있음.

0105

인 명	관심표명인사	비 고
임동규	- Benjamin A. Gilman 의원 각하 앞 법무 장관 앞 서한	- 80 님민전관련 무기형(간첩 방조, 국가보안법 위반) - 600여점의 유죄입증 자료 제출됨.
김현장	- 개인명의 장관앞 서한	- 1982. 미 부산문화원 방화관련 무기형
강종건	- 미국무성, 주한 미대사관	- 1976.12. 대법원에서 국가 보안법 위반혐의로 징역 5년, 자격정지 5년 선고 - 1985.2. 2차 보안감호 연장 (간첩죄를 저질렀던자로 사상 전향 거부, 북괴 찬양지속 - 반국가사범에 대한 보안처분 제도는 여타 선진국에서도 채택되고 있으며 우리나라의 특수한 안보상황을 고려할때 동제도는 필수적임.
우상호	- 국무성	- 87.8.2. NWT 와의 기자회견에서 문제발언 - 87.8.25. 국가모독죄 및 집시법 위반 구속

0106

322 한국 인권문제 제 사안 1

Ⅰ. 인권보장에 관한 국내외적 규정

　1. 인권보장에 관한 국제규약

　　가. 1948년 채택된 세계인권 선언은 1966년 유엔 인권위원회의
　　　초안작성 과정을 거쳐 유엔총회에서 경제적, 사회적및 문화적
　　　권리에 관한 국제규약 (A규약)과 시민적, 정치적 권리에 관한
　　　국제규약 (B규약) 및 선택의정서로 채택되고 1976년부터 동
　　　규약및 선택의정서는 발효되었음.

　　나. 아국도 A. B규약에 가입 (B규약 선택 의정서는 유보)함으로써
　　　인권존중 국가로서의 아국의 대외적 이미지를 고양하였음.

　2. 아국의 인권규약 수용

　　가. A규약에 대한 유보 조항은 없으나 B규약은 몇가지 유보를
　　　두었음.
　　　　1) 4조　　　　: 비상사태하에서 취할수 있는 조치의 한계및
　　　　　　　　　　　　비상조치 내용의 타당사국 통지
　　　　2) 6조5항　: 18세 미만에 대한 사형금지
　　　　3) 9조3항　: 체포, 억류자의 법관에게의 신속한 회부
　　　　4) 23조4항: 혼인중및 혼인해제시의 배우자 평등
　　　　5) 41조1항: 타당사국의 규약 불이행에 대한 일당사국의
　　　　　　　　　　　인권이사회의 통보및 동이사회의 심리권한 인정
　　　　　　　　　　　(아국내 인권문제를 이유로 한국이 국제법상의
　　　　　　　　　　　의무는 지고있지 않음.)

0107

II. 미국의 아국인권문제에 대한 접근방법

1. 미 국무성의 접근유형

가. 공식논평

o 부천서 사건관련 국무성은 공식논평을 통해, 권양의
학대에 대해 " 개탄(deplorable) 과 전율(appalling) 을
금치못한다"고 언급하며 관련책임자 처벌및 재발방지
촉구

나. 주미한국대사관에 미측입장 표시

o 김근태사건 관련, 미국무성은 공식논평 또는 주미
한국대사관을 통하여 미측의 우려표명

다. 주한미대사관을 통한 미측의 입장표시

o 노조운동가 고문사건 관련, 미국무성은 주한미대사관을
통해 아측에 진상설명 요청및 미측의 우려전달

라. 국무성 인권보고서를 통한 한국인권 상황에 주의환기

2. 미의회의 접근법

가. Congressional Friends of Human Rights Monitors Group
(미의회내 인권단체)

o 문익환 목사 구금 해제요청 서한 발송

나. 의원개인 또는 연서 진정서한

1) 각하앞 서한발송

o 양동화, 김성만, 황대권 (미유학생 출신 간첩단 사건
관련 사형및 무기형 확정) 관련, Paul Simon 의원,
Solarz 의원

0108

o 김종삼 (79년 남민전 관련 무기형) 관련, Solarz 의원,
   Mineta 의원

o 임동규 (80년 남민전 관련 무기형) 관련, Gilman 의원

2) 주미대사앞 서한발송
   o 양동화건 관련 Mike Lowry 하원의원
   o 김종삼 관련 Porter 의원, Fascell 의원

3. 인권단체등을 통한 문제 제기
   가. Amnesty International (국제사면협회)
      o A. I 연례보고서를 통해 한국의 집회, 시위관련 구속자,
        정치범에 대한 재판, 구속자에 대한 고문, 학대, 사형제도
        존속등에 관심표명
      o Amnesty international 인사, 주미대사관 수시방문, 특정인물에
        대한 석방 진정 또는 사면요청

   나. 미국변호사협회(American Bar Association)
      o 김근태사건 방청을 위해 입국사증 신청

   다. Helsinki Watch (1975 체결된 Helsinki 협정의 인권조항
       시행을 위해 설립된 민간 인권단체) 산하 Asia Watch
      o 남. 북한 인권보고서 발간을 통해 인권문제 주의환기
      o 김근태, 이을호, 변성수, 임종규등에 대한 진정서한 발송
      o 85. 6 대표단 파한, 인권문제 조사

0109

라. International Human Rights Law Group   (1978설립, 민간인권단체)
   o 서승, 서준식 관련 주미대사관에 제기
   o 사무총장 Amy Young 86. 1 방한, 김근태, 서승등에 대한
     관심표명

마. American Friends Service Committee
   o 서승, 서준식 구명서한

바. Robert Kennedy 추모사업회
   o 매년 인권상 시상을 통해 인권개선 촉구
   o 문익환목사가 86년 수상자 후보에 선정된 바 있음.

4. 개인명의 진정서한
   o 김현장, 김종삼, 차성환등의 서방을 요청하는 각하, 법무장관,
     외무장관앞 개인명의 서한 다수

Ⅲ. 인권문제 제기에 대한 아측의 대응
   1. 기존의 대응방법
      가. 진정서한에 대한 답신 발송
         o 미의회인사, 미인권단체등의 진정서한에 대해서는 법무부에
           의견조회, 관련자료를 주미대사관에 송부, 주미대사
           명의로 회신

         o 개인명의 진정서한에 대해서는 법무부의 관련자료를 관할
           공관에 송부, 공관장 명의로 회신

0110

나. 인권문의에 대한 설명자료 송부

    o 인권단체가 주미대사관 또는 총영사관을 방문, 인권문제에
      대해 문의할 경우, 법무부의 설명자료를 공관에 송부,
      인권문의에 설명토록 조치

다. 주한미대사관 인권담당관 초치, 설명

    o 인권문제 관련한 주한미대사관의 구술문의에 대하여, 인권
      담당관을 초치, 법무부등 관계부처의 설명자료에 입각하여
      설명

2. 기존 대응방법에 대한 평가

  가. 법무부, 안기부등 관련부처의 공식적 입장을 받아 진정서한
    답신시 또는 구두설명시 활용함으로써 부처간의 통일적인
    입장표명 가능

  나. 진정서한을 공람처리만 하고 회신하지 않는 법무부의 처리방침에
    비해 문의자나 문의단체에 대한 당부의 성실한 회답이 긍정적으로
    평가되어질수 있음.

  다. 기존 대응방법으로는 아국 인권문제에 대한 문의나 진정의 빈도를
    줄이는데 기여하지는 못함.

Ⅳ. 인권문제와 관련한 새로운 대응

1. 사전적 홍보강화

  가. 미국등지에서 인권문제로서 제기할만한 소지가 있는 사건, 재판,
    인물을 선별하여 상세한 설명자료를 미국등 주요국가에 송부,
    공식적으로 문제가 제기되는것을 방지

0111

나. 주한미대사관등 주한상주공관에 국내문제와 관련한 관련부처의
　　홍보지침, 설명자료를 조속 입수, 신속한 설명조치를 통해
　　문제화 소지를 극소화

2. 사전적 홍보강화에 대한 평가
　가. 국내주요 문제와 관련하여 안기부등 관계부처가 능동적으로
　　　설명자료, 홍보지침을 외무부에 협조할 경우 정부입장을 신속히
　　　주한상주공관 및 재외공관에 알림으로써 문제가 제거되지 않도록
　　　하는데 상당히 기여하고 있는 것으로 평가됨 (현재 안기부와
　　　당부간에는 facsimille 이 설치되어 신속한 자료협조를
　　　받고있음.)

　나. 그러나 미국 의회인사나 인권단체가 거론하는 아국내 인권문제는
　　　상당수가 법무부의 소관사항이고 법무부의 능동적 자료협조
　　　없이는 사전적으로 신속히 아국정부의 입장을 재외공관이나
　　　주한상주공관에 알릴수 없는 문제점이 있음.

V. 인권문제에 대한 종합적 대책
　1. 기존의 진정서한, 인권단체등의 문의에 대해서는 법무부등의 설명
　　　자료를 활용, 회신 또는 설명하는 현 관행을 지속하되, 문제제기
　　　소지가 있는 아국국내문제, 인권문제에 대해서는 관계부처의 협조를
　　　얻어 사전에 신속히 옹보함으로써 문제제기 소지를 극소화 하는
　　　방향으로 노력

　2. 신문에 보도되지 않는 재판사건등 당부가 사전에 파악할수 없는
　　　경우가 있음에 비추어, 안기부, 법무부와 긴밀한 협조체제를
　　　구축, 문제발생 소지가 있는 구속, 재판등 광범위한 문제에
　　　대한 설명자료 신속 입수가 필요

0112

3. 인권문제는 아국의 정치발전과 밀접한 관계가 있는만큼, 궁극적
   해결은 정치의 민주화및 복지국가의 실현에 있으나 그 과도기중에
   제기될수 있는 인권문제에 대해서는 기존의 대응에 더하여 사전적
   적극적 홍보를 통해 해결해 나가는것이 효과적일 것으로 사료됨.

0113

외 무 부

번 호 : ANW-0211   일 시 : 709031630   종 별 :

수 신 : 장관(미북,영재,사본:주미대사-직송필)

발 신 : 주아틀란타총영사

제 목 : 인권단체면담

대:미북0160-3245

연: ANW-0172

1. 연호 AMNESTY INT. 의 HERRICK (동료2명대등) 는 금 9.3 당관 최영사를 방문, 수감중인 정치범들에대한 고문,가족면담제한,적절한 의료혜택 부족등 문제를 거른한데대하여 최영사는 등단체에서 관심있는 정치범들의 인적사항과 이들에대한 구체적 문의사항을 당관에 브내오면 본국의 관계기관에 문의하여 알려주겠다고 함.

2. 최영사는 한반도분단 현실,복괴의 끊임없는 무력남침 야욕등 아국내 특수한 정치현실과 그럼에도 불구하고 아국정부는 7.9의 사면.복권등과 감한 민주화조치를 취하고 있음을 설명하고,대호의 정부대변인 밥표문을 전달함. 동인들은 어떠한 이유에서건 고문,역압등행위에는 반대타는 입장을 밝히고, 아국정부의 최근의발전적 조치를 환영하면서 한국내 인권문제가 하루속히 국제적수준에 이르게되기를 바란다는 반응이 었음. 끝.

(총영사 김석현-국장)

예고:87.12.31일반

예고문에 의기 재문 (19   )
직위   성

미주국   차관실   1 차보   영교국   청와대   안 기   정보국

87.09.04 09:48
외신 2과 통제관

0114

		기 안 용 지		시 행 상	
분류기호 문서번호	미북0160-	(전화 :	)	특별취급	
보존기간	영구·준영구. 10.5.3.1.	장		관	
수 신 처 보존기간					
시행일자	1987·9·28				

장 관

보조기관	국 장	전결	협조기관			문 서 통 제
	과 장					
기안책임자		노·광일				인

경 유		발신명의	
수 신	법무부장관		
참 조	검찰국장		

제 목	수감자 관계문의

Amnesty International 미 남부지부는 별첨서한을 통해

수감자 ~~함운규~~·이태복·김현종 3인의 석방가능성에 대해 관심을 표명하였

는바, 이에대한 회신안 작성에 필요하니 동인들의 죄명(위반법규)·

재판내용(형량)·현재의 상태(가족·친구 면담허용·건강상태등)을 알려

주시기 바랍니다·

첨부· : 상기서한 및 관련 A.I. 간행물 사본 각 1부· 끝·

0115

1505-25(2-1) 일(1)갑
85. 9. 9. 승인

190mm×268mm 인쇄용지 2급 60g/㎡
가 40-41 1987. 2. 13.

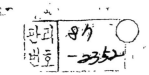

느

주 아 틀 란 타 총 영 사

아틀란타 725 - 286   1987. 9. 10.

수 신 : 장 관

참 조 : 미주국장

제 목 : 인권단체 면담   예고문제 의거
                                        직위

대 : 미북 0160 - 3245

연 : ANW - 0172, - 0211

연호의 인권단체는 9.9자 당관 앞 서한을 통하여 구속중인 김근태, 이태복, 김현종
3인에 관하여 문의하여 왔아오니 이들의 죄상 (위반 법규 내용 포함), 재판 내용 (형량
포함), 현재의 상태 (가족, 친구등 면회 허용 여부, 건강 상태등) 등에 관하여 회시하여
주시기 바랍니다.

첨 부 : 상기 서한 및 Amnesty Int. 간행물 사본 각 1부. 끝.

주 아 틀 란 타 총 영

접수일 1987.9.25			
처 리 과			

0116

730 Peachtree, Suite 982, Atlanta, Georgia 30308 (404) 876-5661

September 9, 1987

Consul Choi Koang Sik
Consulate General of
   The Republic of Korea
229 Peachtree Street NE
Suite 500, Cain Tower
Atlanta, GA 30303

Dear Consul Choi,

On behalf of our Amnesty International delegation, I would like to thank you for taking the time to meet with us on September 3.

I have read with interest the statement by Lee Woong Hee, which you gave to our delegation when we met, and I have passed a copy of it on to the appropriate Amnesty International officials. You mentioned the idea of sending me other such documents as they are issued in the future. I would be very eager to receive them.

You said when we met that you would like to have our concerns in writing so you might pass them on to your government and then forward us its response. That is the purpose of this letter.

In our discussion with you last week, we brought up three prisoner cases which we feel are representative of a much larger number of people who remain prisoners of conscience.- persons detained for political reasons who have neither used nor advocated violence. Twenty-three such prisoners are documented in the Amnesty International publication I gave you when we met. The three of those our delegation mentioned in our discussion with you were Kim Keun-tae, Lee Tae-bok, and Kim Hyon-jang.

While we welcome the many prisoner releases that took place over the summer, we respectfully submit that in accordance with international human rights standards your government should continue releases until there are no more prisoners of conscience in the Republic of Korea.

As a safeguard against possibly detaining prisoners of conscience in the future, we would suggest that the National Security Law, the Law on Assemblies and Demonstrations, the Minor Offenses Law, and Article 104.2 of the Criminal Code be amended so as to exclude from their scope acts which constitute peaceful expression, association, and assembly.

Finally, by eliminating practices that allow several weeks of incommunicado detention to occur, possibilities for torture could be significantly reduced.

The Amnesty International publication I left with you elaborates on these and other recommendations.

I want to thank you again for meeting with us. I look forward to your government's response.

Respectfully yours,

Steve Herrick
Southern Regional Director, AIUSA 0117

POLITICAL IMPRISONMENT
IN THE
REPUBLIC OF KOREA

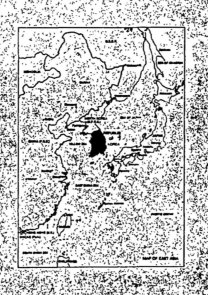

August 1987

THE REPUBLIC OF KOREA

AMNESTY INTERNATIONAL'S CONCERNS AND RECOMMENDATIONS

Contents   Page

I.   INTRODUCTION   1

II.   AMNESTY INTERNATIONAL'S CONCERNS   1

      A. Background to Political Detention   1

      B. The Arrest and Imprisonment of Prisoners   2
              of Conscience

      C. Protection Against Torture and Ill-treatment   3

III   PRISONERS OF CONSCIENCE CASE HISTORIES   4

      A. Introduction   4

      B. Case Histories   4

IV.   RECOMMENDATIONS ON THE IMPLEMENTATION OF HUMAN RIGHTS   22
          SAFEGUARDS

      A. Introduction   22

      B. Recommendations   22

0119

THE REPUBLIC OF KOREA
AMNESTY INTERNATIONAL'S CONCERNS AND RECOMMENDATIONS

I.   INTRODUCTION

Human rights violations became the focus of public protest in South Korea after student Park Chong-chol died under torture on January 14, 1987. A public outcry followed news of the death; two police officers were arrested and the government announced it would take measures to prevent torture. In May, it emerged that five, not two, police officers had been involved in torturing Park Chong-chol and that the two had been offered bribes to take full responsibility. The cover-up triggered a mass wave of street protests across the country.

After almost three weeks of these sometimes violent demonstrations Mr Roh Tae-woo, Chairman of the ruling Democratic Justice Party, announced on June 29 that the government would release political prisoners and guarantee human rights. Two days later, President Chun Doo-hwan endorsed the move.

II.   AMNESTY INTERNATIONAL'S CONCERNS

A.   Background to Political Detention

Since the early 1970s, thousands of people have been arrested and imprisoned in the Republic of Korea for the non-violent exercise of their right to freedom of expression and association despite guarantees of the right to freedom of conscience, speech, press, assembly and association under both the 1972 and 1980 Constitutions. Although a large number of them were released under presidential amnesties, some remain in detention after more than ten years. Some are serving long sentences after being found guilty of endangering national security and of helping or spying for the Democratic People's Republic of Korea (PDRK), North Korea. Of these, a few continue to be held in preventive detention after the expiration of their sentences. People who organize or take part in peaceful anti-government demonstrations are often arrested on the grounds that the demonstration was "likely to cause social unrest" and usually face sentences of one to four years' imprisonment. Another common accusation against government critics is that they "spread distorted or fabricated facts which might cause social unrest or impair public peace and order".

According to official statistics, over 3,400 people were charged with political offenses in 1986. Over 80% were students; others were workers, clergymen, Buddhist monks, members of political organizations, journalists and teachers. Most were released with a warning or detained for less than a month. About a third of them were charged with participating in illegal demonstrations or with pro-communist activities.

In the first part of 1987, mass arrests took place on the occasion of demonstrations on the streets or on university campuses to protest the use of torture and delays in democratic freedoms. The demonstrations were met with severe repression, in particular teargassing, arrests and beatings of detainees.

0120

The demonstrations often resulted in violence and Amnesty International was not able to establish whether the individuals arrested for participation in these demonstrations used or advocated violence.

At the beginning of July over 530 political prisoners were released and on July 10 the government restored the civil rights of 2,335 former political prisoners, including a group of students arrested in 1974 and others tried in 1980 with opposition politician Kim Dae-jung, whom Amnesty International had adopted as prisoners of conscience at the time.

Amnesty International sent a telex to President Chun Doo-hwan on July 16 welcoming the releases, including that of Reverend Moon Ik-kwan, a prisoner of conscience arrested in May 1986, and urged him to release all those prisoners held solely for peacefully exercising their right to freedom of expression and association. In its telex, Amnesty International stressed that many of these prisoners had reportedly been tortured and convicted after unfair trials. It listed 34 prisoners of conscience whose early release was urged.

In an earlier telex dated June 30, 1987, Amnesty International had asked the President to order the release of all prisoners of conscience, to take all measures necessary to prevent torture and to order thorough and impartial investigations into allegations of torture, and to ensure that all detainees were allowed visits from relatives and lawyers.

B.   The Arrest and Imprisonment of Prisoners of Conscience

Over 530 convicted political prisoners were released on 6 and 8 July, including some whom Amnesty International had adopted as prisoners of conscience. But Amnesty International remains concerned that a number of prisoners convicted of "anti-state" activities were not among those set free. Many of these, whom Amnesty International believes are being detained for their peaceful opposition to the government, have been imprisoned for several years. They include people who published or owned books which the authorities regard as "subversive"; people who called for the reunification of Korea or organized groups who non-violently opposed the government; and people who were convicted of espionage for North Korea on the basis of confessions which they testified in court had been obtained under torture. Kim Keun-tae, one of the cases highlighted below, was among those specifically excluded from the amnesty by the Justice Ministry. Sources inside the Republic of Korea suggest that as many as 900 political prisoners are currently imprisoned and believes that some of these may be prisoners of conscience, imprisoned solely for their non-violent opposition activities.

Amnesty International calls on the authorities to release all prisoners detained for the peaceful exercise of their rights of freedom of expression and association, regardless of their political views.

0121

C.   Protection Against Torture and Ill-treatment

An official investigation into Park Chong-chol's death concluded that he died of suffocation after his head was repeatedly held under water and that bruises on his body were also caused by torture. The Minister of Home Affairs and the Head of the National Police resigned, taking responsibility for the death of the student. The President instructed his government to set up a "special commission for the protection of human rights" composed of figures from all walks of life to advise it on how to prevent the occurrence of human rights abuses. While Amnesty International welcomes the setting up of this Commission, the organization is concerned that the Commission will not report until the end of the year, after the proposed adoption of a new Constitution.

For many years Amnesty International has received evidence of the regular use of torture. The South Korean authorities have made a number of statements condemning torture, but its practice has continued and investigations into torture allegations made by political prisoners have rarely been conducted. The trial of police officers for the death of Park Chong-chol was the first prosecution of its kind. To be effective, it is not enough for safeguards against torture and ill-treatment to be written into laws and other regulations; they have to be implemented and monitored, and people should know their rights. When an Amnesty International delegation visited Korea in late May 1987, it found that many, inside and outside the government, agreed with this.

0129

III. PRISONERS OF CONSCIENCE CASE HISTORIES

   A.   Introduction

While Amnesty International welcomes the recent releases of political
prisoners in the Republic of Korea, the organization is concerned that
several prisoners of conscience, some of whom have been imprisoned for
several years, remain in detention.

Given below are case histories of 23 prisoners of conscience, whom
Amnesty International considers are being held solely for their non-
violent opposition to the government. Appeals on behalf of these and
further prisoners have been sent to the South Korean government and
Amnesty International believes that several more prisoners are currently
being held for their non-violent opposition activities.

   B.   Case Histories

Kang Jong-hon, Paik Ok-Kwan, Kim Chul-hyon, Lee Chul, Kang Jong-kon

On 22 November 1975 the Korean Central Intelligence Agency (KCIA)
announced at a press conference that 21 people, many of them Koreans
normally resident in Japan, had been arrested for allegedly infiltrating
South Korean student groups under instructions from the Democratic
People's Republic of Korea (DPRK), North Korea. In December another five
Koreans from Japan were amongst 25 students arrested on the same
charge. It was later reported that around 300 of the 400 Koreans from
Japan who were at that time studying in the Republic of Korea had been
interrogated by the KCIA (now called the National Agency for Security
Planning) in connection with this case.

Paik Ok-kwan, aged 39, was the General Secretary of the Osaka Junior
Chamber of Commerce at the time of his arrest; Kang Jong-hon, aged 36,
was a medical student at Seoul National University; Kim Chul-hyon, aged
42, was a post-graduate student of Korean church history at Hankuk
Theological Seminary in Seoul; Lee Chul, aged 39, was a post graduate
student of politics and diplomacy at Korea University in Seoul; and Kang
Jong-kon, aged 36, was a student of law at Korea University in Seoul.

At their trial, which started in March 1976, all were accused under the
Anti-Communist and National Security laws of working for the North
Korean government and infiltrating student groups to incite demonstrations
against the South Korean government. Kang Jong-hon, Paik Ok-kwan, Lee
Chul and Kim Chul-hyon were alleged to have visited the DPRK for
espionage training: and Kang Jong-hon was alleged to have been recruited
in Japan by a North Korean agent, to whom he allegedly reported about
student demonstrations in the Republic of Korea.

Kang Jong-hon was sentenced to death in May 1976 on charges of visiting
the DPRK, passing information on the Republic of Korea to North Korean
agents in Japan and inciting students to demonstrate against the
government. During his interrogation, he confessed to the charges. At his
trial, however, he rejected his confession and said that he had made it
under torture. He denied having visited the DPRK and his defense lawyer

0123

submitted an alibi in support of his denial. He also denied taking part in student demonstrations and witnesses testified for him. He admitted, however, to having been in contact with members of a pro-North Korean association of Koreans living in Japan called Chochongnyon, and of having read their books and seen their films on the DPRK. He also admitted having talked to them about his personal experience in the Republic of Korea and what he had read in South Korean newspapers, but he denied communicating national secrets. He also said that he had talked to students in the Republic of Korea about information on the DPRK he had acquired in Japan. His death sentence was commuted to life imprisonment in March 1982 and reduced to 20 years' imprisonment in August 1984 under presidential amnesties.

Paik Ok-kwan was sentenced to death in April 1976 on charges of being the ring-leader of a "campus spy-ring", having sent agents posing as students to the Republic of Korea and having visited the DPRK on three occasions to receive espionage training and instructions. His death sentence was commuted to life imprisonment by presidential amnesty in March 1982. Like most of the defendants in this case, he confirmed his confession before the district court. However, evidence that he was in Japan in 1972 and 1975, when the prosecution alleged that he was in the DPRK, which was collected by bar associations in Japan and presented to the court, was ruled inadmissible.

Kim Chul-hyon was sentenced to death in May 1976 on charges of espionage and instigating anti-government demonstrations. Amnesty International believes that he was convicted on the basis of a-confession allegedly made under torture and without corroborative evidence of guilt. He was not allowed to see his lawyer until after the date of the trial was announced. He did not claim to have been tortured but at his trial he appeared abnormally withdrawn, and after being challenged by co-defendants and defense witnesses he admitted to having invented parts of his confession. His death sentence was commuted to life in August 1981 and reduced to 20 years' imprisonment under presidential amnesties.

Lee Chul was sentenced to death on charges of travelling twice to the DPRK, of engaging in espionage activities for the DPRK and of producing and disseminating pamphlets criticizing the South Korean government. He confessed to the charges during the 40 days in which he was held incommunicado and interrogated. He admitted that he was guilty during the trial, but on appeal he denied the charges and said he had confessed under torture and threats that members of his family and fellow-students would also be tortured. Evidence collected by the Tokyo Bar Association, which concluded that a series of alibis showed he was innocent, was submitted in support of his appeal. However, his appeal was rejected by the Seoul High Court on the grounds that he had admitted guilt before the court of first instance.

Kang Jong-kon was charged with reporting on student demonstrations to North Korean agents in Japan and recruiting student sympathizers on behalf of the DPRK, and was sentenced to five years' imprisonment. Since completing his sentence in February 1981 he has been held under the Public Security Law with a series of two-year preventive custody orders. Amnesty International believes he has continued to be detained after the

0121

expiration of his sentence because he refused to sign a statement repudiating the "pro-communist' views he allegedly held at the time of his arrest. In 1983 he brought a court case against the Ministry of Justice (which is responsible for issuing the order) challenging the validity of the preventive custody order. His case was turned down by the Appeal Court in October 1983. In March 1984 the Supreme Court overturned that decision and returned the case to the Appeal Court, saying that the Ministry of Justice's case for continuing to detain Kang Jong-kon did not show "a clear danger that he would repeat the offense". In December 1984 the Appeal Court invalidated the order, but the Minister of Justice appealed against its ruling and has continued to renew the preventive custody order. In March 1987 Kang Jong-kon and another prisoner of conscience went on hunger-strike in protest at their continued detention in preventive custody.

Amnesty International is concerned by reports that the defendants in this case were tortured into making confessions of "pro-communist" activities, which were used in court to secure their convictions, and that there are not sufficient grounds for accepting the court's rulings that they are guilty of espionage. AI urged the South Korean government to allow a fair and open retrial to consider additional evidence which had become available for some of the defendants. After careful consideration AI concluded that these prisoners were detained for the non-violent exercise of their right to freedom of expression and association because they openly discussed political matters and associated with others in the Republic of Korea who were actively involved in criticizing the South Korean government and its policies.

Kim Hyon-jang

Kim Hyon-jang, a freelance journalist and human rights activist, is serving a life sentence in Pusan Prison in the south-east of the Republic of Korea. He was sentenced to death by the courts but the sentence was commuted to life imprisonment by presidential amnesty in March 1983. Kim Hyon-jang was accused of involvement in an arson attack on the American Cultural Center in Pusan in March 1982, in which one student who was using the Center's library died. Leaflets found near the American Cultural Center after the attack criticized the US political and economic support for the South Korean government and called for the removal of US troops from the Republic of Korea. AI has investigated this charge in detail and believes that Kim Hyon-jang was in fact arrested because of his known non-violent criticism of the South Korean government, particularly his criticisms of the government's role in the May 1980 Kwangju disturbances.

At the time of the attack, Kim Hyon-jang was in hiding in the Catholic Education Center in Wonju where he had been for almost two years to avoid arrest for his role in compiling and circulating documents on the death of civilians during the Kwangju disturbances in May 1980 <1>. After

<1> On 18 May 1980 a student demonstration protesting against the imposition of nationwide martial law the day before and mass arrests ended in considerable violence when paratroopers brutally dispersed the demonstrators. In the following days clashes between troops and students

expiration of his sentence because he refused to sign a statement
repudiating the "pro-communist' views he allegedly held at the time of his
arrest. In 1983 he brought a court case against the Ministry of Justice
(which is responsible for issuing the order) challenging the validity of the
preventive custody order. His case was turned down by the Appeal Court
in October 1983. In March 1984 the Supreme Court overturned that
decision and returned the case to the Appeal Court, saying that the
Ministry of Justice's case for continuing to detain Kang Jong-kon did not
show "a clear danger that he would repeat the offense". In December 1984
the Appeal Court invalidated the order, but the Minister of Justice
appealed against its ruling and has continued to renew the preventive
custody order. In March 1987 Kang Jong-kon and another prisoner of
conscience went on hunger-strike in protest at their continued detention
in preventive custody.

Amnesty International is concerned by reports that the defendants in this
case were tortured into making confessions of "pro-communist" activities,
which were used in court to secure their convictions, and that there are
not sufficient grounds for accepting the court's rulings that they are
guilty of espionage. AI urged the South Korean government to allow a fair
and open retrial to consider additional evidence which had become
available for some of the defendants. After careful consideration AI
concluded that these prisoners were detained for the non-violent exercise
of their right to freedom of expression and association because they
openly discussed political matters and associated with others in the
Republic of Korea who were actively involved in criticizing the South
Korean government and its policies.

Kim Hyon-jang

Kim Hyon-jang, a freelance journalist and human rights activist, is
serving a life sentence in Pusan Prison in the south-east of the Republic
of Korea. He was sentenced to death by the courts but the sentence was
commuted to life imprisonment by presidential amnesty in March 1983. Kim
Hyon-jang was accused of involvement in an arson attack on the American
Cultural Center in Pusan in March 1982, in which one student who was
using the Center's library died. Leaflets found near the American Cultural
Center after the attack criticized the US political and economic support
for the South Korean government and called for the removal of US troops
from the Republic of Korea. AI has investigated this charge in detail and
believes that Kim Hyon-jang was in fact arrested because of his known
non-violent criticism of the South Korean government, particularly his
criticisms of the government's role in the May 1980 Kwangju disturbances.

At the time of the attack, Kim Hyon-jang was in hiding in the Catholic
Education Center in Wonju where he had been for almost two years to
avoid arrest for his role in compiling and circulating documents on the
death of civilians during the Kwangju disturbances in May 1980 <1>. After

<1> On 18 May 1980 a student demonstration protesting
against the imposition of nationwide martial law the day
before and mass arrests ended in considerable violence when
paratroopers brutally dispersed the demonstrators. In the
following days clashes between troops and students

the attack, those directly implicated sought refuge at the Center where they were encouraged to surrender to the authorities. Kim Hyon-Jang surrendered a few days later. On 29 April he was charged under the National Security Law with planning the arson attack and with carrying out other pro-communist activities.

At the trial, which began in June 1982, Moon Pu-shik, the leading participant in the arson attack, and a number of other defendants admitted the charge of arson but denied all charges of "pro-communist" acts. Kim Hyon-Jang, supported by Moon Pu-shik, totally denied any knowledge of, or involvement in, the arson attack. Kim Hyon-Jang testified that he had been forced under torture to make a false confession admitting his involvement. He said : "They tied my hands behind my back and poured mustard into my nose. This was done a total of six times. Then I wrote what they told me to." The prosecution's evidence that he was involved in the incident reportedly rested on an alleged meeting between himself and Moon Pu-shik in 1981, when, according to the prosecution, the attack was planned. However, both men testified that months before the attack took place, Kim Hyong-Jang had forcefully tried to dissuade Moon Pu-shik from plans to attack the Cultural Center. To Amnesty International's knowledge no evidence other than Kim Hyon-Jang's confession was presented in support of the charge that he had incited others to commit arson.

A large part of the trial proceedings was devoted to establishing that the defendants, including Kim Hyon-Jang, were communists, which they denied. Kim Hyon-Jang was accused of speaking at "consciousness-raising" seminars organized by the Catholic Education Center.

Kim Hyon-Jang is said to have been arrested on political charges in 1977, but AI has no details of the case. In 1979 he was reportedly working with the Kwangju Dismissed Students Association which aimed to help students dismissed from college or university for political reasons. Possibly he was also working with a self-help group for farmers. In the late 1970's Kim Hyon-Jang wrote and article for the magazine Dialogue, published by the Korea Christian Academy, about a young man executed for killing a government official during the clearance of an illegal slum area. He also wrote an article on "prostitution tourism" on Cheju Island for the magazine Deeper Roots.

Kim Keun-tae

Kim Keun-tae, the founding chairman of the National Youth Alliance for Democracy (NYAD) is serving a five year prison sentence in Kyongju prison on charges of having organized or participated in a series of meetings and demonstrations "feared to cause social unrest" and of

continued. By 21 May, the demonstrators were virtually in control of the city, but on 27 May troops retook the city with great brutality. Official statistics indicate that around 200 people were killed. However, reports from other sources put the figure of civilian dead at at least 1,200.

0127

promoting North Korean propaganda. AI has adopted him as a prisoner of conscience and is also concerned about his claims that he was tortured.

Kim Keun-tae, now aged 40, graduated in economics from Seoul National University where he is reported to have been very actively involved in organizing support for Kim Dae-jung, the opposition candidate in the April 1971 presidential elections. Wanted by the authorities for his anti-government activities, he went into hiding for most of the rest of the decade, working in factories and with the Urban Industrial Mission, a protestant group which helps factory workers to defend their rights.

The NYAD was set up in September 1983. Its objectives were to bring about the democratization of politics in the Republic of Korea, the reunification of North and South Korea, an independent economy "from which corruption and gross inequality in the distribution of wealth have been eliminated" and an independent education system and culture.

To promote its objectives the NYAD distributed leaflets and a journal, The Road to Democratization, and organized and took part in demonstrations. On several occasions members of the Alliance were arrested for their peaceful activities in support of the Alliance's objectives. Kim Keun-tae himself is said to have served seven sentences in police custody for "spreading groundless rumors". In May 1985 for example, he was arrested and sentenced to 10 days' police detention after the Alliance organized a series of demonstrations calling on the government to give a full account of the quelling of the insurrection in Kwangju in 1980 in which a large number of civilians were killed.

Kim Keun-tae was arrested on 4 September 1985 and interrogated at the headquarters of the Anti-Communist Bureau of the National Police in Namyoung-dong, in Seoul, until his transfer to the Seoul prosecutor's office on 26 September. He was indicted on 25 October and his trial started on 9 December. On 6 March he was sentenced to seven years' imprisonment. His sentence was reduced to five years on appeal.

On 26 September, as he was being taken for the first time to the prosecutor's office, Kim Keun-tae met his wife by chance and told her that he had been tortured during interrogation. In October 1985 his lawyers applied twice for a court order to have him examined by a judge and a doctor to document evidence of torture. The court ruled that there was no need for such an examination, without making public the grounds for this ruling. On 7 November the court granted a prosecution request to ban Kim Keun-tae from meeting his relatives for fear that he would ask them to remove evidence. When the Supreme Prosecutor's office issued a statement on its investigation into reports of his torture, they found that "there was no sign of torture in his walk or other physical and mental (?) movements", but there was no indication that a thorough investigation had been conducted and no details were given about the date or means of the investigation or whether it included a medical examination. Kim Keun-tae was not allowed to see his lawyers until 10 December, 10 days before the start of his trial. Prison guards reportedly prevented Kim Keun-tae from giving them the scab he had preserved as evidence of injuries inflicted under torture.

At his trial, Kim Keun-tae gave a long testimony in which he claimed to have been tortured during his interrogation and complained of a number of illegalities, including his detention without an arrest warrant for about 36 hours. He also complained that his letters to the prosecution authorities and the court, requesting an investigation into his treatment during interrogation, had remained unanswered, as had his request to the court for a medical examination.

He described how he had been tortured with electric shocks on many occasions between 4 and 20 September. Each torture session lasted about five hours. He said he was given no food on the days of torture, and found it impossible to eat after 13 September because of the torture. In his testimony he said : "When I think about what happened in the torture cell, I tremble with anger and humiliation. The police forced me to surrender. They repeatedly said they were going to break me and that is exactly what they did...By 20 September I became covered all over with wounds and couldn't stand any more. At last, on 25 September, I gave in to them. In groups they beat me up and asked me to beg for my life by crawling on the floor naked. I did what I was told. I wrote in the interrogation records as they demanded."

The charges against him included organizing and participating in meetings such as the Alliance's third general assembly where speeches were made calling for an end to the "military dictatorship" and for the release of political prisoners, and of making speeches critical of the authorities in terms similar to those used by the Democratic People's Republic of Korea (DPRK), North Korea, in its propaganda against the Republic of Korea. He was also charged with buying a book entitled Capitalism : Yesterday and Today, by British author Maurice Dobb, which the prosecution argued "advanced the interests of the DPRK".

In August 1986, Kim Keun-tae and 17 student prisoners in Kyongju prison were reportedly seriously beaten by prison officers. He was held at the time in a very small isolation cell. According to reports, the students were beaten after protesting about his treatment and Kim was later beaten when he complained to the prison authorities of the ill-treatment of the students. He was later visited by his wife who reported that his face was swollen and bruised and that there was considerable bruising on his body. He is said to be in poor health and is suffering from headaches, digestion problems and anal bleeding.

Kim Yong

Kim Yong was a student in the philosophy department of Pusan National University when he was arrested on 19 May 1980, for distributing leaflets criticizing the extension of martial law two days earlier. Hundreds of students were detained at that time on similar grounds. Amnesty International received reports that he was tortured during the first two months of his detention. In August 1980 he was sentenced to three years' imprisonment, but this was later reduced to two years.

At an appeal court hearing in November 1980, Kim Yong was offered the choice between serving the prison sentence or being conscripted into the military. He chose to do his military service. In the second half of 1981

0129

Kim Yong learned of the arrest of a number of his friends in the Purim (Pusan Good Books Association) case <2> and that he was wanted in connection with it. According to reports received by Amnesty International, Kim Yong was on guard duty on 28 October 1981 when believing that military intelligence officers had come to arrest him, he decided to desert, but after four days he gave himself up to the authorities. A court martial sentenced Kim Yong to ten years' imprisonment on charges of praising and supporting the Democratic People's Republic of Korea (DPRK), North Korea, and of deserting the army. His appeal against this sentence was rejected He is currently detained in Taegu Prison.]

Amnesty International received reports that during his interrogation by the military police and military intelligence in 1981 Kim Yong was tortured to make him admit to having praised the North Korean leader Kim Il-sung and the more equal distribution of wealth under communism. Amnesty International is concerned at these reports and that his confession was used to convict him of the charges, undermining the fairness of his trial.

Amnesty International does not contest the authorities right to imprison Kim Yong for desertion but it is concerned that his conviction relates largely to his holding non-violent political views and to that extent Amnesty International considers him to be a prisoner of conscience. The maximum sentence under Article 28.3 of the Military Penal Code, on desertion of a guard post by a sentry, is two years' imprisonment. Although Amnesty International does not know the length of the sentence imposed on Kim Yong for desertion, it is very likely that he has now finished serving this sentence and is currently serving the sentence imposed on him under the National Security Law for his political views and activities. Amnesty International is now calling for his immediate and unconditional release.

Lee Tae-bok

Lee Tae-bok, a publisher, has been detained since 1981 for publishing "pro-communist" books such as translations of texts on economics and social sciences. He was originally sentenced to life imprisonment but the sentence was later reduced under a presidential amnesty to 20 years' imprisonment. During his trial he testified that he had been tortured to force him to confess to the accusations against him. Amnesty International has adopted him as a prisoner of conscience.

After graduating from Kukmin University in the mid-1970s, Lee Tae-bok, now 36 years old, reportedly worked for two years in a factory before

<2> In this case. sixteen people. who were said to have met to discuss social and political issues and to have organized study groups to help workers demand their rights, were charged with activities aimed at overthrowing the government and bring about a communist society. Amnesty International considered them to be prisoners of conscience. They have all now been released.

setting up a small publishing company, called Kwangminsa. He was also involved in the work of the Ileungsadan Academy, which organized lectures and various activities aimed at raising students' and young people's awareness of the Republic of Korea's social, political and economic problems.

Lee Tae-bok was taken away by police on 10 June 1981, although the warrant for his arrest was not issued until 31 July. During these seven weeks of illegal detention he was reportedly held and interrogated at the Anti-Communist Bureau of the National Police in Namyoung-dong, Seoul. He was transferred to Seoul Detention Center in Sudaemoon in the first week of August when his interrogation by a public prosecutor started. On 8 September, he was charged under the National Security Law (NSL) with organizing two "anti-state" groups, the Democratic Students' Federation (DSF) and the Democratic Labor Federation (DLF), and of publishing books which the authorities regarded as pro-communist, in an "attempt to create unrest and prepare for a communist revolution". He was not allowed access to his relatives until mid-September, more than three months after his arrest, and he did not see a lawyer appointed by his family until some time in October.

Lee Tae-bok's trial started on 29 October 1981, together with 27 other defendants, including students, trade unionists and church workers, who faced charges of belonging to the same two groups, the DSF and the DLF. Among the books which were used by the prosecution as evidence that Lee Tae-bok disseminated communist ideas and tried to inspire students and workers to overthrow the government, were several translations of books by foreign authors such as Studies in the Development of Communism by Maurice Dobb, and works by G.D.H. Cole, Herbert Marcuse and Christopher Hill. Some of these books were said to be standard reading recommended by university professors in the Republic of Korea to their students, and Lee Tae-bok was said to have received official permission for their publication.

In the course of his trial, Lee Tae-bok reportedly described being tied naked to a coffin and beaten, threatened with death, immersed in water, given electric shocks, and beaten on the soles of his feet. Often, he said, the torture would be repeated and he would lose consciousness. Finally, he said : "...because nothing could be gained by continued denial, I felt there was nothing I could do but agree to their charges..."

On 22 January 1982, Lee Tae-bok was sentenced to life imprisonment by Seoul District Criminal Court. The prosecution had earlier asked for the death penalty. (His co-defendants received prison sentences ranging from one to ten years : all have now been released, either on expiration of their sentences or under presidential amnesties). Lee Tae-bok's life sentence was reduced to 20 years' imprisonment under a presidential amnesty, on 12 August 1983.

Lee Tae-bok is currently detained in Taejon Prison. He is said to have suffered injury to his genitals during torture and recent reports state that he has a testicular infection with genital pain and haematuria. He also suffers from hemorrhoids. Although he had received permission earlier

0131

this year for hospital examination following which some medication was prescribed, there is concern that he may still be in ill-health.

Yu Sang-dok

On 4 September 1986, the Agency for National Security Planning announced that it had arrested four people, including Yu Sang-dok, under the National Security Law on suspicion of being members of a "spy ring" working for the Democratic People's Republic of Korea (DPRK), North Korea. The alleged leader of the "spy ring", Professor Lee Pyong-sol, aged 48 and a professor of geography at Seoul National University, was accused of having incited campus and labor unrest and of organizing four underground cells among students, workers and teachers for the purpose of collecting information to give to North Korea agents and to carry out activities benefiting the DPRK. On 24 January 1987, he was sentenced to 15 years' imprisonment by the Seoul District Court, reduced on appeal to 12 years' imprisonment on 28 May 1987.

Yu Sang-dok, aged 37, was a high-school teacher and the chairperson of the Young Men's Christian Association's Council for the Realization of Democratic Education (CRDE).

The YMCA Council for the Realization of Democratic Education is working towards changes in the South Korean educational system. It has a network of branches and members nationwide, holds seminars for teachers, publishes a bulletin entitled Democratic Education five times a year, as well as the monthly Teachers' Newspaper, which has a circulation of around 5,000. It also organizes groups of parents interested in education issues. On 10 May 1986 the YMCA issued a "Declaration for the Democratization of Education", said to be 86 pages long, which called for, amongst other things, (1) a guarantee in the country's Constitution of the political independence of the educational system; (2) the right of teachers, parents and students to be involved in decisions regarding education; (3) the right for teachers to form independent teachers' organizations; and (4) an end to obligatory non-academic activities for students and teachers. The Declaration was signed by over 920 primary and secondary school teachers in various cities. A number of them were subsequently arrested and prosecuted; others who refused to withdraw their signatures were reportedly forced to resign from their jobs, given pay cuts, transferred to other schools, or given warnings.

Yu Sang-dok is also a practicing member of the Presbyterian Church of the Republic of Korea (PROK) and graduated from the PROK's Mission and Education Center. He has been active in the Young Men's Christian Association teachers' movement since 1981, and under its auspices organized the CRDE. He was forced to resign from his job at a high school in Seoul in 1983, apparently because of his involvement in the CRDE.

Yu Sang-dok was taken into custody by the Agency for National Security Planning (ANSP) on 15 July 1986. He was detained illegally until 28 July when a warrant of arrest was issued against him. It is believed that he was held in an ANSP facility in Namean, Seoul, until 14 August when he was transferred to Yongdungpo Detention Center. To Amnesty

0132

International's knowledge, he was not allowed to see his relatives or a lawyer during his interrogation. When his wife visited him on 11 September, he told her that he had been subjected to physical and mental torture to make him confess that he knew that Professor Lee Pyong-sol was a spy for the DPRK.

In September 1986, reports were received that Yu Sang-dok went on hunger-strike for over 13 days to demand that the Director of the ANSP and the Secretary of the Ministry of Education apologize for the "distorted reporting" of his case and that of the others arrested with him.

Yu Sang-dok was indicted on 12 September 1986. He was charged under Articles 7(1) and 7(5) of the NSL with praising the DPRK and under Article 8(1) with communicating with a North Korean agent. The first charge refers to his possessing some books; the second to his having been in contact with Professor Lee Pyong-sol, who was accused of providing information on the Republic of Korea to the DPRK.

Amnesty International has been informed that Yu Sang-dok had known Professor Lee Pyong-sol while he was a student at Seoul National University, but had not been in contact with him for over ten years until September 1984, when he approached him to discuss his plans to go to Japan to study law. Professor Lee Pyong-sol had received his degree in Japan and knew the Japanese university system well. In March 1985 Professor Lee Pyong-sol introduced Yu Sang-dok to a visiting Japanese professor, but by this time, Yu Sang-dok had reportedly decided not to go to Japan. On another occasion, Lee Pyong-sol and Yu Sang-dok met in a coffee shop; Professor Lee told Yu Sang-dok that he was going to Japan and asked if there was anything he could do for him while he was there. Yu Sang-dok asked Professor Lee to buy him books published by a third world education center in Tokyo but he did not specify which ones. Professor Lee brought him back several books which included Education for National Liberation, How To Educate Korean Residents in Japan, What An Agricultural Country Should Be Like, and The Education Theory About Koreans Resident in Japan. Some of these books had been published by Chochongnyon, the pro-North Korean General Federation of Korean Residents in Japan, and others referred to the situation on the DPRK in their text.

During Yu Sang-dok's trial the prosecutor argued that Yu Sang-dok had ordered these books to praise the DPRK. The prosecution further argued that Yu Sang-dok had agreed with comments favorable to the DPRK made to him by Professor Lee Pyong-sol during their conversation. Yu Sang-dok admitted in court that they had discussed aerial photos of North Korean land reclamation work, but denied having praised the DPRK. Yu Sang-dok also claimed that other evidence of him having praised the DPRK had been obtained from him by torture when he was beaten with a wooden stick, threatened with death and deprived of sleep.

The prosecution did not have evidence that Yu Sang-dok knew Professor Lee Pyong-sol to be working for the DPRK, but argued that he should have been alerted by Professor Lee's keenness to help him study in Japan and that he should have been aware that Chochongnyon tries to attract

0133

Korean students to Japan to train them as spies <3>. On 24 January 1987 the Seoul District Court found Yu Sang-dok guilty of the charges and sentenced him to three years' imprisonment. On 28 May 1987 his sentence was reduced to two years' imprisonment by Seoul High Court.

Amnesty International believes that Yu Sang-dok is detained for the peaceful exercise of his right to freedom of opinion and expression and is calling for his immediate and unconditional release. It is also concerned about reports that he was tortured and urges the South Korean authorities to initiate an immediate and impartial investigation into the allegations that Yu Sang-dok was tortured and requests that the result of the investigation be made available to it.

Soh Sung, Soh Joon-shik

Soh Sung was a post-graduate student in sociology at Seoul National University and his brother, Soh Joon-shik, was a law student at Seoul National University when they were arrested in April 1971. The brothers were born in Japan and normally resided there. They were tried on charges of spying for the Democratic People's Republic of Korea (DPRK), North Korea, and instigating anti-government student demonstrations under North Korean instruction. Both were also charged with travelling to DPRK. Soh Sung was sentenced to death by the Seoul District Court, but his sentence was reduced to life imprisonment on appeal. Soh Joon-shik was sentenced to 15 years' imprisonment, reduced to seven years' on appeal, but he has continued to be detained after the expiration of his sentence in May 1978 under a series of preventive custody orders.

Travel of nationals of the Republic of Korea to the DPRK is prohibited and punishable under the National Security Law. Amnesty International considers that the mere fact of traveling to the DPRK without evidence either of espionage activities or of the use or advocacy of violence cannot justify imprisonment.

During his trial, Soh Sung admitted visiting the DPRK but denied carrying out espionage activities or inciting students to demonstrate against the government. He explained that as a second-generation Korean living in Japan his search for national identity led him to be interested in both the Democratic People's Republic of Korea and the Republic of Korea, and that his studies at a South Korean university and his visits to the DPRK were aimed at understanding the political realities in both countries which he felt should be reunified by peaceful means.

Soh Sung's trial was delayed because he needed hospital treatment for severe burns to 16 per cent of his body after trying to commit suicide, reportedly to avoid further torture during his interrogation. In court, he

<3> Professor Lee Pyong-sol is said to have confessed to the charges against him, saying that he had not visited the DPRK, but had communicated periodically with Chochongnyon. Amnesty International is seeking further information on the case of Lee Pyong-sol to ascertain whether he is a prisoner of conscience and whether he was given a fair trial.

claimed to have written a confession under torture, in which he admitted having collected and transmitted national secrets of the Republic of Korea to the DPRK and having organized underground student Communist groups in the Republic of Korea. He is said to have signed his confession about six weeks later, while in the hospital recovering from his suicide attempt, by affixing the imprint of his big toe. To the district court judges and when appealing against his conviction, Soh Sung explained that he attempted suicide as he "could not endure the mental and physical pains during interrogation."

In his appeal to the Supreme Court, dated 31 January 1983, he wrote "... the prosecutor's indictment resulted from my involuntary statement, forced by torture, and from the investigation which was deceptively done under unsatisfactory physical and psychological conditions..." During an interview, which however was not private, Soh Sung told an Amnesty International delegate who had come to observe the hearing of his appeal, that he had been beaten with clubs during his interrogation. In a response to a query, the Amnesty International observer was informed by the prosecution that it had not conducted an investigation into the prisoner's claims that a confession had been illegally obtained from him. The court accepted Soh Sung's confession as primary evidence of his guilt, although there are no indications that they conducted a thorough and impartial investigation to establish its validity.

In July 1985, Amnesty International received reports that, following a protest against conditions at Taejon Prison, Soh Sun was tied with rope, hung from the ceiling and beaten. After this incident, he was reportedly detained in a "punishment cell" measuring less that three by six feet with only a small air vent and no windows.

Amnesty International believes that Soh Sung's brother, Soh Joon-shik, was also wrongly convicted of espionage after an unfair trial on the basis of a confession allegedly made under torture and without corroborative evidence of guilt, and that he was in fact imprisoned because of his non-violent political views. Since the expiration of his sentence in May 1978, Soh Joon-shik has been detained in preventive custody under the Public Security Law. Under this law, "any person with a strong possibility of committing a crime again" may be held in preventive custody. The term of detention is two years, renewable by the Minister of Justice.

Amnesty International believes that the reason for Soh Joon-shik's continued detention is his refusal to sign a declaration of conversion to anti-Communism. Soh Joon-shik reportedly claimed that while serving his sentence, he was ill-treated and restrictions were imposed on his rights to receive visitors, exercise, read, or write letters, in an attempt to make him sign such a declaration. In 1974 he stated in a conversation with a member of the Japanese Diet who visited him in prison that he had been tortured since his conviction. He claimed that he had been stripped naked and tied up in the open air on a cold winter day while water was thrown over him, and that prison staff trampled on his stomach after he had been forced to drink four kettles of water.

On 11 June 1982 Soh Joon-shik filed an administrative appeal against the third preventative detention order imposed on him. In a written

0135

statement to the Seoul High Court, the Ministry of Justice reportedly argued that Soh Joon-shik's continued detention under the Public Security Law was justified because he had refused to convert to anti-Communism and had incited other prisoners to go on hunger-strike in protest against their detention, and that he was therefore likely to commit an offense similar to that of which he was originally convicted. On 30 May 1983 the Seoul High Court rejected Soh Joon-shik's appeal. In May 1986 the preventive custody order against Soh Joon-shik was renewed for a further two years.

In March and April 1987 Soh Joon-shik staged a 51 day hunger-strike in protest at his continued detention in preventive custody. He is held in Chongju Detention Center.

Park Hyon-su

Park Hyon-su, a student of Yonsei University and a member of its student council, was arrested in June 1986 after anti-government leaflets were found on high-school grounds in Seoul or received at home by high-school students. The authorities had announced that they were looking for members of the student councils of Yonsei and Seoul National Universities in Seoul whom they held responsible for distributing the leaflets and letters. Park Hyon-su was accused of sending about 2,000 letters to students of middle and high schools across the Republic of Korea. He was sentenced on 10 December 1986 to 18 months' imprisonment for mailing "impure" letters to high-school students in an attempt to foment "class struggle".

The Korea Herald reported that the letters contained such statements as "Your friend's daddy is a company president who has a good sedan. Your father is a manual worker at a construction site. What a contrast! Isn't it absurd to say that communism is simply bad?"

The leaflets were said to describe the objectives of the university student councils and to explain their views on issues such as the revision of the Constitution, the role of the United States in the division of the Korean peninsula after World War II as well as the criticisms of "anti-Communist education" given in schools.

Amnesty International is concerned that Park Hyon-su is detained for his peaceful criticism of the government of the Republic of Korea and considers him to be a prisoner of conscience.

0136

Koh Song-guk, Lee Pom, Kim Sang-bok, Koh Kyong-dae, Park Sung-in

These five men were among twelve people taken into custody on 25 March 1986 following a series of raids by South Korean police on bookstores around university campuses in Seoul in which large numbers of books were seized. The twelve were reportedly charged with violating the National Security Law by publishing and distributing "subversive" books and by giving ideological support to "radical" student activities.

Three of those arrested were prominent in unlicensed publication groups: Koh Song-guk, a 28 year old part time lecturer in diplomacy at Korea University, was the chairman of the Tasan Kihwoek company. Koh Kyong-dae, a 28 year old graduate of Yonsei University, was chairman of the Poim Kihwoek company. Lee Pom, who had previously been detained for political reasons in 1978 and 1979, was the 28 year old president of the Paeksan Sodang publication company at the time of his arrest. Kim Sang-bok, aged 30, was the former head of the cultural section of the Ecumenical Youth Council. No personal details are known about Park Sung-in.

Following their arrest, the twelve men were taken to the Anti Communist Bureau of the National Police in Seoul. Official detention notices were reportedly not issued until 29 March, and did not reach relatives until 1 April. Lee Pom was denied family visits for 10 days, while others were allowed to see their relatives at the beginning of April. The prisoners' relatives alleged that the detainees were tortured by the police in order to force them to "confess" to the charges made against them and that they showed signs of having been seriously ill-treated. The sister of Koh Kyong-dae has reportedly stated that when she visited him on 29 March he "was unable to walk properly" because of ill-treatment inflicted on him. Kim Sang-bok is reported to have told a relative in early April that he had been subjected to torture by electric shock. During this visit his eyes were said to have been dazed and had difficulty focusing. He also had apparent difficulty in walking and keeping his balance.

On 27 September 1986, the Seoul District Criminal Court sentenced ten of the prisoners to terms of imprisonment ranging between three months to four years. In January 1987 the Seoul High Court reduced some of the sentences. AI has adopted these five men as prisoners of conscience and is urging the authorities to investigate the allegations of torture.

0137

Im Kyu-yong, Im Tong-kyu, Kim Chong-sam, Noh Jae-chang

Im Kyu-yong, Im Tong-kyu, Kim Chong-sam, and Noh Jae-chang were arrested in 1979 and convicted under the Anti-Communist Law and the National Security Law of membership in an "anti-state" organization called the Preparatory Committee of the South Korean National Liberation Front (SKNLF). The prosecution claimed it was an underground group planning to "establish a Communist regime through a violent anti-government struggle." They were arrested at a time of growing opposition to the government of President Park Chung-hee and widespread dissatisfaction with the domestic economic situation. More that 100 people were detained for investigation in connection with this case, and 73 were brought to trial in December 1979. Fourteen of them are still detained.

Kim Chong-sam, the son of a farmer, is a graduate in veterinary medicine. As a student he had been active in an organization which provided education services and seasonal labor to farmers. From 1976 onwards, he worked in the research department of the Catholic Farmers' Association, of which, at the time of his arrest, he was the Director. He was associated with research studies which concluded that the impoverishment of farmers resulted from government controls on the price of agricultural products and with studies pointing out the health hazards of working with pesticides and chemical fertilizers. He was sentenced to 15 years' imprisonment. In May 1986 he went on a 17 day hunger-strike in protest at the conditions of detention in Chonju Prison. In early June his sister, who had visited him in prison, said he was in a weak condition, that he had suffered damage to his throat as a result of force-feeding, and that his body was covered with bruises, probably sustained when he resisted force-feeding. He went on another hunger-strike in August 1986 in protest at his ill-treatment following his first protest. He is now held in Taegu Prison and is said to suffer from a heart complaint for which he is taking medication.

Im Tong-kyu is serving two sentences of life imprisonment. Originally from a farming family near Kwangju, he had been actively involved, as a student at Seoul National University, in organizing students' labor services to farmers. At the time of his arrest he was working in the Labor Research Institute of Korea University in Seoul. His first life sentence was imposed in October 1979 for allegedly trying to set up a group working towards a Communist revolution in the Republic of Korea and carrying out espionage activities for the Democratic Peoples' Republic of Korea. He was accused of "having attempted to instill anti-government and pro-Communist ideas among intellectuals through the publication of an agricultural magazine and lecture meetings, and of helping a journalist from Japan to meet the wife of poet Kim Chi-ha, then in prison, thereby assisting him to write articles benefiting the DPRK." A few days after his first life sentence was imposed, the authorities announced that he was being interrogated in connection with the SKNLF; he was later given another life sentence in connection with this case. Im Tong-kyu is now held in Taejon Prison.

Noh Jae-chang, also a farmer's son, studied economics at Seoul National University. Throughout his studies he maintained an active interest in

0138

the problems faced by farmers. In 1979 he took part in student protests against the government and reportedly went into hiding to avoid arrest. He is serving a 10-year prison sentence in Chonju Prison.

Im Kyu-yong was a history student when he was first arrested in 1974 in connection with the National Democratic Youth and Student Federation, an organization which the government accused of planning to overthrow the government. AI adopted all those detainees in this case as prisoners of conscience. He was sentenced to 20 years' imprisonment but was released a few years later. He was working as an automobile mechanic when he was arrested in 1979. He is now serving a 10-year prison sentence in Kwanju Prison.

Amnesty International has collected information which it believes shows convincingly that these four men have been imprisoned for the non-violent exercise of their rights to freedom of expression and association. Information from many sources shows that these four prisoners held views that were critical of the Government of the Republic of Korea and its policies, in particular with regard to the rural sector, but that they did not support violence as a means of political change. AI's request to the government for information on the evidence used to convict them was refused, but a number of legal documents relating to the trial indicate that the charges of advocacy of violence and participation in robberies were supported mainly by confessions made by prisoners and by their co-defendants in circumstances which place serious doubt about their voluntary and genuine nature.

Amnesty International is concerned that all the prisoners in this case were convicted after unfair trials. They were detained in October and November 1979 by the police without warrant of arrest for longer that legally permitted, in some cases for up to a month. Their relatives were not informed of their whereabouts until their detention was authorized by a judge and they were moved to regular police stations. The prisoners were held in isolation for six to nine weeks; reportedly they were not allowed to see a lawyer of their choice before the day they were formally charged, 26 December 1979, six to eleven weeks after the beginning of their detention. Their families were allowed to see them for the first time on the day of the first trial.

The defendants testified in court that they had been tortured by police interrogators to make them confess to the charges and that their statements to the prosecutor were made under threat of further torture and were false. Some described their torture to the courts; others reportedly showed injuries which were said to be the result of torture. They referred to beatings, electric shocks and "water torture" where a person is forcibly immersed in water or water is forcibly poured into the victim's nose. To Amnesty International's knowledge, the judges' investigation into the claims of torture was limited to a statement made in court on behalf of the prosecution that there had been no torture. Amnesty International believes that the circumstances of the defendant's interrogation place serious doubts on the validity of their confessions, and has urged the government to reopen their case.

0139

sentenced to three years' imprisonment. He is currently detained in Chonju Prison.

Reverend Kang Hee-nam

Reverend Kang Hee-nam is aged 67 and is the Presbyterian minister of Namsan Church in Chonju, North Cholla Province. He was arrested on November 7, 1986 after addressing a student rally at Chunbuk National University in Chonju. In his speech, entitled "Democracy and Pro-Communist Organizations", he reportedly accused the authorities of labelling students arrested after a three-day occupation of Konkuk University in Seoul at the end of October 1986 as "Communists", while in his view they were simply advocating the democratization of politics. On October 28, over 2,000 students from 26 colleges and universities had taken part in a rally at Konkuk University to establish a "patriotic student committee against foreign power and dictatorship". After riot police broke up the rally and arrested over 200 participants, other participants occupied several university buildings and arrested over 1,200 students. Around 400 were eventually tried and indicted for taking part in the protest: some 140 were eventually charged under the National Security Law (NSL) with using slogans the authorities said were similar to North Korean propaganda; the others were charged with taking part in an illegal assembly.

Reverend Kang Hee-nam was charged under the NSL with "benefiting" the Democratic People's Republic of Korea. On April 7, 1987, he was sentenced to three years' imprisonment. He is currently detained in Chonju Prison.

Amnesty International has adopted Reverend Kang Hee-nam as a prisoner of conscience, detained for the peaceful expression of his political views, and is calling for his immediate and unconditional release.

Reverend Kang Hee-nam has been involved in social and political issues for a number of years. He was adopted by Amnesty International as a prisoner of conscience during his imprisonment from May 1977 to December 1979. His arrest on that occasion had been prompted by a speech he had made at a Democratic Unification Party convention in Chonju. He was sentenced to ten years' imprisonment under the Anti-Communist Law and Emergency Regulation No. 9. In 1978 he was reported to have been insulted and beaten by prison guards for not standing to attention during an investigation of his cell. Reverend Kang Hee-nam was released in December 1979 when Emergency Regulation No. 9 was repealed.

Reverend Kang Hee-nam is the chairman of the Korea National Federation of Christian Farmers Associations which was set up in 1978 to improve the political, economic and social status of peasants and to promote the participation of farmers in the democratization movement. He was also chairman of the Central Committee of Mintongnyon, the United Minjung Movement for Democratization and Unification, an umbrella organization of 26 dissident groups set up in March 1985. Mintongnyon's aim was to involve the public in protests against the government: it organized street demonstrations and published a newsletter Voice of the People. It was closed by the authorities in November 1986 and most of its leaders are currently in detention.

0140

356 한국 인권문제 제 사안 1

From April 24 to June 3, 1987, Reverend Kang Hee-nam undertook a
hunger-strike in protest at the decision by President Chun Doo-hwan on
April 13 to suspend debate on constitutional reform until after the 1988
Seoul Olympics.

0141

IV. RECOMMENDATIONS ON THE IMPLEMENTATION OF HUMAN RIGHTS SAFEGUARDS

A. Introduction

Discussions are currently underway in South Korea, within the government, political parties, the legal profession and other circles, on how best to protect human rights. Amnesty International would like to make its contribution to this debate on human rights safeguards. Below are the measures it considers should be implemented at the earliest opportunity. They are based on international human rights standards and bring up to date the recommendations it submitted to the Government of the Republic of Korea in August 1985.

B. Recommendations

1. Freedom of expression and association

International human rights standards provide that everyone has the rights to freely hold and express opinions and to associate and assemble peacefully with others. These rights are set out in the Universal Declaration of Human Rights and in the International Covenant on Civil and Political Rights (ICCPR).

The 1980 Constitution of the Republic of Korea guarantees the rights to freedom of conscience, freedom of speech and of the press, and freedom of assembly and association and the right of workers to collective action. The Constitution allows restrictions on these freedoms and rights "when necessary for national security, the maintenance of public order or public welfare" but stipulates that "even when such restriction is imposed, no essentials of the freedom or right shall be violated."

To further guarantee the rights of freedom of expression, assembly and association, Amnesty International recommends that:

1.1 the Government of the Republic of Korea should release all prisoners detained for the non-violent exercise of their rights of freedom of conscience, expression, association and peaceful assembly, regardless of their political views and of whether their trials have been completed;

1.2 the Government of the Republic of Korea should ratify, without reservations and at the earliest opportunity, the International Covenant on Civil and Political Rights and its Optional Protocol and the International Covenant on Economic, Social and Cultural Rights;

1.3 the National Security Law, the Law on Assemblies and Demonstrations, the Minor Offences Law and Article 104.2 of the Criminal Code should be amended so as to define clearly the offenses contained in them and exclude from their scope acts which constitute the peaceful exercise of the rights of freedom of opinion, expression, association and peaceful assembly. These laws have been used to hold prisoners of conscience;

1.4 the Public Security Law should also be amended so as to stop it being used to detain people for their non-violent political opinions;

0142

1.6   the practice of placing people under house arrest or restricting the freedom of movement of people because of their peaceful political views and activities should be made illegal.

2.   Torture

Torture and other cruel, inhuman or degrading treatment or punishment of prisoners is prohibited by the Universal Declaration of Human Rights and a number of other international human rights instruments. These include the International Covenant on Civil and Political Rights and the Convention against Torture and Other Cruel, Inhuman or Degrading Treatment or Punishment, adopted by the United Nations on 10 December 1984. International standards emphasize that torture can never be justified, even in exceptional circumstances such as a state of war, internal political instability or other public emergency.

The 1980 Constitution of the Republic of Korea specifically prohibits the use of torture and the Code of Criminal Procedure contains a number of provisions which, if implemented, would help to protect detainees against torture and ill-treatment. Amnesty International has found that in many cases of torture and ill-treatment the main safeguards provided by international standards and by the laws of the Republic of Korea had not been respected.

To ensure the protection of all detainees against torture and ill-treatment, Amnesty International recommends that:

2.1.   the Government of the Republic of Korea should ratify without reservations the Convention against Torture and Other Cruel, Inhuman or Degrading Treatment or Punishment at the earliest opportunity;

2.2.   laws of the Republic of Korea and other regulations should be amended or reinforced to end the practice of incommunicado detention and interrogation and to guarantee that anyone arrested or detained should be brought promptly before a judicial authority and should have prompt and regular access to relatives, the detainee's own lawyer and a doctor.

Accurate information on a detainee's whereabouts should be made available to relatives immediately after arrest; early and regular communications and visits should be allowed, subject only to restrictions and supervision necessary in the interests of the administration of justice. Legal recourse should be available to detainees and families denied the right to communicate and meet.

Regular communication and consultation with a lawyer are of the utmost importance to ensure, among other legal guarantees, that statements taken in evidence from the detainee are given freely and not as a result of coercion. Such consultations must occur at a minimum before and between interrogation sessions and in a degree of privacy if the lawyer's presence is to serve as a credible restraint on the interrogators' potential abuse of power.

Detainees should be allowed to be examined, in private, on arrival at any detention center before interrogation begins and regularly afterwards, by medical officers not responsible to the agencies interrogating or detaining the suspects. Records of these examinations should be treated as confidential but should be communicated at the detainee's request to his or her lawyer or family.

0143

The laws of the Republic of Korea should ensure that detainees be brought promptly before a judge or other judicial officer. The right to have the courts to review the legality of arrest or detention should be available to all detainees.

2.3. the relevant regulations and the practice regarding the detention of suspects should be reviewed so as to separate the authorities responsible for interrogation from those responsible for detention. This is particularly important when the interrogation is conducted by the Anti-Communist Bureau of the National Police, the Agency for National Security Planning and the Military Security Command which have been linked in numerous cases to torture.

Detaining authorities should be directed to keep detailed records on the suspects in their care. Such records should include information on, for instance, the time and duration of each interrogation session, requests or complaints made by the detainees or on their behalf, instances of legitimate use of force against a detainee or of violence by the detainee against guards or against him or herself. The burden should be on the authorities to prove through such records that injuries to prisoners were not sustained through ill-treatment in custody at the hands of officials. All records should be made available to the detainees and his or her legal counsel as well as to the prosecutor supervising the interrogation of the suspect;

2.4. procedures should be established to ensure that all and well-founded reports, complaints of torture and ill-treatment are investigated by competent authorities and that prisoners are informed of their rights to lodge complaints about their treatment. Places of detention should be visited regularly for inspection by independent and competent authorities;

2.5. the relevant authorities should conduct impartial and thorough investigations into all claims of torture and ill-treatment and, depending on the results of the investigations, should review the legal position of the prisoners, compensate the victims and bring to justice any officials found to have assaulted prisoners;

2.6. training procedures should be introduced for all officials involved in the custody, interrogation or treatment of prisoners in which it is stressed that torture is a criminal act, that any orders to commit torture should be refused and abuses reported to superiors or to the authorities vested with reviewing or remedial powers. Amnesty International recommends that a code of conduct based on the United Nations Code of Conduct for Law Enforcement Officials should be adopted and made public.

3.   The right to a fair trial

Amnesty International seeks to ensure that the trials of all political prisoners conforms to internationally recognized norms, such as those of the Universal Declaration of Human Rights and of the ICCPR. These norms include the right to a fair and public hearing by a competent, independent and impartial tribunal and the right to be presumed innocent until proved guilty.

0144

Amnesty International recommends that laws of the Republic of Korea and other regulations should be amended so as to guarantee a fair trial to all political detainees. It also calls for all the cases of political prisoners still in custody to be reviewed whenever there were irregularities in pre-trial or trial procedures, such as illegal detention without a warrant of arrest, prolonged incommunicado detention and interrogation, claims of torture or ill-treatment, denial of prompt and regular access to a lawyer, and the use as evidence of confessions said by the defendants to have been extracted under torture.

4.   The right to life

Amnesty International opposes the death penalty in all cases without reservation on the grounds that it is a violation of the right to life and the right not to be subjected to cruel, inhuman or degrading punishment as proclaimed in the Universal Declaration of Human Rights and in other international human rights instruments;

4.1.   Amnesty International urges the President of the Republic of Korea to commute all death sentences and urges the government to take steps for the abolition of the death penalty;

4.2.   In preparation for abolition, the Government should inform the public about criminological and penal issues related to the death penalty, including its lack of proven special deterrent effect. This is in line with a recommendation of the United Nations Secretariat in 1980 that "It...seems to be an important task of governments, the academic community, the mass media, and other publicly minded organizations...to educate the public as to the uncertainty of the deterrent effect of capital punishment.."

Amnesty International Urges Seoul to Free Political Prisoners

By MARVINE HOWE

As Korean-Americans marked South Korean Liberation Day yesterday with rallies for democracy, Amnesty International urged the South Korean Government to release all prisoners of conscience and provide new guarantees for human rights.

In its latest report on dissent in South Korea, the international human rights organization expressed concern that as many as 900 political prisoners were still being held, including dozens imprisoned for their peaceful opposition to the Government.

Welcoming the recent release of prisoners in South Korea, John G. Healey, executive director of Amnesty International U.S.A., called for "the immediate unconditional freedom of the remaining prisoners of conscience," as a demonstration of the Government's commitment to safeguard human rights.

In what was described as their first nationwide demonstration, Korean-Americans held rallies here and in ten other United States cities to demand that the Chun Doo Hwan regime carry out its promised reforms.

A common resolution adopted by the rallies called for the release of all political prisoners, specifically: Lee Poo

Young, Chang Ki Pyo and Kim Keum Tae. The resolution also urged the Reagan Administration not to support the regime's Presidential candidate, General Roh Tai Woo, and asked for the discharge of South Korean Chief of Staff, General Park Hee Do, who reportedly made a veiled threat against opposition leader, Kim Dae Jung.

With traditional drums and cymbals, some 70 demonstrators gathered in front of the South Korean Consulate in midtown Manhattan, brandishing signs in Korean and English with slogans such as: "No more military dictatorship" and "U.S. Stop Supporting General Roh."

The rally was organized by the New York Coalition for Democracy in Korea, formed recently by Korean community and religious groups. Expressing disappointment in the low turnout, the Rev. Kyung Suk Soh of the Korean Church of Brooklyn, said: "People here tend to think the crisis in Korea is over but we have to put continuous pressure on the regime to get real democracy."

Amnesty International's report, "Political Imprisonment in the Republic of Korea" was said to be timed to coincide with discussions underway for the preparation of a new constitution.

Noting that human rights violations continue, despite prior constitutional safeguards, Amnesty International makes a number or recommendations to the South Korean Government, including:

*amend security laws to guarantee the rights of freedom of opinion, expression, association and peaceful assembly;

*end practices of incommunicado detention and interrogation to ensure protection against torture;

*guarantee the right to prompt and fair trial, access to counsel and investigation of all claims of ill-treatment;

*commute all death sentences and take steps to abolish the death penalty.

Detention and Ill-Treatment

Expressing concern over the continued detention and ill-treatment of a number of prisoners of conscience, Amnesty International presents case histories of 23 Koreans being held "solely for their non-violent opposition to the Government."

It cites the case of Kim Hyon Jang, a free-lance journalist, serving a life sentence on charges of involvement in an arson attack on the American Cultural Center in Pusan in March, 1982. Denying any knowledge of the attack, Mr.

Kim testified that he had been forced to make a false confession under torture.

There is also the case of the publisher, Lee Tae Bok, sentenced to life imprisonment for publishing "pro-communist books" such as translations of texts on economics and social sciences. During his trial, which began Oct. 29, 1981, Mr. Lee reportedly described being tied naked to a coffin and beaten, threatened with death, immersed in water, given electric shocks and beaten on the soles of his feet..."until I felt there was nothing I could do but agree to their charges."

Bomb in Basque City Kills 2

SAN SEBASTIAN, Spain, Aug. 15 (R ers) — Two people were killed whe.. a bomb exploded near their car in this northern Basque city today, the police said. They said the two victims were burned beyond recognition, and it was not immediately known whether they were police officers or civilians.

0146 乙 - 1b - 근기

법   무   부

보안이 0160-   14062   (503-9928)   1987. 10. 20.

수신 외무부장관

참조 미북 과장

제목 수감자 관계 문의에 대한 회신

　　　1. 미북 0160-39040 (87. 9. 28)과 관련임.

　　　2. 귀부에서 문의 하신 이태복등에 대한 수용 상황에 대하여 다음과
같이 회보 합니다.

　　　　　가. 이태복은 집시법위반 국가보안법위반 죄로 징역20년을 받아
복역중이며 관계 규정에 따라 가족등 접견이 허용되고 있고 건강상태 양호하며
수용생활 잘 적응 하고 있음.

　　　　　나. 김현장은 현주건조물방화 치상 국가보안법위반 등으로 징역
무기를 받아 복역중이며 관계 규정에 따라 가족등 접견이 허용 되고 있고 건강
상태 양호하며 수용 생활에 잘 적응하고 있음. 끝.

법   무   부   장

교정국장 전결

선 결			결재(홍람)	
수일시 1987.10.21				
처 리 과				

0147

관리 번호 87-2593

발 신 전 보

번 호: WAN-0311 일 시: 91022 19° 전보종별: _____

수 신: 주 아틀란타 (때사) 총영사

발 신: 장 관 (미북)

제 목: 수감자 관계문의 회신

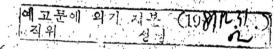

대 : 아틀란타 725-286

　　1. 대호 김근태·이태복은 집시법·국가보안법 위반죄로 징역5년
(김근태)·징역 20년(이태복)을 각각 선고받아 복역 중이며 김현장은
현주 건조물 (사람이 거주하고 있는 건물) 방화·치상 및 국가보안법 위반
등으로 무기징역을 선고받아 복역중임.

　　2. 상기 3인은 관계규정에 따라 가족 등 접견이 허용되고 있고,
건강상태 양호하며 수용생활에도 잘 적응하고 있음.

　　　　　　　　　　　　　　　　(미주국장　신두병)

0148　　보안통제

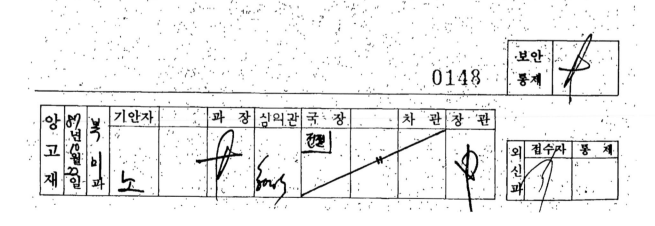

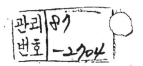

기 안 용 지

분류기호 문서번호	미북 202- ㅃㅂㄱ	(전화 :　　　　　)	시 행 상 특별취급	
보존기간	영구·준영구. 10. 5. 3. 1.		장　　　관	
수 신 처 보존기간				
시행일자	1987. 11. 4.			

보 조 기 관	국장	전　결	협 조 기 관		문 서 통 제
	심의관				
	과장				
기안책임자		노강일			

경 유			발 신 명 의	
수 신	법무부			
참 조	검찰국장			

제 목	수감자 법규 위반내용 문의

Amnesty International 미남북지부측은 국가보안법 및

집시법 위반죄로 수감중인 김근태와 이태복에 대한 집시법 위반 내용

상세를 문의하고 있는 바, 통보가능한 범위내에서 동 위반내용을 당부로

알려 주시기 바랍니다. 끝.

검토 88. 6. 30

검토필 (1) 87. 12. 11.

첨부 : 관련전보사본 1건.

0149

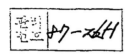

외 무 부

번 호 : ANW-0260   일 시 : 710301600   종 별 :

수 신 : 장 관(미북)

발 신 : 주 아틀란타 총영사

제 목 : 수감자관계

대 : WAN-0311

연 : 아틀란타725-286

글 10.30 당관은 AMNESTY INT. 의 미국남부지역담당 DIRECTOR 인 HERRICK 에게
대호 내용을 전달한데대하여 동인은 김근태와 이태복의 집시법위반 내용상세를 문의
하고있사오니 회시바람.끝.

(총영사김석현-국장)

예고 : 88.12.31일반

검토필 (1) 87.12.31.) 안

검토필 (1) 88 6 30.) 서

예고문에 의거 재분(1988 안)
직위   성 명

───

미주국   차관실   1 차보   정둔국   청와대   안 기. 법우부 (11/2)

PAGE   1   87.10.31 09:15
                                                외신 2과 등제관

                                                    0150

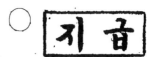

45393

기 안 용 지

분류기호 문서번호	미북 20002-	(전화 :)	시 행 상 특별취급	
보존기간	영구·준영구. 10.5.3.1.	장 관		
수 신 처 보존기간		ↄ		

시행일자 1987.11.6.

보조기관	국장	전 결	협조기관		문 서 통 제
	심의관				
	과장				

기안책임자 노광일

발 송 인

경 유 수 신 참 조	법무부장관	발신 명의	

제 목 수감자 관계문의

미국 시카고 Amnesty International 지부장 Reichard는

87.11.16.(월) 주 시카고 총영사 면담시 현재 복역중인 백옥관에 대해

문의할 예정이라 하는 바、동인의 범법사항、재판경과 및 현황 등

관계 자료를 지급 송부하여 주시기 바랍니다.

첨부: 관련 전문 사본 1부. 끝.

0151

1505-25(2-1) 일(1)갑
85. 9. 9. 승인

190㎜×268㎜ 인쇄용지 2급 60g /㎡
가 40-41 1987. 2. 13.

ㄴ

법   무   부

보안이 2002- 15102   (503-9928)   1987· 11· 11·

수신 외무부장관

참조 미북 과장

제목 수용자 관계 문의에 대한 회신

1· 미북 2002-45393 (87· 11· 6)와 관련임·

2· 귀부에서 문의하신 백옥광의 수형사항 및 근황을 다음과 같이 통보

합니다·

가· 백옥광은 국가보안법위반 등으로 입소하여 건강한 몸으로 수형

생활에 잘 적응 하고 있음·   끝

법   무   부   장

(교정심의관 대결)

선 결			결재 (관람)		
접수일시 1987.11.12.	번호				
처리과	27933				

87· 11· 16
보안이과- 김섬기· 건협의

0152

재리
번호 87-209

외 무 부 착 신 전

번 호 : CGW-1105   일 시 : 711041600   종 별 :

수 신 : 장관(미북)

발 신 : 주 시카고 총영사

제 목 : AMNESTY INTERNATIONAL면담자료 요청

당지 AMNESTY INTERNATIONAL U.S.A DR. RICHARD W. REICHARD 는 본직앞 서한을 등
해 한국내 정치범 문제 및 이와는 별도로 북역증인 백욱관 (오사카 청년 상공회의스
사무총장) 문제에 대해 관심을 표명하면서 면담을 요청, 본직은 11.16(월) 등인을
면담할 예정인바, 상기 백욱관의 범법 사항, 재판경과 및 현황등을 지급 회시 바람.
(총영사 이승곤-국장)
88.6.30일반

검토필 (87.12.31.)

예꾜문제 의기 재부 (198.6.30)
직위   성

미주국   차관실   1 차보   청와대   안 기   정문국~ 법무부 11/5

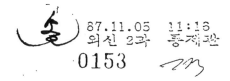

87.11.05 11:16
외신 2과 통제관
0153

발 신 전 보

번 호 : WCG-0###   입 시 : 71116 1130   전보종별 : 지 급

수 신 : 주   시카고   / 대사 / 총영사

발 신 : 장   관 (미북)

제 목 : 수감자 자료

         대 : CGW - 1105

       대호 백옥강은 간첩활동을 한 자로서 국가 보안법 위반으로
입소 하여 현재 건강한 몸으로 수형생활에 잘 적응하고 있음.

(미주국장 대리 송영식)

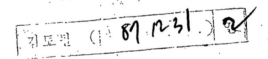

검토필 (87 12 31.)

예고문에 의거 재분류 (198. 6 .)
직위   성명

0154

보안 통제	#

		기안자		과 장	심의관	국 장		차 관	장 관			접수자	통 제
앙 고 재	87 년4 월 일	북 미 과	노			신결						외 신 과		

공 란

공 란

공 란

공 란

기 안 용 지

분류기호 문서번호	미북0160-440	(전화 :)	시 행 상 특별취급	
보존기간	영구·준영구. 10. 5. 3. 1.	장 관		
수 신 처 보존기간				문서통제
시행일자	87. 11. 21.			

보 조 기 관	국 장	전결	협 조 기 관		비밀문서 1987. 11. 23 통제실
	과 장				
기안책임자	노 광 일			발 송 인

| 경 유
수 신
참 조 | 주 아틀란타 총영사 | 발
신
명
의 | 발송
1987. 11. 23
외무부 |
| 제 목 | 수감자 문의 | | |

검토필 (87. 12. 3.)   인

대 : ANW - 0260

대호 김근태 및 이태복의 집시법 위반 관계자료를 별첨

송부합니다.

첨 부 : 상기자료 2건.   끝.

0159

김근태 반정부 활동사항

ㅇ 83.9.   민주화 운동 청년연합 (민청련)을 조직, 불온 유인물
민주화의 길을 90여회 발간, 배포하고 20여차례나 반정부
시위 활동을 선동

ㅇ 85.3.   민청련을 민족 민주혁명 이론에 따른 반제.반파쇼 투쟁을
표방하는 이적 단체화

ㅇ 85.1-85.6. 민청련 회원등에게 북괴 대남 혁명 노선에 동조하는
민족 민주주의 혁명이론 전파

ㅇ 노학 연대 투쟁(84.9-85.9), 신한 당사 점거 농성 (85.1.16)
서울 미문화원 점거 농성(85.5.23), 깃발 등 14종의 불온유인물
제작.배포(84.8-85.6)등을 배후 조정

ㅇ 김근태는 국가보안법 및 집시법 위반으로 1985.9.4. 검거(10.25. 기소)
86.9.23. 대법원에서 5년징역, 5년 자격정지 형이 확정 되었음.
 - 수용고도소 : 경주교도소
 - 건강상태   : 식사.운동.독서 등 수용생활 정상이며 건강 양호

0160

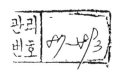

주 시 카 고 총 영 사 관

주시카고(정) 750-4089   1987. 11. 25.

수신 장관

참조 미주국장, 정보문화국장

제목 Amnesty International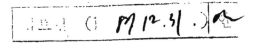

　　　당지 Amnesty International (USA) 의   Dr. Richard W.
Reichard 등 3명은 11.24. 본직을 방문, 한국내 정치범에 대한 동단체의 일반적
관심내용을 밝히고 백옥광, 이철, 강종헌에 대한 특별한 관심을 표명해 왔는 바,
동 요지를 아래 보고합니다.

1.   Amnesty International 측 표명 요지

　　가. 일반적 관심 표명

　　　　ㅇ 한국정부는 72년 및 80년의 헌법에서 양심, 언론, 표현, 집회,
　　　　　　결사의 자유를 보장하고 있음에도 불구하고 70년대 초반이후 비폭력
　　　　　　표현의 자유를 행사한 사람들이 체포 구속되었으며, 그후 대통령
　　　　　　특사등으로 상당수가 석방되었으나, 아직도 국가보안법 위반 및
　　　　　　스파이죄로 10년이상 수감중인 자가 있음.

　　　　ㅇ Amnesty International 은 지난 7월 전대통령에게 Telex
　　　　　　를 보내 문익환 목사등 양심수 석방 조치에 대해 환영의 뜻을
　　　　　　표하면서 더 많은 양심수들을 석방해 줄것을 촉구하였으며, 특히
　　　　　　이들중 상당수가 고문을 받은후 부당한 재판으로 유죄가 확정된
　　　　　　사실을 강조한 바 있음. 이에 앞서 지난 6월에는 모든 양심수를
　　　　　　석방하고 고문을 중지할 것과 구금자의 가족 및 변호사 방문등 조치를
　　　　　　취해 줄 것을 요청한바도 있음.

참고문에 의거 재분
직위　　　　　성

접수일시 1987.12

처리과

0161

o   양심수에 대한 취급은 UN 인권협약등의 기준이 최소한은 지켜져야
     하며 어떠한 경우라도 고문 또는 학대 (ill-treatment) 가
     있어서는 안됨.

o   80년 헌법은 물론 기타 형법등 관계법도 고문을 금지하는 규정이
     명시되어 있음에도 불구하고, 정치범에 대한 물고문, 전기고문,
     구타등을 통한 허위 자백 강요가 사실상 존재하고 있으며, 나아가서는
     변호사접근 저지등 재판절차가 공정성을 잃고 있음.

o   이상의 고문 및 학대로부터 보호하기 위하여 한국정부는 다음과 같은
     조치를 하여 줄것을 요청함.

     -    UN 고문 방지협약은 유보없이 비준할것

     -    격리수감 (incommunicado detention)   을 방지하기
          위한 법적 조치를 할것

     -    체포후 가족에게 구금자에 관한 정확한 정보를 알리고 가족과의
          면담이 허용되도록 할것

     -    변호사와의 적정한 협의가 가능하도록 할것

     -    구금장소 도착시 의료진찰을 받게하고 가족 또는 변호사에게
          알리도록 할 것

     -    구금시에는 즉시 공정한 사법절차를 받도록 할것

나. 한편 동인들은 백옥광, 이철, 강종헌의 사례를 언급 방북 및 학생선동으로
     구속되어 현재 11년째 복역중이라고 말하면서, 아국 정부의 사면 가능성등을
     타진함.

0162

2. 본직 표명 요지

    ○ 본직은 관심내용은 잘 알겠다고 전제하고 일단 서울에 보고는 하겠으나
       아국 사정에 대한 이해가 필요하다고 말함.

    ○ 아국은 기본적으로 인권을 존중하는 나라이며 사법절차도 선진국과
       대동소이하나 법제도는 각국 특유한 문화의 산물이므로 부분적으로
       다룰수는 있는 것이라고 말함.

    ○ 특히 버마사건, 땅굴등 그간의 북한의 만행을 설명하면서 남북한이
       군사적으로 냉엄하게 대치하고 있는 한반도의 현실을 이해할 필요가
       있음을 주지시킴.

    ○ 이와 같이 한국은 미국이 처한 여건과는 다른 점을 직시하여, 미국 사회의
       관점에서 다른 나라에 동일한 rule 을 적용할수는 없다는 점을
       설명하면서, 정치범 입장만 일방적으로 들을 것이 아니라 한국정부의
       입장에서도 이해하는 것이 사리를 판단하는데 좀더 객관적이고 도움이
       될 것임을 부연하였음.

    ○ 백옥광등에 대하여는 방북하여 밀봉교육을 받은후 입국하여 스파이활동을
       한자임을 설명하고, 현재 동인들이 모든 적정한 사법절차를 끝내고
       복역중이며 사면여부의 문제는 동인들의 복역태도 및 회개여부등 구체적
       정황을 보고 사법당국이 판단하여 조치할 문제라고 말함. 끝.

주 시 카 고 총 영

0163

주 미 대 사 관

미국(정)700-375   1987. 12. 4.

수 신 : 장 관
참 조 : 미주국장
제 목 : 사면청원

　　　당지　Amnesty Int'l　미 동부지부는 출판인 이태복의
사면을 청원하는 2,700명의 연서 청원서와 아국 인권에 관한 보고서를
당관에 송부하여 왔는바, 동 연서 청원서중 견본 1매와 보고서를 별첨송부
합니다.

　　　첨 부 : 청원서 및 보고서 1부. 끝.

　　　　　　　주　　　　미　　　　대

0164

AN APPEAL TO THE REPUBLIC OF KOREA FOR THE RELEASE OF LEE TAE-BOK

ATTENTION: KYUNG-WON KIM, THE REPUBLIC OF KOREA AMBASSADOR TO THE UNITED STATES

*We call for the immediate release of Lee Tae-bok, a prisoner of conscience, currently serving a 20-year sentence in Taejon prison.

*We believe that Lee Tae-bok is being held solely for his publication of books on econmics and the social sciences and has suffered severe injury as a result of torture.

*We stress the universal right of all individuals to freely express their opinion as described in the United Nations Convenant on Civil and Political Rights.

*We take no position on any government, political party, or ideology concerning the Republic of Korea.

WE URGE the government of the Republic of Korea respond to our appeal for the release of Lee Tae-bok for the sake of furthering human rights in the Republic of Korea.

Name	Address	Zip
Harold Tritt	P.O. Box 1600	20002
James Byrne	P.O. Box 2005	20002
Joseph Lenaghan	P.O Box 982	''
Kim Raeus	PO BOX 1386	''
Amy Belden	P.O. Box 232	''
Elizabeth Butcher	PO Box 2923	''
Mario Hernandez	PO BX 687	''
Pamela Jordan	P.O. Bx 2899	''
Lori O'Neil	P.O. Box 1208	''
Debbie Harison	P.O. Box 758	0165

POLITICAL IMPRISONMENT
IN THE
REPUBLIC OF KOREA

August 1987

THE REPUBLIC OF KOREA

AMNESTY INTERNATIONAL'S CONCERNS AND RECOMMENDATIONS

Contents   Page

I.   INTRODUCTION   1

II.   AMNESTY INTERNATIONAL'S CONCERNS   1

      A.   Background to Political Detention   1

      B.   The Arrest and Imprisonment of Prisoners   2
                of Conscience

      C.   Protection Against Torture and Ill-treatment   3

III   PRISONERS OF CONSCIENCE CASE HISTORIES   4

      A.   Introduction   4

      B.   Case Histories   4

IV.   RECOMMENDATIONS ON THE IMPLEMENTATION OF HUMAN RIGHTS   22
                SAFEGUARDS

      A.   Introduction   22

      B.   Recommendations   22

0167

THE REPUBLIC OF KOREA
AMNESTY INTERNATIONAL'S CONCERNS AND RECOMMENDATIONS

I. INTRODUCTION

Human rights violations became the focus of public protest in South Korea after student Park Chong-chol died under torture on January 14, 1987. A public outcry followed news of the death; two police officers were arrested and the government announced it would take measures to prevent torture. In May, it emerged that five, not two, police officers had been involved in torturing Park Chong-chol and that the two had been offered bribes to take full responsibility. The cover-up triggered a mass wave of street protests across the country.

After almost three weeks of these sometimes violent demonstrations Mr Roh Tae-woo, Chairman of the ruling Democratic Justice Party, announced on June 29 that the government would release political prisoners and guarantee human rights. Two days later, President Chun Doo-hwan endorsed the move.

II. AMNESTY INTERNATIONAL'S CONCERNS

A. Background to Political Detention

Since the early 1970s, thousands of people have been arrested and imprisoned in the Republic of Korea for the non-violent exercise of their right to freedom of expression and association despite guarantees of the right to freedom of conscience, speech, press, assembly and association under both the 1972 and 1980 Constitutions. Although a large number of them were released under presidential amnesties, some remain in detention after more than ten years. Some are serving long sentences after being found guilty of endangering national security and of helping or spying for the Democratic People's Republic of Korea (PDRK), North Korea. Of these, a few continue to be held in preventive detention after the expiration of their sentences. People who organize or take part in peaceful anti-government demonstrations are often arrested on the grounds that the demonstration was "likely to cause social unrest" and usually face sentences of one to four years' imprisonment. Another common accusation against government critics is that they "spread distorted or fabricated facts which might cause social unrest or impair public peace and order".

According to official statistics, over 3,400 people were charged with political offenses in 1986. Over 80% were students; others were workers, clergymen, Buddhist monks, members of political organizations, journalists and teachers. Most were released with a warning or detained for less than a month. About a third of them were charged with participating in illegal demonstrations or with pro-communist activities.

In the first part of 1987, mass arrests took place on the occasion of demonstrations on the streets or on university campuses to protest the use of torture and delays in democratic freedoms. The demonstrations were met with severe repression, in particular teargassing, arrests and beatings of detainees.

0168

The demonstrations often resulted in violence and Amnesty International was not able to establish whether the individuals arrested for participation in these demonstrations used or advocated violence.

At the beginning of July over 530 political prisoners were released and on July 10 the government restored the civil rights of 2,335 former political prisoners, including a group of students arrested in 1974 and others tried in 1980 with opposition politician Kim Dae-Jung, whom Amnesty International had adopted as prisoners of conscience at the time.

Amnesty International sent a telex to President Chun Doo-hwan on July 16 welcoming the releases, including that of Reverend Moon Ik-kwan, a prisoner of conscience arrested in May 1986, and urged him to release all those prisoners held solely for peacefully exercising their right to freedom of expression and association. In its telex, Amnesty International stressed that many of these prisoners had reportedly been tortured and convicted after unfair trials. It listed 34 prisoners of conscience whose early release was urged.

In an earlier telex dated June 30, 1987, Amnesty International had asked the President to order the release of all prisoners of conscience, to take all measures necessary to prevent torture and to order thorough and impartial investigations into allegations of torture, and to ensure that all detainees were allowed visits from relatives and lawyers.

B.   The Arrest and Imprisonment of Prisoners of Conscience

Over 530 convicted political prisoners were released on 6 and 8 July, including some whom Amnesty International had adopted as prisoners of conscience. But Amnesty International remains concerned that a number of prisoners convicted of "anti-state" activities were not among those set free. Many of these, whom Amnesty International believes are being detained for their peaceful opposition to the government, have been imprisoned for several years. They include people who published or owned books which the authorities regard as "subversive"; people who called for the reunification of Korea or organized groups who non-violently opposed the government; and people who were convicted of espionage for North Korea on the basis of confessions which they testified in court had been obtained under torture. Kim Keun-Tae, one of the cases highlighted below, was among those specifically excluded from the amnesty by the Justice Ministry. Sources inside the Republic of Korea suggest that as many as 900 political prisoners are currently imprisoned and believes that some of these may be prisoners of conscience, imprisoned solely for their non-violent opposition activities.

Amnesty International calls on the authorities to release all prisoners detained for the peaceful exercise of their rights of freedom of expression and association, regardless of their political views.

C.   Protection Against Torture and Ill-treatment

An official investigation into Park Chong-chol's death concluded that he died of suffocation after his head was repeatedly held under water and that bruises on his body were also caused by torture. The Minister of Home Affairs and the Head of the National Police resigned, taking responsibility for the death of the student. The President instructed his government to set up a "special commission for the protection of human rights" composed of figures from all walks of life to advise it on how to prevent the occurrence of human rights abuses. While Amnesty International welcomes the setting up of this Commission, the organization is concerned that the Commission will not report until the end of the year, after the proposed adoption of a new Constitution.

For many years Amnesty International has received evidence of the regular use of torture. The South Korean authorities have made a number of statements condemning torture, but its practice has continued and investigations into torture allegations made by political prisoners have rarely been conducted. The trial of police officers for the death of Park Chong-chol was the first prosecution of its kind. To be effective, it is not enough for safeguards against torture and ill-treatment to be written into laws and other regulations; they have to be implemented and monitored, and people should know their rights. When an Amnesty International delegation visited Korea in late May 1987, it found that many, inside and outside the government, agreed with this.

0170

III. PRISONERS OF CONSCIENCE CASE HISTORIES

A. Introduction

While Amnesty International welcomes the recent releases of political prisoners in the Republic of Korea, the organization is concerned that several prisoners of conscience, some of whom have been imprisoned for several years, remain in detention.

Given below are case histories of 23 prisoners of conscience, whom Amnesty International considers are being held solely for their non-violent opposition to the government. Appeals on behalf of these and further prisoners have been sent to the South Korean government and Amnesty International believes that several more prisoners are currently being held for their non-violent opposition activities.

B. Case Histories

Kang Jong-hon, Paik Ok-Kwan, Kim Chul-hyon, Lee Chul, Kang Jong-kon

On 22 November 1975 the Korean Central Intelligence Agency (KCIA) announced at a press conference that 21 people, many of them Koreans normally resident in Japan, had been arrested for allegedly infiltrating South Korean student groups under instructions from the Democratic People's Republic of Korea (DPRK), North Korea. In December another five Koreans from Japan were amongst 25 students arrested on the same charge. It was later reported that around 300 of the 400 Koreans from Japan who were at that time studying in the Republic of Korea had been interrogated by the KCIA (now called the National Agency for Security Planning) in connection with this case.

Paik Ok-kwan, aged 39, was the General Secretary of the Osaka Junior Chamber of Commerce at the time of his arrest; Kang Jong-hon, aged 36, was a medical student at Seoul National University; Kim Chul-hyon, aged 42, was a post-graduate student of Korean church history at Hankuk Theological Seminary in Seoul; Lee Chul, aged 39, was a post graduate student of politics and diplomacy at Korea University in Seoul; and Kang Jong-kon, aged 36, was a student of law at Korea University in Seoul.

At their trial, which started in March 1976, all were accused under the Anti-Communist and National Security laws of working for the North Korean government and infiltrating student groups to incite demonstrations against the South Korean government. Kang Jong-hon, Paik Ok-kwan, Lee Chul and Kim Chul-hyon were alleged to have visited the DPRK for espionage training; and Kang Jong-hon was alleged to have been recruited in Japan by a North Korean agent, to whom he allegedly reported about student demonstrations in the Republic of Korea.

Kang Jong-hon was sentenced to death in May 1976 on charges of visiting the DPRK, passing information on the Republic of Korea to North Korean agents in Japan and inciting students to demonstrate against the government. During his interrogation, he confessed to the charges. At his trial, however, he rejected his confession and said that he had made it under torture. He denied having visited the DPRK and his defense lawyer

0171

submitted an alibi in support of his denial. He also denied taking part in student demonstrations and witnesses testified for him. He admitted, however, to having been in contact with members of a pro-North Korean association of Koreans living in Japan called <u>Chochongnyon</u>, and of having read their books and seen their films on the DPRK. He also admitted having talked to them about his personal experience in the Republic of Korea and what he had read in South Korean newspapers, but he denied communicating national secrets. He also said that he had talked to students in the Republic of Korea about information on the DPRK he had acquired in Japan. His death sentence was commuted to life imprisonment in March 1982 and reduced to 20 years' imprisonment in August 1984 under presidential amnesties.

Paik Ok-kwan was sentenced to death in April 1976 on charges of being the ring-leader of a "campus spy-ring", having sent agents posing as students to the Republic of Korea and having visited the DPRK on three occasions to receive espionage training and instructions. His death sentence was commuted to life imprisonment by presidential amnesty in March 1982. Like most of the defendants in this case, he confirmed his confession before the district court. However, evidence that he was in Japan in 1972 and 1975, when the prosecution alleged that he was in the DPRK, which was collected by bar associations in Japan and presented to the court, was ruled inadmissible.

Kim Chul-hyon was sentenced to death in May 1976 on charges of espionage and instigating anti-government demonstrations. Amnesty International believes that he was convicted on the basis of a confession allegedly made under torture and without corroborative evidence of guilt. He was not allowed to see his lawyer until after the date of the trial was announced. He did not claim to have been tortured but at his trial he appeared abnormally withdrawn, and after being challenged by co-defendants and defense witnesses he admitted to having invented parts of his confession. His death sentence was commuted to life in August 1981 and reduced to 20 years' imprisonment under presidential amnesties.

Lee Chul was sentenced to death on charges of travelling twice to the DPRK, of engaging in espionage activities for the DPRK and of producing and disseminating pamphlets criticizing the South Korean government. He confessed to the charges during the 40 days in which he was held incommunicado and interrogated. He admitted that he was guilty during the trial, but on appeal he denied the charges and said he had confessed under torture and threats that members of his family and fellow-students would also be tortured. Evidence collected by the Tokyo Bar Association, which concluded that a series of alibis showed he was innocent, was submitted in support of his appeal. However, his appeal was rejected by the Seoul High Court on the grounds that he had admitted guilt before the court of first instance.

Kang Jong-kon was charged with reporting on student demonstrations to North Korean agents in Japan and recruiting student sympathizers on behalf of the DPRK, and was sentenced to five years' imprisonment. Since completing his sentence in February 1981 he has been held under the Public Security Law with a series of two-year preventive custody orders. Amnesty International believes he has continued to be detained after the

0172

expiration of his sentence because he refused to sign a statement
repudiating the "pro-communist' views he allegedly held at the time of his
arrest. In 1983 he brought a court case against the Ministry of Justice
(which is responsible for issuing the order) challenging the validity of the
preventive custody order. His case was turned down by the Appeal Court
in October 1983. In March 1984 the Supreme Court overturned that
decision and returned the case to the Appeal Court, saying that the
Ministry of Justice's case for continuing to detain Kang Jong-kon did not
show "a clear danger that he would repeat the offense". In December 1984
the Appeal Court invalidated the order, but the Minister of Justice
appealed against its ruling and has continued to renew the preventive
custody order. In March 1987 Kang Jong-kon and another prisoner of
conscience went on hunger-strike in protest at their continued detention
in preventive custody.

Amnesty International is concerned by reports that the defendants in this
case were tortured into making confessions of "pro-communist" activities,
which were used in court to secure their convictions, and that there are
not sufficient grounds for accepting the court's rulings that they are
guilty of espionage. AI urged the South Korean government to allow a fair
and open retrial to consider additional evidence which had become
available for some of the defendants. After careful consideration AI
concluded that these prisoners were detained for the non-violent exercise
of their right to freedom of expression and association because they
openly discussed political matters and associated with others in the
Republic of Korea who were actively involved in criticizing the South
Korean government and its policies.

Kim Hyon-jang

Kim Hyon-jang, a freelance journalist and human rights activist, is
serving a life sentence in Pusan Prison in the south-east of the Republic
of Korea. He was sentenced to death by the courts but the sentence was
commuted to life imprisonment by presidential amnesty in March 1983. Kim
Hyong-jang was accused of involvement in an arson attack on the
American Cultural Center in Pusan in March 1982, in which one student
who was using the Center's library died. Leaflets found near the American
Cultural Center after the attack criticized the US political and economic
support for the South Korean government and called for the removal of US
troops from the Republic of Korea. AI has investigated this charge in
detail and believes that Kim Hyon-jang was in fact arrested because of
his known non-violent criticism of the South Korean government,
particularly his criticisms of the government's role in the May 1980
Kwangju disturbances.

At the time of the attack, Kim Hyong-jang was in hiding in the Catholic
Education Center in Wonju where he had been for almost two years to
avoid arrest for his role in compiling and circulating documents on the
death of civilians during the Kwangju disturbances in May 1980 <1>. After

<1> On 18 May 1980 a student demonstration protesting
against the imposition of nationwide martial law the day
before and mass arrests ended in considerable violence when

0173

the attack, those directly implicated sought refuge at the Center where they were encouraged to surrender to the authorities. Kim Hyon-jang surrendered a few days later. On 29 April he was charged under the National Security Law with planning the arson attack and with carrying out other pro-communist activities.

At the trial, which began in June 1982, Moon Pu-shik, the leading participant in the arson attack, and a number of other defendants admitted the charge of arson but denied all charges of "pro-communist" acts. Kim Hyon-jang, supported by Moon Pu-shik, totally denied any knowledge of, or involvement in, the arson attack. Kim Hyon-jang testified that he had been forced under torture to make a false confession admitting his involvement. He said : "They tied my hands behind my back and poured mustard into my nose. This was done a total of six times. Then I wrote what they told me to." The prosecution's evidence that he was involved in the incident reportedly rested on an alleged meeting between himself and Moon Pu-shik in 1981, when, according to the prosecution, the attack was planned. However, both men testified that months before the attack took place, Kim Hyong-jang had forcefully tried to dissuade Moon Pu-shik from plans to attack the Cultural Center. To Amnesty International's knowledge no evidence other than Kim Hyong-jang's confession was presented in support of the charge that he had incited others to commit arson.

A large part of the trial proceedings was devoted to establishing that the defendants, including Kim Hyon-jang, were communists, which they denied. Kim Hyon-jang was accused of speaking at "consciousness-raising" seminars organized by the Catholic Education Center.

Kim Hyon-jang is said to have been arrested on political charges in 1977, but AI has no details of the case. In 1979 he was reportedly working with the Kwangju Dismissed Students Association which aimed to help students dismissed from college or university for political reasons. Possibly he was also working with a self-help group for farmers. In the late 1970's Kim Hyong-jang wrote and article for the magazine Dialogue, published by the Korea Christian Academy, about a young man executed for killing a government official during the clearance of an illegal slum area..He also wrote an article on "prostitution tourism" on Cheju Island for the magazine Deeper Roots.

---

paratroopers brutally dispersed the demonstrators. In the following days clashes between troops and students continued. By 21 May, the demonstrators were virtually in control of the city, but on 27 May troops retook the city with great brutality. Official statistics indicate that around 200 people were killed. However, reports from other sources put the figure of civilian dead at at least 1,200.

0174

Kim Keun-tae

Kim Keun-Tae, the founding chairman of the National Youth Alliance for Democracy (NYAD) is serving a five year prison sentence in Kyongju prison on charges of having organized or participated in a series of meetings and demonstrations "feared to cause social unrest" and of promoting North Korean propaganda. AI has adopted him as a prisoner of conscience and is also concerned about his claims that he was tortured.

Kim Keun-tae, now aged 40, graduated in economics from Seoul National University where he is reported to have been very actively involved in organizing support for Kim Dae-jung, the opposition candidate in the April 1971 presidential elections. Wanted by the authorities for his anti-government activities, he went into hiding for most of the rest of the decade, working in factories and with the Urban Industrial Mission, a protestant group which helps factory workers to defend their rights.

The NYAD was set up in September 1983. Its objectives were to bring about the democratization of politics in the Republic of Korea, the reunification of North and South Korea, an independent economy "from which corruption and gross inequality in the distribution of wealth have been eliminated" and an independent education system and culture.

To promote its objectives the NYAD distributed leaflets and a journal, The Road to Democratization, and organized and took part in demonstrations. On several occasions members of the Alliance were arrested for their peaceful activities in support of the Alliance's objectives. Kim Keun-tae himself is said to have served seven sentences in police custody for "spreading groundless rumors". In May 1985 for example, he was arrested and sentenced to 10 days' police detention after the Alliance organized a series of demonstrations calling on the government to give a full account of the quelling of the insurrection in Kwangju in 1980 in which a large number of civilians were killed.

Kim Keun-tae was arrested on 4 September 1985 and interrogated at the headquarters of the Anti-Communist Bureau of the National Police in Namyoung-dong, in Seoul, until his transfer to the Seoul prosecutor's office on 26 September. He was indicted on 25 October and his trial started on 9 December. On 6 March he was sentenced to seven years' imprisonment. His sentence was reduced to five years on appeal.

On 26 September, as he was being taken for the first time to the prosecutor's office, Kim Keun-tae met his wife by chance and told her that he had been tortured during interrogation. In October 1985 his lawyers applied twice for a court order to have him examined by a judge and a doctor to document evidence of torture. The court ruled that there was no need for such an examination, without making public the grounds for this ruling. On 7 November the court granted a prosecution request to ban Kim Keun-tae from meeting his relatives for fear that he would ask them to remove evidence. When the Supreme Prosecutor's office issued a statement on its investigation into reports of his torture, they found that "there was no sign of torture in his walk or other physical and mental (?) movements", but there was no indication that a thorough investigation had been conducted and no details were given about the date or means of

0175

the investigation or whether it included a medical examination. Kim Keun-tae was not allowed to see his lawyers until 10 December, 10 days before the start of his trial. Prison guards reportedly prevented Kim Keun-tae from giving them the scab he had preserved as evidence of injuries inflicted under torture.

At his trial, Kim Keun-tae gave a long testimony in which he claimed to have been tortured during his interrogation and complained of a number of illegalities, including his detention without an arrest warrant for about 36 hours. He also complained that his letters to the prosecution authorities and the court, requesting an investigation into his treatment during interrogation, had remained unanswered, as had his request to the court for a medical examination.

He described how he had been tortured with electric shocks on many occasions between 4 and 20 September. Each torture session lasted about five hours. He said he was given no food on the days of torture, and found it impossible to eat after 13 September because of the torture. In his testimony he said : "When I think about what happened in the torture cell, I tremble with anger and humiliation. The police forced me to surrender. They repeatedly said they were going to break me and that is exactly what they did...By 20 September I became covered all over with wounds and couldn't stand any more. At last, on 25 September, I gave in to them. In groups they beat me up and asked me to beg for my life by crawling on the floor naked. I did what I was told. I wrote in the interrogation records as they demanded."

The charges against him included organizing and participating in meetings such as the Alliance's third general assembly where speeches were made calling for an end to the "military dictatorship" and for the release of political prisoners, and of making speeches critical of the authorities in terms similar to those used by the Democratic People's Republic of Korea (DPRK), North Korea, in its propaganda against the Republic of Korea. He was also charged with buying a book entitled Capitalism : Yesterday and Today, by British author Maurice Dobb, which the prosecution argued "advanced the interests of the DPRK".

In August 1986, Kim Keun-tae and 17 student prisoners in Kyongju prison were reportedly seriously beaten by prison officers. He was held at the time in a very small isolation cell. According to reports, the students were beaten after protesting about his treatment and Kim was later beaten when he complained to the prison authorities of the ill-treatment of the students. He was later visited by his wife who reported that his face was swollen and bruised and that there was considerable bruising on his body. He is said to be in poor health and is suffering from headaches, digestion problems and anal bleeding.

Kim Yong

Kim Yong was a student in the philosophy department of Pusan National University when he was arrested on 19 May 1980, for distributing leaflets criticizing the extension of martial law two days earlier. Hundreds of students were detained at that time on similar grounds. Amnesty International received reports that he was tortured during the first two

0176

months of his detention. In August 1980 he was sentenced to three years' imprisonment, but this was later reduced to two years.

At an appeal court hearing in November 1980, Kim Yong was offered the choice between serving the prison sentence or being conscripted into the military. He chose to do his military service. In the second half of 1981 Kim Yong learned of the arrest of a number of his friends in the Purim (Pusan Good Books Association) case <2> and that he was wanted in connection with it. According to reports received by Amnesty International, Kim Yong was on guard duty on 28 October 1981 when believing that military intelligence officers had come to arrest him, he decided to desert, but after four days he gave himself up to the authorities. A court martial sentenced Kim Yong to ten years' imprisonment on charges of praising and supporting the Democratic People's Republic of Korea (DPRK), North Korea, and of deserting the army. His appeal against this sentence was rejected. He is currently detained in Taegu Prison.

Amnesty International received reports that during his interrogation by the military police and military intelligence in 1981 Kim Yong was tortured to make him admit to having praised the North Korean leader Kim Il-sung and the more equal distribution of wealth under communism. Amnesty International is concerned at these reports and that his confession was used to convict him of the charges, undermining the fairness of his trial.

Amnesty International does not contest the authorities right to imprison Kim Yong for desertion but it is concerned that his conviction relates largely to his holding non-violent political views and to that extent Amnesty International considers him to be a prisoner of conscience. The maximum sentence under Article 28.3 of the Military Penal Code, on desertion of a guard post by a sentry, is two years' imprisonment. Although Amnesty International does not know the length of the sentence imposed on Kim Yong for desertion, it is very likely that he has now finished serving this sentence and is currently serving the sentence imposed on him under the National Security Law for his political views and activities. Amnesty International is now calling for his immediate and unconditional release.

Lee Tae-bok

Lee Tae-bok, a publisher, has been detained since 1981 for publishing "pro-communist" books such as translations of texts on economics and social sciences. He was originally sentenced to life imprisonment but the

---

<2> In this case, sixteen people, who were said to have met to discuss social and political issues and to have organized study groups to help workers demand their rights, were charged with activities aimed at overthrowing the government and bring about a communist society. Amnesty International considered them to be prisoners of conscience. They have all now been released.

0177

sentence was later reduced under a presidential amnesty to 20 years' imprisonment. During his trial he testified that he had been tortured to force him to confess to the accusations against him. Amnesty International has adopted him as a prisoner of conscience.

After graduating from Kukmin University in the mid-1970s, Lee Tae-bok, now 36 years old, reportedly worked for two years in a factory before setting up a small publishing company, called Kwangminsa. He was also involved in the work of the Ileungsadan Academy, which organized lectures and various activities aimed at raising students' and young people's awareness of the Republic of Korea's social, political and economic problems.

Lee Tae-bok was taken away by police on 10 June 1981, although the warrant for his arrest was not issued until 31 July. During these seven weeks of illegal detention he was reportedly held and interrogated at the Anti-Communist Bureau of the National Police in Namyoung-dong, Seoul. He was transferred to Seoul Detention Center in Sudaemoon in the first week of August when his interrogation by a public prosecutor started. On 8 September, he was charged under the National Security Law (NSL) with organizing two "anti-state" groups, the Democratic Students' Federation (DSF) and the Democratic Labor Federation (DLF), and of publishing books which the authorities regarded as pro-communist, in an "attempt to create unrest and prepare for a communist revolution". He was not allowed access to his relatives until mid-September, more than three months after his arrest, and he did not see a lawyer appointed by his family until some time in October.

Lee Tae-bok's trial started on 29 October 1981, together with 27 other defendants, including students, trade unionists and church workers, who faced charges of belonging to the same two groups, the DSF and the DLF. Among the books which were used by the prosecution as evidence that Lee Tae-bok disseminated communist ideas and tried to inspire students and workers to overthrow the government, were several translations of books by foreign authors such as Studies in the Development of Communism by Maurice Dobb, and works by G.D.H. Cole, Herbert Marcuse and Christopher Hill. Some of these books were said to be standard reading recommended by university professors in the Republic of Korea to their students, and Lee Tae-bok was said to have received official permission for their publication.

In the course of his trial, Lee Tae-bok reportedly described being tied naked to a coffin and beaten, threatened with death, immersed in water, given electric shocks, and beaten on the soles of his feet. Often, he said, the torture would be repeated and he would lose consciousness. Finally, he said : "...because nothing could be gained by continued denial, I felt there was nothing I could do but agree to their charges..."

On 22 January 1982, Lee Tae-bok was sentenced to life imprisonment by Seoul District Criminal Court. The prosecution had earlier asked for the death penalty. (His co-defendants received prison sentences ranging from one to ten years : all have now been released, either on expiration of their sentences or under presidential amnesties). Lee Tae-bok's life

0178

sentence was reduced to 20 years' imprisonment under a presidential amnesty, on 12 August 1983.

Lee Tae-bok is currently detained in Taejon Prison. He is said to have suffered injury to his genitals during torture and recent reports state that he has a testicular infection with genital pain and haematuria. He also suffers from hemorrhoids. Although he had received permission earlier this year for hospital examination following which some medication was prescribed, there is concern that he may still be in ill-health.

Yu Sang-dok

On 4 September 1986, the Agency for National Security Planning announced that it had arrested four people, including Yu Sang-dok, under the National Security Law on suspicion of being members of a "spy ring" working for the Democratic People's Republic of Korea (DPRK), North Korea. The alleged leader of the "spy ring", Professor Lee Pyong-sol, aged 48 and a professor of geography at Seoul National University, was accused of having incited campus and labor unrest and of organizing four underground cells among students, workers and teachers for the purpose of collecting information to give to North Korea agents and to carry out activities benefiting the DPRK. On 24 January 1987, he was sentenced to 15 years' imprisonment by the Seoul District Court, reduced on appeal to 12 years' imprisonment on 28 May 1987.

Yu Sang-dok, aged 37, was a high-school teacher and the chairperson of the Young Men's Christian Association's Council for the Realization of Democratic Education (CRDE).

The YMCA Council for the Realization of Democratic Education is working towards changes in the South Korean educational system. It has a network of branches and members nationwide, holds seminars for teachers, publishes a bulletin entitled Democratic Education five times a year, as well as the monthly Teachers' Newspaper, which has a circulation of around 5,000. It also organizes groups of parents interested in education issues. On 10 May 1986 the YMCA issued a "Declaration for the Democratization of Education", said to be 86 pages long, which called for, amongst other things, (1) a guarantee in the country's Constitution of the political independence of the educational system; (2) the right of teachers, parents and students to be involved in decisions regarding education; (3) the right for teachers to form independent teachers' organizations; and (4) an end to obligatory non-academic activities for students and teachers. The Declaration was signed by over 920 primary and secondary school teachers in various cities. A number of them were subsequently arrested and prosecuted; others who refused to withdraw their signatures were reportedly forced to resign from their jobs, given pay cuts, transferred to other schools, or given warnings.

Yu Sang-dok is also a practicing member of the Presbyterian Church of the Republic of Korea (PROK) and graduated from the PROK's Mission and Education Center. He has been active in the Young Men's Christian Association teachers' movement since 1981, and under its auspices organized the CRDE. He was forced to resign from his job at a high

0179

school in Seoul in 1983, apparently because of his involvement in the CRDE.

Yu Sang-dok was taken into custody by the Agency for National Security Planning (ANSP) on 15 July 1986. He was detained illegally until 28 July when a warrant of arrest was issued against him. It is believed that he was held in an ANSP facility in Namean, Seoul, until 14 August when he was transferred to Yongdungpo Detention Center. To Amnesty International's knowledge, he was not allowed to see his relatives or a lawyer during his interrogation. When his wife visited him on 11 September, he told her that he had been subjected to physical and mental torture to make him confess that he knew that Professor Lee Pyong-sol was a spy for the DPRK.

In September 1986, reports were received that Yu Sang-dok went on hunger-strike for over 13 days to demand that the Director of the ANSP and the Secretary of the Ministry of Education apologize for the "distorted reporting" of his case and that of the others arrested with him.

Yu Sang-dok was indicted on 12 September 1986. He was charged under Articles 7(1) and 7(5) of the NSL with praising the DPRK and under Article 8(1) with communicating with a North Korean agent. The first charge refers to his possessing some books; the second to his having been in contact with Professor Lee Pyong-sol, who was accused of providing information on the Republic of Korea to the DPRK.

Amnesty International has been informed that Yu Sang-dok had known Professor Lee Pyong-sol while he was a student at Seoul National University, but had not been in contact with him for over ten years until September 1984, when he approached him to discuss his plans to go to Japan to study law. Professor Lee Pyong-sol had received his degree in Japan and knew the Japanese university system well. In March 1985 Professor Lee Pyong-sol introduced Yu Sang-dok to a visiting Japanese professor, but by this time, Yu Sang-dok had reportedly decided not to go to Japan. On another occasion, Lee Pyong-sol and Yu Sang-dok met in a coffee shop; Professor Lee told Yu Sang-dok that he was going to Japan and asked if there was anything he could do for him while he was there. Yu Sang-dok asked Professor Lee to buy him books published by a third world education center in Tokyo but he did not specify which ones. Professor Lee brought him back several books which included Education for National Liberation, How To Educate Korean Residents in Japan, What An Agricultural Country Should Be Like, and The Education Theory About Koreans Resident in Japan. Some of these books had been published by Chochongnyon, the pro-North Korean General Federation of Korean Residents in Japan, and others referred to the situation on the DPRK in their text.

During Yu Sang-dok's trial the prosecutor argued that Yu Sang-dok had ordered these books to praise the DPRK. The prosecution further argued that Yu Sang-dok had agreed with comments favorable to the DPRK made to him by Professor Lee Pyong-sol during their conversation. Yu Sang-dok admitted in court that they had discussed aerial photos of North Korean land reclamation work, but denied having praised the DPRK. Yu Sang-dok also claimed that other evidence of him having praised the DPRK

0180

had been obtained from him by torture when he was beaten with a wooden stick, threatened with death and deprived of sleep.

The prosecution did not have evidence that Yu Sang-dok knew Professor Lee Pyong-sol to be working for the DPRK, but argued that he should have been alerted by Professor Lee's keenness to help him study in Japan and that he should have been aware that Chochongnyon tries to attract Korean students to Japan to train them as spies <3>. On 24 January 1987 the Seoul District Court found Yu Sang-dok guilty of the charges and sentenced him to three years' imprisonment. On 28 May 1987 his sentence was reduced to two years' imprisonment by Seoul High Court.

Amnesty International believes that Yu Sang-dok is detained for the peaceful exercise of his right to freedom of opinion and expression and is calling for his immediate and unconditional release. It is also concerned about reports that he was tortured and urges the South Korean authorities to initiate an immediate and impartial investigation into the allegations that Yu Sang-dok was tortured and requests that the result of the investigation be made available to it.

Soh Sung, Soh Joon-shik

Soh Sung was a post-graduate student in sociology at Seoul National University and his brother, Soh Joon-shik, was a law student at Seoul National University when they were arrested in April 1971. The brothers were born in Japan and normally resided there. They were tried on charges of spying for the Democratic People's Republic of Korea (DPRK), North Korea, and instigating anti-government student demonstrations under North Korean instruction. Both were also charged with travelling to DPRK. Soh Sung was sentenced to death by the Seoul District Court, but his sentence was reduced to life imprisonment on appeal. Soh Joon-shik was sentenced to 15 years' imprisonment, reduced to seven years' on appeal, but he has continued to be detained after the expiration of his sentence in May 1978 under a series of preventive custody orders.

Travel of nationals of the Republic of Korea to the DPRK is prohibited and punishable under the National Security Law. Amnesty International considers that the mere fact of traveling to the DPRK without evidence either of espionage activities or of the use or advocacy of violence cannot justify imprisonment.

During his trial, Soh Sung admitted visiting the DPRK but denied carrying out espionage activities or inciting students to demonstrate against the government. He explained that as a second-generation Korean living in Japan his search for national identity led him to be interested in both the Democratic People's Republic of Korea and the Republic of Korea, and

---

<3> Professor Lee Pyong-sol is said to have confessed to the charges against him, saying that he had not visited the DPRK, but had communicated periodically with Chochongnyon. Amnesty International is seeking further information on the case of Lee Pyong-sol to ascertain whether he is a prisoner of conscience and whether he was given a fair trial.

0181

that his studies at a South Korean university and his visits to the DPRK were aimed at understanding the political realities in both countries which he felt should be reunified by peaceful means.

Soh Sung's trial was delayed because he needed hospital treatment for severe burns to 15 per cent of his body after trying to commit suicide, reportedly to avoid further torture during his interrogation. In court, he claimed to have written a confession under torture, in which he admitted having collected and transmitted national secrets of the Republic of Korea to the DPRK and having organized underground student Communist groups in the Republic of Korea. He is said to have signed his confession about six weeks later, while in the hospital recovering from his suicide attempt, by affixing the imprint of his big toe. To the district court judges and when appealing against his conviction, Soh Sung explained that he attempted suicide as he "could not endure the mental and physical pains during interrogation."

In his appeal to the Supreme Court, dated 31 January 1983, he wrote "... the prosecutor's indictment resulted from my involuntary statement, forced by torture, and from the investigation which was deceptively done under unsatisfactory physical and psychological conditions..." During an interview, which however was not private, Soh Sung told an Amnesty International delegate who had come to observe the hearing of his appeal, that he had been beaten with clubs during his interrogation. In a response to a query, the Amnesty International observer was informed by the prosecution that it had not conducted an investigation into the prisoner's claims that a confession had been illegally obtained from him. The court accepted Soh Sung's confession as primary evidence of his guilt, although there are no indications that they conducted a thorough and impartial investigation to establish its validity.

In July 1985, Amnesty International received reports that, following a protest against conditions at Taejon Prison, Soh Sun was tied with rope, hung from the ceiling and beaten. After this incident, he was reportedly detained in a "punishment cell" measuring less that three by six feet with only a small air vent and no windows.

Amnesty International believes that Soh Sung's brother, Soh Joon-shik, was also wrongly convicted of espionage after an unfair trial on the basis of a confession allegedly made under torture and without corroborative evidence of guilt, and that he was in fact imprisoned because of his non-violent political views. Since the expiration of his sentence in May 1978, Soh Joon-shik has been detained in preventive custody under the Public Security Law. Under this law, "any person with a strong possibility of committing a crime again" may be held in preventive custody. The term of detention is two years, renewable by the Minister of Justice.

Amnesty International believes that the reason for Soh Joon-shik's continued detention is his refusal to sign a declaration of conversion to anti-Communism. Soh Joon-shik reportedly claimed that while serving his sentence, he was ill-treated and restrictions were imposed on his rights to receive visitors, exercise, read, or write letters, in an attempt to make him sign such a declaration. In 1974 he stated in a conversation with a member of the Japanese Diet who visited him in prison that he had been

0182

tortured since his conviction. He claimed that he had been stripped
naked and tied up in the open air on a cold winter day while water was
thrown over him, and that prison staff trampled on his stomach after he
had been forced to drink four kettles of water.

On 11 June 1982 Soh Joon-shik filed an administrative appeal against the
third preventative detention order imposed on him. In a written
statement to the Seoul High Court, the Ministry of Justice reportedly
argued that Soh Joon-shik's continued detention under the Public Security
Law was justified because he had refused to convert to anti-Communism
and had incited other prisoners to go on hunger-strike in protest against
their detention, and that he was therefore likely to commit an offense
similar to that of which he was originally convicted. On 30 May 1983 the
Seoul High Court rejected Soh Joon-shik's appeal. In May 1986 the
preventive custody order against Soh Joon-shik was renewed for a further
two years.

In March and April 1987 Soh Joon-shik staged a 51 day hunger-strike in
protest at his continued detention in preventive custody. He is held in
Chongju Detention Center.

Park Hyon-su

Park Hyon-su, a student of Yonsei University and a member of its student
council, was arrested in June 1986 after anti-government leaflets were
found on high-school grounds in Seoul or received at home by high-school
students. The authorities had announced that they were looking for
members of the student councils of Yonsei and Seoul National Universities
in Seoul whom they held responsible for distributing the leaflets and
letters. Park Hyon-su was accused of sending about 2,000 letters to
students of middle and high schools across the Republic of Korea. He was
sentenced on 10 December 1986 to 18 months' imprisonment for mailing
"impure" letters to high-school students in an attempt to foment "class
struggle".

The Korea Herald reported that the letters contained such statements as
"Your friend's daddy is a company president who has a good sedan. Your
father is a manual worker at a construction site. What a contrast! Isn't
it absurd to say that communism is simply bad?"

The leaflets were said to describe the objectives of the university student
councils and to explain their views on issues such as the revision of the
Constitution, the role of the United States in the division of the Korean
peninsula after World War II as well as the criticisms of "anti-Communist
education" given in schools.

Amnesty International is concerned that Park Hyon-su is detained for his
peaceful criticism of the government of the Republic of Korea and
considers him to be a prisoner of conscience.

0183

Koh Song-guk, Lee Pom, Kim Sang-bok, Koh Kyong-dae, Park Sung-in

These five men were among twelve people taken into custody on 25 March 1986 following a series of raids by South Korean police on bookstores around university campuses in Seoul in which large numbers of books were seized. The twelve were reportedly charged with violating the National Security Law by publishing and distributing "subversive" books and by giving ideological support to "radical" student activities.

Three of those arrested were prominent in unlicensed publication groups: Koh Song-guk, a 28 year old part time lecturer in diplomacy at Korea University, was the chairman of the Tasan Kihwoek company. Koh Kyong-dae, a 28 year old graduate of Yonsei University, was chairman of the Polm Kihwoek company. Lee Pom, who had previously been detained for political reasons in 1978 and 1979, was the 28 year old president of the Paeksan Sodang publication company at the time of his arrest. Kim Sang-bok, aged 30, was the former head of the cultural section of the Ecumenical Youth Council. No personal details are known about Park Sung-in.

Following their arrest, the twelve men were taken to the Anti Communist Bureau of the National Police in Seoul. Official detention notices were reportedly not issued until 29 March, and did not reach relatives until 1 April. Lee Pom was denied family visits for 10 days, while others were allowed to see their relatives at the beginning of April. The prisoners' relatives alleged that the detainees were tortured by the police in order to force them to "confess" to the charges made against them and that they showed signs of having been seriously ill-treated. The sister of Koh Kyong-dae has reportedly stated that when she visited him on 29 March he "was unable to walk properly" because of ill-treatment inflicted on him. Kim Sang-bok is reported to have told a relative in early April that he had been subjected to torture by electric shock. During this visit his eyes were said to have been dazed and had difficulty focusing. He also had apparent difficulty in walking and keeping his balance.

On 27 September 1986, the Seoul District Criminal Court sentenced ten of the prisoners to terms of imprisonment ranging between three months to four years. In January 1987 the Seoul High Court reduced some of the sentences. AI has adopted these five men as prisoners of conscience and is urging the authorities to investigate the allegations of torture.

0184

Im Kyu-yong, Im Tong-kyu, Kim Chong-sam, Noh Jae-chang

Im Kyu-yong, Im Tong-kyu, Kim Chong-sam, and Noh Jae-chang were
arrested in 1979 and convicted under the Anti-Communist Law and the
National Security Law of membership in an "anti-state" organization called
the Preparatory Committee of the South Korean National Liberation Front
(SKNLF). The prosecution claimed it was an underground group planning
to "establish a Communist regime through a violent anti-government
struggle." They were arrested at a time of growing opposition to the
government of President Park Chung-hee and widespread dissatisfaction
with the domestic economic situation. More that 100 people were detained
for investigation in connection with this case, and 73 were brought to
trial in December 1979. Fourteen of them are still detained.

Kim Chong-sam, the son of a farmer, is a graduate in veterinary medicine.
As a student he had been active in an organization which provided
education services and seasonal labor to farmers. From 1976 onwards, he
worked in the research department of the Catholic Farmers' Association, of
which, at the time of his arrest, he was the Director. He was associated
with research studies which concluded that the impoverishment of farmers
resulted from government controls on the price of agricultural products
and with studies pointing out the health hazards of working with
pesticides and chemical fertilizers. He was sentenced to 15 years'
imprisonment. In May 1986 he went on a 17 day hunger-strike in protest
at the conditions of detention in Chonju Prison. In early June his sister,
who had visited him in prison, said he was in a weak condition, that he
had suffered damage to his throat as a result of force-feeding, and that
his body was covered with bruises, probably sustained when he resisted
force-feeding. He went on another hunger-strike in August 1986 in
protest at his ill-treatment following his first protest. He is now held in
Taegu Prison and is said to suffer from a heart complaint for which he is
taking medication.

Im Tong-kyu is serving two sentences of life imprisonment. Originally
from a farming family near Kwangju, he had been actively involved, as a
student at Seoul National University, in organizing students' labor
services to farmers. At the time of his arrest he was working in the
Labor Research Institute of Korea University in Seoul. His first life
sentence was imposed in October 1979 for allegedly trying to set up a
group working towards a Communist revolution in the Republic of Korea
and carrying out espionage activities for the Democratic Peoples' Republic
of Korea. He was accused of "having attempted to instill anti-government
and pro-Communist ideas among intellectuals through the publication of
an agricultural magazine and lecture meetings, and of helping a journalist
from Japan to meet the wife of poet Kim Chi-ha, then in prison, thereby
assisting him to write articles benefiting the DPRK." A few days after his
first life sentence was imposed, the authorities announced that he was
being interrogated in connection with the SKNLF; he was later given
another life sentence in connection with this case. Im Tong-kyu is now
held in Taejon Prison.

Noh Jae-chang, also a farmer's son, studied economics at Seoul National
University. Throughout his studies he maintained an active interest in

0185

the problems faced by farmers. In 1979 he took part in student protests against the government and reportedly went into hiding to avoid arrest. He is serving a 10-year prison sentence in Chonju Prison.

Im Kyu-yong was a history student when he was first arrested in 1974 in connection with the National Democratic Youth and Student Federation, an organization which the government accused of planning to overthrow the government. AI adopted all those detainees in this case as prisoners of conscience. He was sentenced to 20 years' imprisonment but was released a few years later. He was working as an automobile mechanic when he was arrested in 1979. He is now serving a 10-year prison sentence in Kwanju Prison.

Amnesty International has collected information which it believes shows convincingly that these four men have been imprisoned for the non-violent exercise of their rights to freedom of expression and association. Information from many sources shows that these four prisoners held views that were critical of the Government of the Republic of Korea and its policies, in particular with regard to the rural sector, but that they did not support violence as a means of political change. AI's request to the government for information on the evidence used to convict them was refused, but a number of legal documents relating to the trial indicate that the charges of advocacy of violence and participation in robberies were supported mainly by confessions made by prisoners and by their co-defendants in circumstances which place serious doubt about their voluntary and genuine nature.

Amnesty International is concerned that all the prisoners in this case were convicted after unfair trials. They were detained in October and November 1979 by the police without warrant of arrest for longer that legally permitted, in some cases for up to a month. Their relatives were not informed of their whereabouts until their detention was authorized by a judge and they were moved to regular police stations. The prisoners were held in isolation for six to nine weeks; reportedly they were not allowed to see a lawyer of their choice before the day they were formally charged, 26 December 1979, six to eleven weeks after the beginning of their detention. Their families were allowed to see them for the first time on the day of the first trial.

The defendants testified in court that they had been tortured by police interrogators to make them confess to the charges and that their statements to the prosecutor were made under threat of further torture and were false. Some described their torture to the courts; others reportedly showed injuries which were said to be the result of torture. They referred to beatings, electric shocks and "water torture" where a person is forcibly immersed in water or water is forcibly poured into the victim's nose. To Amnesty International's knowledge, the judges' investigation into the claims of torture was limited to a statement made in court on behalf of the prosecution that there had been no torture. Amnesty International believes that the circumstances of the defendant's interrogation place serious doubts on the validity of their confessions, and has urged the government to reopen their case.

0186

Reverend Kang Hee-nam

Reverend Kang Hee-nam is aged 67 and is the Presbyterian minister of Namsan Church in Chonju, North Cholla Province. He was arrested on November 7, 1986 after addressing a student rally at Chunbuk National University in Chonju. In his speech, entitled "Democracy and Pro-Communist Organizations", he reportedly accused the authorities of labelling students arrested after a three-day occupation of Konkuk University in Seoul at the end of October 1986 as "Communists", while in his view they were simply advocating the democratization of politics. On October 28, over 2,000 students from 26 colleges and universities had taken part in a rally at Konkuk University to establish a "patriotic student committee against foreign power and dictatorship". After riot police broke up the rally and arrested over 200 participants, other participants occupied several university buildings and arrested over 1,200 students. Around 400 were eventually tried and indicted for taking part in the protest: some 140 were eventually charged under the National Security Law (NSL) with using slogans the authorities said were similar to North Korean propaganda; the others were charged with taking part in an illegal assembly.

Reverend Kang Hee-nam was charged under the NSL with "benefiting" the Democratic People's Republic of Korea. On April 7, 1987, he was sentenced to three years' imprisonment. He is currently detained in Chonju Prison.

Amnesty International has adopted Reverend Kang Hee-nam as a prisoner of conscience, detained for the peaceful expression of his political views, and is calling for his immediate and unconditional release.

Reverend Kang Hee-nam has been involved in social and political issues for a number of years. He was adopted by Amnesty International as a prisoner of conscience during his imprisonment from May 1977 to December 1979. His arrest on that occasion had been prompted by a speech he had made at a Democratic Unification Party convention in Chonju. He was sentenced to ten years' imprisonment under the Anti-Communist Law and Emergency Regulation No. 9. In 1978 he was reported to have been insulted and beaten by prison guards for not standing to attention during an investigation of his cell. Reverend Kang Hee-nam was released in December 1979 when Emergency Regulation No. 9 was repealed.

Reverend Kang Hee-nam is the chairman of the Korea National Federation of Christian Farmers Associations which was set up in 1978 to improve the political, economic and social status of peasants and to promote the participation of farmers in the democratization movement. He was also chairman of the Central Committee of Mintongnyon, the United Minjung Movement for Democratization and Unification, an umbrella organization of 26 dissident groups set up in March 1985. Mintongnyon's aim was to involve the public in protests against the government: it organized street demonstrations and published a newsletter Voice of the People. It was closed by the authorities in November 1986 and most of its leaders are currently in detention.

0187

From April 24 to June 3, 1987, Reverend Kang Hee-nam undertook a hunger-strike in protest at the decision by President Chun Doo-hwan on April 13 to suspend debate on constitutional reform until after the 1988 Seoul Olympics.

IV. RECOMMENDATIONS ON THE IMPLEMENTATION OF HUMAN RIGHTS SAFEGUARDS

A. Introduction

Discussions are currently underway in South Korea, within the government, political parties, the legal profession and other circles, on how best to protect human rights. Amnesty International would like to make its contribution to this debate on human rights safeguards. Below are the measures it considers should be implemented at the earliest opportunity. They are based on international human rights standards and bring up to date the recommendations it submitted to the Government of the Republic of Korea in August 1985.

B. Recommendations

1. Freedom of expression and association

International human rights standards provide that everyone has the rights to freely hold and express opinions and to associate and assemble peacefully with others. These rights are set out in the Universal Declaration of Human Rights and in the International Covenant on Civil and Political Rights (ICCPR).

The 1980 Constitution of the Republic of Korea guarantees the rights to freedom of conscience, freedom of speech and of the press, and freedom of assembly and association and the right of workers to collective action. The Constitution allows restrictions on these freedoms and rights "when necessary for national security, the maintenance of public order or public welfare" but stipulates that "even when such restriction is imposed, no essentials of the freedom or right shall be violated."

To further guarantee the rights of freedom of expression, assembly and association, Amnesty International recommends that:

1.1   the Government of the Republic of Korea should release all prisoners detained for the non-violent exercise of their rights of freedom of conscience, expression, association and peaceful assembly, regardless of their political views and of whether their trials have been completed;

1.2   the Government of the Republic of Korea should ratify, without reservations and at the earliest opportunity, the International Covenant on Civil and Political Rights and its Optional Protocol and the International Covenant on Economic, Social and Cultural Rights;

1.3   the National Security Law, the Law on Assemblies and Demonstrations, the Minor Offences Law and Article 104.2 of the Criminal Code should be amended so as to define clearly the offenses contained in them and exclude from their scope acts which constitute the peaceful exercise of the rights of freedom of opinion, expression, association and peaceful assembly. These laws have been used to hold prisoners of conscience;

1.4   the Public Security Law should also be amended so as to stop it being used to detain people for their non-violent political opinions;

0189

1.5   the practice of placing people under house arrest or restricting the freedom of movement of people because of their peaceful political views and activities should be made illegal.

2.   Torture

Torture and other cruel, inhuman or degrading treatment or punishment of prisoners is prohibited by the Universal Declaration of Human Rights and a number of other international human rights instruments. These include the International Covenant on Civil and Political Rights and the Convention against Torture and Other Cruel, Inhuman or Degrading Treatment or Punishment, adopted by the United Nations on 10 December 1984. International standards emphasize that torture can never be justified, even in exceptional circumstances such as a state of war, internal political instability or other public emergency.

The 1980 Constitution of the Republic of Korea specifically prohibits the use of torture and the Code of Criminal Procedure contains a number of provisions which, if implemented, would help to protect detainees against torture and ill-treatment. Amnesty International has found that in many cases of torture and ill-treatment the main safeguards provided by international standards and by the laws of the Republic of Korea had not been respected.

To ensure the protection of all detainees against torture and ill-treatment, Amnesty International recommends that:

2.1.   the Government of the Republic of Korea should ratify without reservations the Convention against Torture and Other Cruel, Inhuman or Degrading Treatment or Punishment at the earliest opportunity;

2.2.   laws of the Republic of Korea and other regulations should be amended or reinforced to end the practice of incommunicado detention and interrogation and to guarantee that anyone arrested or detained should be brought promptly before a judicial authority and should have prompt and regular access to relatives, the detainee's own lawyer and a doctor.

Accurate information on a detainee's whereabouts should be made available to relatives immediately after arrest; early and regular communications and visits should be allowed, subject only to restrictions and supervision necessary in the interests of the administration of justice. Legal recourse should be available to detainees and families denied the right to communicate and meet.

Regular communication and consultation with a lawyer are of the utmost importance to ensure, among other legal guarantees, that statements taken in evidence from the detainee are given freely and not as a result of coercion. Such consultations must occur at a minimum before and between interrogation sessions and in a degree of privacy if the lawyer's presence is to serve as a credible restraint on the interrogators' potential abuse of power.

Detainees should be allowed to be examined, in private, on arrival at any detention center before interrogation begins and regularly afterwards, by medical officers not responsible to the agencies interrogating or detaining the suspects. Records of these examinations should be treated as confidential but should be communicated at the detainee's request to his or her lawyer or family.

0190

The laws of the Republic of Korea should ensure that detainees be brought promptly before a judge or other judicial officer. The right to have the courts to review the legality of arrest or detention should be available to all detainees.

2.3.   the relevant regulations and the practice regarding the detention of suspects should be reviewed so as to separate the authorities responsible for interrogation from those responsible for detention. This is particularly important when the interrogation is conducted by the Anti-Communist Bureau of the National Police, the Agency for National Security Planning and the Military Security Command which have been linked in numerous cases to torture.

Detaining authorities should be directed to keep detailed records on the suspects in their care. Such records should include information on, for instance, the time and duration of each interrogation session, requests or complaints made by the detainees or on their behalf, instances of legitimate use of force against a detainee or of violence by the detainee against guards or against him or herself. The burden should be on the authorities to prove through such records that injuries to prisoners were not sustained through ill-treatment in custody at the hands of officials. All records should be made available to the detainees and his or her legal counsel as well as to the prosecutor supervising the interrogation of the suspect;

2.4.   procedures should be established to ensure that all and well-founded reports, complaints of torture and ill-treatment are investigated by competent authorities and that prisoners are informed of their rights to lodge complaints about their treatment. Places of detention should be visited regularly for inspection by independent and competent authorities;

2.5.   the relevant authorities should conduct impartial and thorough investigations into all claims of torture and ill-treatment and, depending on the results of the investigations, should review the legal position of the prisoners, compensate the victims and bring to justice any officials found to have assaulted prisoners;

2.6.   training procedures should be introduced for all officials involved in the custody, interrogation or treatment of prisoners in which it is stressed that torture is a criminal act, that any orders to commit torture should be refused and abuses reported to superiors or to the authorities vested with reviewing or remedial powers. Amnesty International recommends that a code of conduct based on the United Nations Code of Conduct for Law Enforcement Officials should be adopted and made public.

3.   The right to a fair trial

Amnesty International seeks to ensure that the trials of all political prisoners conforms to internationally recognized norms, such as those of the Universal Declaration of Human Rights and of the ICCPR. These norms include the right to a fair and public hearing by a competent, independent and impartial tribunal and the right to be presumed innocent until proved guilty.

0191

Amnesty International recommends that laws of the Republic of Korea and other
regulations should be amended so as to guarantee a fair trial to all political
detainees. It also calls for all the cases of political prisoners still in custody
to be reviewed whenever there were irregularities in pre-trial or trial
procedures, such as illegal detention without a warrant of arrest, prolonged
incommunicado detention and interrogation, claims of torture or ill-treatment,
denial of prompt and regular access to a lawyer, and the use as evidence of
confessions said by the defendants to have been extracted under torture.

4.   The right to life

Amnesty International opposes the death penalty in all cases without
reservation on the grounds that it is a violation of the right to life and the
right not to be subjected to cruel, inhuman or degrading punishment as
proclaimed in the Universal Declaration of Human Rights and in other
international human rights instruments;

4.1.   Amnesty International urges the President of the Republic of Korea to
commute all death sentences and urges the government to take steps for the
abolition of the death penalty;

4.2.   In preparation for abolition, the Government should inform the public
about criminological and penal issues related to the death penalty, including its
lack of proven special deterrent effect. This is in line with a recommendation
of the United Nations Secretariat in 1980 that "It...seems to be an important
task of governments, the academic community, the mass media, and other
publicly minded organizations...to educate the public as to the uncertainty of
the deterrent effect of capital punishment.."

46. 김대중에 대한 조치 또는 인권상 수여

0193

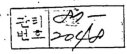

외 무 부

착신전보

번 호 : USW-4352
일 시 : 708181620
증 별 :

수 신 : 장관(미북,통일,노동부)

발 신 : 주미대사

제 목 : 한국노총 위원장 방미

대 : USW-3594.

1. 87.8.14-18 AFL-CIO 초청으로 당지를 방문하고 있는 김동인 한국노총 위원장 일행(강석호 노총사무차장,최강석 AAFLI 계획관)은 8.16 AFL-CIO,KIRKLAND 위원장, DO NAHUE 사무총장등 산하간부 50여 명이 참석한 동단체 집행위에 참석,기조연설을 통하여

가. 아국 노총과의 협력에 사의를 표하고 한국 노총의 발전 현황과 앞으르의 노동권 신장에 대한 한국 노총의 입장을 설명하였다함.

나. 또한 최근 격화되고 있는 노사분규에 관심을 가지고 있는 참석자들로부터 노조결성에 따른 장애 요인과 자동차 산업의 부품 생산 하청업체에 노조 결성 제한여부등에 질문을 받고 6.29 발표이후 노조결성에 제한이 없음을 설명하였으며,저임금 및 년소 근로자 고용, 산업안전 보건에관하여는 질문이 없었다함.

2. AFL-CIO 및 UAW 가 아국의 GSP 혜택배제 청원과 관련,지금한국은 민주화조치가 진행중에 있으며,노동권 역시 제도개선과 근로조건이 점차 개선되어가고 있으므로 GSP 혜택을 배제하게된다면 중소기업 근로자들의 실적은 물론,생활 안정에도 큰장애를 받게되기때문에 제고하여주도록 요청하였다함.

3. 또한 동 집행위의 발표에 따르면,87.10.26 마이애미에서 개최되는 AFL-CIO 연차대회시 김대중 씨에게 조지-미니-인권상을 수여키로 결정되었음을 발표하였다하며,동 조지 미니상은 국적에 관계없이 인권 및 노동관련 분야에 공이 많은자에게 수여하여왔다고 하였다함

(대사 김경원-장관)

예고문에 의거 자. 재분류(19. .)

직위_____ 성명 _____

√미주국   차관실   2차보   통상국   청와대   안기   노동부

1차보

PAGE 1

87.08.19   09:04
외신 2과   통제관

0194

410 한국 인권문제 제 사안 1

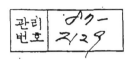

외 무 부

번 호 : USW-4505   일 시 : 708261936   종 별 : 지급

수 신 : 장관(미북)사본:노동부장관

발 신 : 주미대사

제 목 : 조지미니 인권상

대 : WUS-3838,3794

연 : USW-4432

1. 대호 인권상의 정식명칭은 -조지미니 인권상(GEORGE MEANY HUMAN RIGHTS AWARD)
- 이며,87년도 수상 예정자는 김대중 1명임.

2.동건 관련 8.26(수)당관 노무관이 업무관계에 있는   AFL-CIO 의   PAUL SOMOGYI
국제부차장과 면담,현재 여야간에 원활히 진행되고 있는 개헌협상과 정치일정을
상세히 설명하고,이같이 대통령선거를 앞둔 민감한 정치적 전환기에 특정 정치인에게
동상을 시상하는것은 국민의 여망속에 추진되고 있는 민주화과정에 바람직하지못한
영향을 가져올 수 있다는 점과 수상 추천당시와 현재의 상황에는 현저한 차이가 있음
을 감안할때 개인적 생각으로는 시상을 취소 또는 연기하는것이 오히려 아국의 민주
발전과정에 도움이 될것으로 본다고 설명하였음.

3.이에 대해 동 차장은 개인적으로는 그러한 사정을 이해할수 있으나,동시상이 집행
이사회에서 DONAHUE   사무총장의 발의와 KIRKLAND 위원장의 재청으로 결정된
배경을 감안할때,이를 변경 또는 번복하기위해서는 집행이사회를 재소집해야할뿐 아
니라, DONAHUE 사무총장과 KIRKLAND 위원장 및 KAHN 국제부장의 김대중과
의 친분관계에 비추어 시상의 취소나 연기는 사실상 불가능할것으로 본다고 언급하였
음.

4. SOMOGYI 국제부 차장은 또한 AFL-CIO 와 김대중과의 관계 및 관련사항에
관해 아래 설명하였음.

가.김대중과의 관계

미주국   차관실   청와대   안 기   노동부

PAGE   1   87.08.28 13:30
                                              외신 2과   통제관

0195

-김대중이 미국 체류중이던 85년도 KIRKLAND 위원장 사무실을 방문,아국 인권문제와 자신의 이력등에관해 설명한바있음.

-또한 DONAHUE 사무총장(AFL-CIO 의 2인자)과 KAHN 국제부장등 일행은 87.1월 방한시 김대중의 집을 방문하기도 하였음(소모기 차장은 동 방문시의 기념 사진 및 김대중이 KAHN 부장에게 써준 -근하신년-족자를 보여줌)

나.시상대상 및 시상제도

-시상대상은 인권 및 노동권에 관한 공적뿐만아니라 자유평화 추호 업적등 광범위한 고려하에 집행위에서 결정됨.

-집행위는 AFL-CIO 위원장,사무총장등 간부,산업별노도 위원장등 23명으로 구성됨.

-동상은 81년부터 매년 시상하여왔으며,매년 개최되는 총회에서 시상함(동 차장은 연호 시상제도를 정정 설명함)

-지금까지 년도별 수상기록은 다음임

86 ANDREI SAKHAROV(쏘련)

85 ERNESTO HERRERA(비율빈)

84 ANDRE BERGERON,FORECE OUVIERE(불란서)

83 INTERNATIONAL RESCUE COMMITTEE(단체)

82 GOTSHA BUTHELEZI AND NEIL AGGETT(남아공)

81 LECH WALESA(폴랜드)

다.8.18 집행위후 발표된 시상결정에 대한 NEWS RELEASE 는 다음임.

  IN ADDITION,THE COUNCIL VOTEDTHIS MORNING TO AWARD THE 1987 GEORGE MEANY HUMAN RIGHTS AWARD TO SOUTH KOREA S KIM DAE JUNG.IN MAKING THE AWARD,THE COUNCIL NOTED THAT KIM HAS PAID A HEAVY PRICE IN HIS FIGHT FOR DEMOCRACY. HE UNDERWENT KIND ANPPING,IMPRISONMENT,A DEATH SENTENCE,EXILE AND HOUSE ARREST.THIS IMPROVED CHANCE THAT SOUTH KOREAN HAVE TODAY OF ACHIEVING REAL WORKER AND HUMAN RIGHTS IS LARGELY TRACEABLE TO KIM S EFFORTS.

5. 당관 관찰 및 건의

PAGE   2

0196

가. 금번 시상 결정은 AFL-CIO 의 핵심인물인 KIRKLAND 위원장, DONAHUE 사무총장, KAHN 국제부장(조지 미니상 이주로 외국인을 대상으로 하는점에서)등 3 인이 중심이되어 집행위에서 의결시킨것으로 나타나고 있음.

나. 또한 주로 외국인을 대상으로하기 때문에 AFL-CIO 가 주요국에 설치하고 있는 <u>AAFLI</u> 사무소의 현지 보고 또는 건의가 공식적으로는 동시상 결정과정의 기초가 되고 있는것으로 관찰 됨.

다. AFL-CIO 의 독립적인 성격과 또한 동 기구가 지금까지 아국의 노동권 및 인권상황에 대해 매우 비판적인 잣세를 취해왔으며, 시상결정이 공식 의결기구에서 결정, 발표된점과 동 결정의 핵심인물들이 김대중과의 개인적 관계를 가져왔다는점에 비추어, 현재 상황에서 시상결정의 취소 또는 연기를 위해 정부 차원에서 직접 관여하는 인상을 줄경우 <u>오히려 더큰 부작용을 초래 할 가능성이 큰것으로 판단됨</u>(이러한 고려에서 당관 노무관은 직업상의 자연스런 관심차원에서 동 조직의 평소 접촉선을 통해 견해를 표시하는것으로 해오고 있음)

라. 따라서 상기 핵심인물들을 설득할수 있는 제 3자를 통해 정부 개입 인상을 주지 않도록 하면서 이들을 설득, 시상 결정의 취소 또는 연기를 유도하는 방안을 강구해야 할것이나, 상기 결정 배경 및 절차등을 고려할때 현실적으로 <u>그 가능성은 극히 희박한</u> 것으로 보임.

마. 연이나 AFL-CIO 조직내에서 아국 실정을 공식적으로 대변할수있는 <u>AAFLI</u>? 의 서울 사무소측이 상황 변경을 이유로하여 공식경로를 통해 시상결정의 취소 또는 연기를 건의할 경우 혹시라도 어떤 효과를 기대할수는 있을것으로 보이는바, 아국 노총으로 하여금 동 사무소측과 적극 접촉토록함이 좋을것으로 사료됨.

바. 또한 아국 노총이 AFL-CIO 본부와 직접 접촉하는것도 고려할 필요가 있다고 생각됨.

ⓐ 아울러 당관은 상기 핵심인물과의 친분이 있는 인사중 당관이 이문제로 상의할수 있는 인사를 물색하는등 가능한 방안을 계속 강구할것임.

6. 한편 본직은 내주초(8.31 또는 9.1중)국무성 SIGUR 차관보와 단독 면담을 갖고 이문제에 대한 동 차관보의 사적인 의견과 자문을 요청할 예정임. *(대사 김경원)*

예고문앤 의함. 재분류 61년 (. . .)
직위 성명

PAGE 3

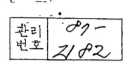

외 무 부

착신전

번 호 : USW-4559　　　일 시 : 8709011923　　종 별 :

수 신 : 장관(미북 사본:노동부장관)

발 신 : 주미대사

제 목 : 조지미니 인권상

연 : USW-4505

　　본직은 금 9.1(화) 표제관련　SIGUR　국무부 동아태 담당 차관보와 오찬면담을
가졌는바 동요지 아래 보고함

1. 본직은　SIGUR　차관보에게　AFL-CIO　가 87년도 조지미니 인권상을 김대중
씨에게 수여하기로 결정하였다는 사실을 알리면서 아국정부가 미국 느조 결정에 간여
하려는 것은 아니나 아국에서 진행되고 있는 개헌협상과 향후 정치일정과 관련하여
김대중씨가 정치인으로 차기 대통령 선거의 입후보자가 될수 있는 위치에 있기 때문
에　AFL-CIO　의 금번 결정은 한국 내정에 간섭하는 인상을 매우 강하게 풍기고 있
다고 지적함

2. 또한 본직은 상기관련 미국무부에서　AFL-CIO　측과 동문제에 관해 협의 또는
충고할수 있는 방법이 있다면 동 수상결정을 취소케 하던가 적어도 10월예정으로 있
는 수상일자를 아국 대통령 선거가 끝난후로 연기하도록 미 국무부가　AFL-CIO　을
설득하여 줄것을 요청함.

3.　SIGUR　차관보는 김대중씨의 동 조지미니상 수상 사실에 대해 전혀 알지못했
다고 말하고 한국정부가　AFL-CIO　측에게 상기 요청을 정식제기 하였는지 묻고
본직이 아직 제기 하지 않았다고 대답하자 예상되는　AFL-CIO　측의 반발을 감안할
때 전달 않하기를 잘했다고 말함. 또한 사안의 성격상 미 국무부가　AFL-CIO　의
득자적 결정에 대해 충고할수 있는입장이 되지 못하는 미국무부의 어려운 입장을 아
측이 이해해 줄것을 희망하였음. 그러나 미 국무부는 동문제가 현재의 한국정치 상황
과 관련 정치적으로 민감한 문제라는 것은 인식하고 있으며 이를 유의하고 적절한

미주국　차관실　1차보　청와대　안기

방안에 대하여 연구해 보겠다고 답변함

(대사 김경원)

美 労総의 金大中에 대한 授賞 計劃 報告
- 죠지. 미니 人權賞 -

87. 8

外　務　部

駐美大使 報告에 의하면 美國 勞動總聯盟은 87.10.26-29 마이애미 開催 豫定인 總會에서 金大中에게 죠지. 미니 人權賞을 授與키로 하였다고 하는 바 다음 報告드립니다.

授賞 経緯

o 죠지. 미니 人權賞을 金大中에게 授與하기로 한 經緯는 美 勞總執行委에서 金大中과 평소 接触이 있는 도나휴 事務總長의 發議와 커클랜드 委員長의 再請으로 決定됨

- 85. 金大中 滯美時 커클랜드 委員長을 訪問, 自身의 經歷紹介 및 紐帶 構築
- 87.2 도나휴 事務總長 一行 訪韓時 金大中 自宅 訪問, 人權 및 勞動問題等 協議

죠지. 미니 人権賞

o 美 勞總 죠지. 미니 初代委員長의 生存時 業績을 追慕 하기 위해 同 죠지. 미니 人權賞을 制定, 1981年 부터 每年 開催되는 總會에서 授與함

- 受賞者를 總會에 招請, 紀念牌와 5,000美弗의 賞金 支給

0201

- 美國 勞組幹部 및 各國 勞組關係者等 約 1,500名 總會 參席

ㅇ 죠지. 미니 人權賞은 制定된지 얼마되지 않기 때문에 國際的으로 널리 알려져 있지 않음

- 끝 -

Int'l Rescue Committee 개요

○ 사무국 소재지 : 파리

○ 사무국장 : Charles Steinberg (뉴욕거주)

○ 설립년도 : 1933년

○ 구 조 : 이사회(Board), 집행이사회(Executive Committee)

○ 재 정 : 기부금 (주로 미국인),

　　　　　　　　정부 및 정부간 국제기구 지원금

○ 설립취지 및 목적

　- 나치즘, 파시즘에 대항하는 민주인사에 대한 지원

　- 종교, 인종, 국적에 관계없이 모든 전체주의의 희생자에 대한

　　재정적 지원

　- 전체주의 희생자에 대한 지원을 도모키 위해 동 희생자들이 처한

　　곤경, 실상 등을 홍보

○ 주요활동

　- 난민지원

　- 장학금 및 기술습득 지원

　- 긴급 재난 구호

0203

As Bangladesh, Hon..... ., Indonesia, Korea Rep (2), Malaysia (2), Nepal, Philippines (2), Singapore, Sri Lanka, Thailand. Au Fiji.
**1983.10

♦ F0045 International Institute of Andragogy
Institut international d'andragogie — Instituto internacional de Andragogia (INSTIA)
Pres Felix Adam, Ave Veracruz, Edificio Capaya P H7, Las Mercedes, Caracas 1060, Venezuela. T. 926 811. C. INSTIA.
Aims Serve the Latin American needs for training and research in adult education.
Language English; French, Spanish. Publication INSTIA Magazine (monthly).
Members Individuals in 5 countries:
Am Costa Rica; Dominican Rep; Peru, USA, Venezuela. .
*1984.09.25

♦ F0050 Defence for Children — International (DCI)
Défense des enfants — International (DEI) — Defensa de los Niños — International (DNI)
SG Nigel Cantwell, PO Box 359, CH-1211 Genève 4, Switzerland. T. (022) 20 83 45.
Founded 5 July 1979, Geneva, as Defence for Children. Present name adopted 1982.
Aims Ensure on-going practical, systematic and concerted action internationally for the promotion and protection of children's rights by monitoring and reacting to violations and seeking the most effective means of preventing them, as well as spreading information on the issues and problems involved.
Structure General Assembly of all members; executive Council elected by assembly. Languages English, French, Spanish. Staff 5 paid, 2 voluntary. Finance Members' dues; grants from international and national bodies.
Consultative status ECOSOC (Ros). NGO Relations Member organization of Council of International Organizations Directly Interested in Children and Youth (COIDIEA); International Association for the Child's Right to Play (IPA); World Federation of Mental Health (WFMH). Biennial General Assembly Geneva 1980, Paris 1982, Netherlands 1984. Publications International Children's Rights Monitor (quarterly) in English and French.
Members Individual and organisational members in 37 countries:
Af Egypt, Ghana, Kenya, Madagascar, Niger, Nigeria, Tunisia, Zambia, Zimbabwe. Am Argentina, Bolivia, Brazil, Canada, Colombia, Costa Rica, Mexico, Peru, USA. As Bangladesh, India, Israel, Japan. Au Australia, New Zealand. Eu Belgium, Denmark, Finland, France, Greece, Italy, Monaco, Netherlands, Norway, Poland, Sweden, Switzerland, Uk.
**1983.11

♦ F0054 International Rescue Committee (IRC)
Comité international de sauvetage
Exec Dir Charles Sternberg, 386 Park Ave S, New York NY 10016, USA. T. (212) 679 0010.
Headquarters: Bd des Capucines 35, F-75002 Paris, France.
Office in Switzerland G G Ackerson, 7 rue Gautier, CH-1201 Genève, Switzerland.
Founded 1933, as International Rescue and Relief Committee, originally to aid the democratic opponents of nazism and fascism. Registered according to US law. Aims Assist, resettle and rehabilitate victims of totalitarian oppression and persecution and administer such relief without regard to race, nationality or religion; conduct programmes of public education regarding the situation, circumstances, needs and plight of such victims of totalitarianism for the purpose of mobilizing assistance on their behalf. Structure Board; Executive Committee. Finance Contributions (mainly from the USA); grants from governments and intergovernmental agencies. IGO Relations Intergovernmental Committee for Migration; UNHCR. NGO Relations Conference of Nongovernmental Organizations interested in Migration; Agency for International Development (AID); American Council of Voluntary Agencies for Foreign Service (ACVAFS); International Council of Voluntary Agencies (ICVA). Activities Assistance to refugees; student scholarships and apprentice assistance; emergency relief.
***1986

♦ F0065j Transnational Institute (TNI)
Dir Basker Vashee, Paulus Potterstraat 20, 1071 DA Amsterdam, Netherlands. T. (020) 72 66 08. C. TRANSNAT Amsterdam.
Contact Institute for Policy Studies, 1901 Q Street NW, Washington DC 20009, USA. T. (202) 234-9382 C. IPSWASH Washington DC.
Founded 1973, as the International programme of the Institute for Policy Studies (IPS) — Institut d'études politiques. Aims Search for alternatives to imperialism; study transnational political economy and the problems of those exploited by it; study development, militarism, and forms of resistance to imperialism. Consultative Status ECOSOC (II). Activities Functions as a contact point in an international network to provide information on multinational/transnational enterprises in Europe. Conferences and seminars.
Members Individuals.
***1985

♦ F0074 Eco Theo Group
Contact Ave d'Auderghem 23, B-1040 Bruxelles, Belgium.
Aims Reflect on various subjects of common interest to economists and theologians; discuss matters of economic and social policy with civil servants of the Commission of the European Communities; endeavour to bring before the Churches the questions of international economic policy moves – especially as taking shape within the European Community institutions. Activities Meeting in Brussels twice a year. Publications Working papers.
***1986

♦ F0077g Asian Development Bank (AsDB)
Banque asiatique de développement (BAsD) — Banco Asiático de Desarrollo — Asiatische Entwicklungs Bank (AEB)
Pres Masao Fujioka, 2330 Roxas Blvd, PO Box 789, Pasay City, Manila 2800, Philippines. T. 831 72 51 – 831 7211 C. ASIANBANK Manila. Tx 23103 ADB PH RCA – 40571 ADB PM ITT – 63587 ADB PN ETPI.
Sec Wilfred A Vawdrey, same address.
Established 22 Aug 1966, Manila, when Articles of Agreement establishing the Asian Development Bank were drawn up under the auspices of the then United Nations Economic Commission for Asia and the Far East (ECAFE), currently United Nations Economic and Social Commission for Asia and the Pacific (ESCAP). Articles of agreement were adopted at 2nd Ministerial Conference on Asian Economic Cooperation, Nov-Dec 1965, Manila, and entered into force with the ratification or acceptance by 15 Signatories. Establishment followed recommendations of the first Ministerial Conference on Asian Economic Cooperation, Dec 1963, Manila, also under the auspices of ECAFE which set up a Working Group of Experts; and of the 25th Session of ECAFE, Mar 1965, Wellington, when a Consultative Committee was set up to prepare a draft agreement. Bank commenced operations 19 Dec 1966, Manila, following inaugural Meeting of the Board of Governors, Nov 1966, Tokyo. Known also under English initials ADB and French initials BAD.
Aims Foster economic growth and cooperation in the Asian and Pacific region and contribute to economic development of the developing member countries in the region, including the South Pacific.
Structure Board of Governors, composed of one Governor and one Alternate Governor appointed by each member elects President; Board of Directors, composed of

Directors elected by Board of Governors, 8 by regional non-regional countries; Each Director appoints an Alternate [Presidents (Operations; Projects; Finance and Administration) ap Directors on the recommendation of President. Under Vice-Pr there are 4 Departments: 'Agriculture', including 3 Divisions: Forestry; Fisheries and Livestock; Agricultural Support Servic Rural Development', including 3 geographical Divisions. 'Infrast. Divisions: Airports and. Highways; Port, Railways and Telecom Supply; Social Infrastructure; Education 'Industry and Developme Energy-Planning Unit and 4 Divisions: Industry and Minerals; I (West); Development Finance. In all there are 21 departments and resident office in Bangladesh and a regional office in Vanuatu. . Manila: Asian Development Fund (ADF) — Fonds Asiático de Desar Assistance Special Fund. Languages English. Staff 1,492 paid. capital as at 31 dec 1983 was US $ 15,461 million; subscribe 11,510 million. Special funds resources at that time were (total re $ 4,207.2 million and (contributions) for Technical Assistance 59.2 million. Total assets as at 31 Dec 1983: US $ 8,127.582 IGO Relations Close working relationship with the United Natic and in particular with: FAO; WHO; IMF; World Bank Group. Act IFAD following cooperation agreement Apr 1978. Member c Agency for UNDP for specific national or regional projects.
Activities Promotes investment in the region of public and private ment purposes; utilizes the resources at its disposal for giving lc ment of member countries; provides assistance in the coordinat policies and plans and for the preparation, financing and execut projects and programs; cooperates with the United Nations, its or bodies, and with public international organizations and other inter as well as national entities whether public or private, which are investment of development funds in the region; interests such Inst in new opportunities for investment and assistance. Loan approval covered 53 projects and amounted to US $ 1,893.2 million. By projects and 377 technical assistance projects had been comp! Board of Governors Annual Meeting Manila 1968, Sydney Singapore 1971, Vienna 1972, Manila 1973, Kuala Lumpur Jakarta 1976, Manila 1977, Vienna 1978, Manila 1979, Manila (USA) 1981, Manila 1982, Manila 1983, Amsterdam 1984, Ba 1986.
Publications Operational Information on Proposed Projects (mon Review in English, French, German, Japanese. Annual Reports; su ings; regional surveys, studies and reports; case studies; occasion . staff papers; statistical publications; sector papers; information l Members Governments of 31 countries and territories in the rep As Afghanistan, Bangladesh, Bhutan, Burma, Hong Kong, India, Indo chea, Korea Rep, Laos, Malaysia, Maldives, Nepal, Pakistan, Philippines, . Taiwan, Thailand, Viet Nam. Au Australia, Cook Is, Fiji, Kiribati, New Guinea, Samoa, Solomon Is, Tonga, Vanuatu.
Governments of 14 countries outside the region:
Am Canada, USA. Eu Austria, Belgium, Denmark, Finland, France, Germ lands, Norway, Sweden, Switzerland, UK.

♦ F0079g Asian Highway Co-ordinating Committee
Comité de coordination pour les routes d'Asie
Secretariat c/o Economic and Social Commission, for Asia a Sanitham, Bangkok 2, Thailand. T. 813544. C. ESCAP.
Established Also referred to as Asian Highway Network Project. coordinate the Asian Highway project aimed at developing inter national highway traffic for trade and commerce, for tourism and better understanding between the peoples of Asia. Structure C least once a year; Executive Secretary of United Nations Economic Asia Pacific (ESCAP) is ex-officio member; elects its own chairman Asian Highway Transport Technical Bureau, set up by United Na Programme (UNDP), acts as administrative organ. Finance Pro concerned, with additional external aid.
Members Governments of 14 countries:
As Afghanistan, Burma, India, Indonesia, Iran, Kampuchea, Laos, Mala Singapore, Sri Lanka, Thailand, Viet Nam.

♦ F0080v League International for Creditors (LIC)
Ligue internationale pour la protection du crédit — Liga Internacio ción del Crédito — Liga für Internationalen Creditschutz — Lega In Tutela del Credito
Contact LIC Int Collection Ltd, Nordstrasse 23, PO Box, CH-80 land. T. (01) 363 00 56.
Founded 1962, as an association of independent commercial de cies located all over the world. Structure Subsidiary commercial o in Zürich: LICInternational Collection Ltd; Collecta LIC (Switzerlan Members Experts in over 130 countries.
Membership countries not specified.

♦ F0084 World Assembly of First Nations (WAFN)
Assemblée internationale des nations premières — Asamblea In Naciones Primas
Pres David Ahenakew, 222 Queen Street, Ottawa ON, Canada. Contact R Ramirez, University of Regina, Classroom Bldg C-4, Regina T. (306) 584 8333.
Assembly Regina (Canada) 1982.

♦ F0093gf European Monetary Cooperation Fund (EMCF)
Fonds européen de coopération monétaire (FECOM) — Europäisch rungspolitische Zusammenarbeit (EFWZ) — Fondo Europeo di Coo aria
Secretariat of Board of Governors: c/o Bank for International, tralbahnplatz 2, CH-4002 Basel, Switzerland. T. 20 81 11. Tx E Established 3 Apr 1973, Luxembourg, with separate legal persons (EEC) No 907/73 of the Council of the European Communities, v force on 6 Apr 1973.
Aims Promote the proper functioning of the Basel Agreement of 24 narrowing of the margins of fluctuations between community cur tions in community currencies on the exchange markets, and the positions resulting from those interventions. Administer, under the ary System (EMS), the pooling of the Community's gold and do eventually become a European Monetary Fund. Activities Keeps term borrowings made by national Central Banks to support curr Board of Governors of the 10 central banks of EEC Member States Commission of the European Communities participates. Finance C

0204

관리
번호 87-2208

외　두　부　착신전

번　호 : USW-4923　　　일　시 : 709211128　　종 별 :

수　신 : 장관(미북,노동부)

발　신 : 주미대사

제　목 : 죠지미니 인권상

대 : WUS-4024

1. AFL-CIO 연차총회에 아국 공관 관계관이 초청을 받았거나, 참석한 전례가 없음.

2. 다만, 금년들어 당관에 노무관이 신설되어, AFL-CIO 와 AAFLI 등을 접촉함에 따라, 노무관 총회참석을 요청하여왔으며, 매년차 총회시에는 외국 노초위원장및 미국 주재 공관 노무관을 초청하는것이 관례이나 동남아 국가중에서는 일본, 대만, 비올빈 노무관 이 참석한바 있다함

(대사 김경원-장관)

예고문에 의거 재분류 (19 . .)
직위 : 12.31 일 보통　성명

안기백위와 별도

미주국　차관실　2차보　청와대　안기　노등부

87.09.22　09:08
외신 2과　통제관

(토)

0205

87.9.22. 17:50.
복미과 파직원 : 북장→외요장관 전화, 불관이 함께 인장.
87.9.23. 16:15. 송실버관, 안거북3국 송 박록장통화. 수송시거가 국내정치 종요시거와 원리. 노무는 파견은 별허

분류번호	보존기간

발 신 전 보

번 호 : *WUS-4481*   일 시 : *71006 1620*   전보종별 : _____

수 신 : 주   미   대사 *(총영사)*

발 신 : 장   관 (미북)

제 목 : 죠 지미니 인권상

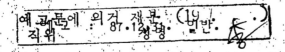

대 : USW - 4611, 4923

연 : WUS - 4024

대호, 관계부처와 협의한 바 AFL-CIO 연차총회에

귀관 노무관의 참석은 불필요한 것으로 사료되니 참석하지 말기바람.

(미주국장 신두병)

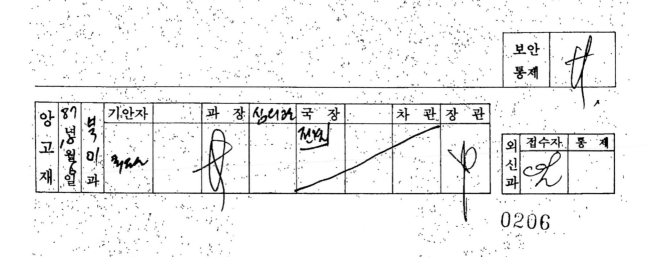

		기안자	과 장	국 장	차 관	장 관	보안통제
앙고재	87년월일 북미과						외신과 접수자 / 통제

0206

외 무 부

번 호 : USW-5239   일 시 : 710081825   종 별 : 지급

수 신 : 장관(미북)사본:노동부장관

발 신 : 주 미 대사

제 목 : 죠지미니 인권상 수상

당관 고인래 노무관이 표제건에 관하여 10.8. AAFLE 의 HUTCHISON 사무차장
에게 탐문한바에 의하면, 김대중씨가 한국내 정치 일정으로해서 방미할수 없는 경우
에는 L.A. 에 거주하는 김대중씨 차남이 대리 수상하도록 10.7. 김대중 씨측과
협의 결정하였다함.

(대사 김경원)

미주국   차관실   1차보   정문국   청와대   안 기   노동부

PAGE   1

87.10.09 11:17
외신 2과 통제관

0207

착신전보

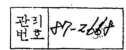

외 무 부

번 호 : USW-5666   일 시 : 710291602   종 별 : 지급

수 신 : 장관(미북) 사본 노동부장관

발 신 : 주미대사

제 목 : 죠지미니 인권상

연 : USW-5239

1. 10.26. 부터 마이애미에서 총회를 개최중인 미 AFL-CIO 는 10.27.김대중에 수여되는 죠지미니 인권상을 김대중 차남 김홍업 에게 대리 수여하였음.

2. 동 수상식에서 김대중은 비디오 테입을 통해 국내사정상 수상식에 참석치 못하는 것을 유감으로 생각한다고 말하고 인권 및 노동권 향상에 전력을 다하겠다고 언급 하였음. 또한 대리수상자인 김홍업은 현재 한국내에는 시간당 50센트에도 못미치는 저임금 노동자가 많이 있다고 하면서 노동법 개정등 노동운동에 앞장 서겠다고 말함.

3. 동 인권상 수상 후 AFL-CIO 국제부장 MR.KHAN 은 한국 노총 민오기 사무총장에게 동 인권상 수상에 대해 COMMENT 하여줄것을 요청한바, 민 사무총장은 현역 정치인이며 12월 대통령선거 출마자에게 인권상을 수여하는 것은 AFL-CIO 가 한국정치에 관여하는 인상을 줄것이라고 답변함. MR.KHAN 은 민 사무총장의 언급에 수긍하면서 김대중이 동 인권상 수상후보로 추천될 당시에는 김대중의 위치와 상황이 현재와는 달랐다고 언급하였음.

(대사 김경원)

예고문에 의거 재분류 (19   )
작위   88.6.30

마주국   차관실   1차보   청와대   안 기   노동부

PAGE 1

87.10.30 10:01
외신 2과 통제관
0208

424 한국 인권문제 제 사안 1

외교문서 비밀해제: 한국 인권문제 1
한국 인권문제 제 사안 1

초판인쇄 2024년 03월 15일
초판발행 2024년 03월 15일

지은이 한국학술정보(주)
펴낸이 채종준
펴낸곳 한국학술정보(주)
주 소 경기도 파주시 회동길 230(문발동)
전 화 031-908-3181(대표)
팩 스 031-908-3189
홈페이지 http://ebook.kstudy.com
E-mail 출판사업부 publish@kstudy.com
등 록 제일산-115호(2000. 6. 19)

ISBN 979-11-7217-055-4 94340
     979-11-7217-054-7 94340 (set)